Nam-Sense

Surviving Vietnam
with the 101st Airborne Division

Nam-Sense

Surviving Vietnam
with the 101st Airborne Division

Arthur Wiknik, Jr.

CASEMATE
Havertown, PA

Published by
CASEMATE
2114 Darby Road, Havertown, PA
Phone: 610-853-9131

Typeset and design by
Savas Publishing & Consulting Group

ISBN 1-932033-40-8

Printed in the United States of America

To the families and friends of the 58,209 men and women
who sacrificed their all in Vietnam;

To Tommy Shay, Jimmy Manning and Ray Contino,
boys from my childhood who died in the war.

And to the thousands of men and women who so proudly and bravely served
in the military during one of the most turbulent times in our nation's history.

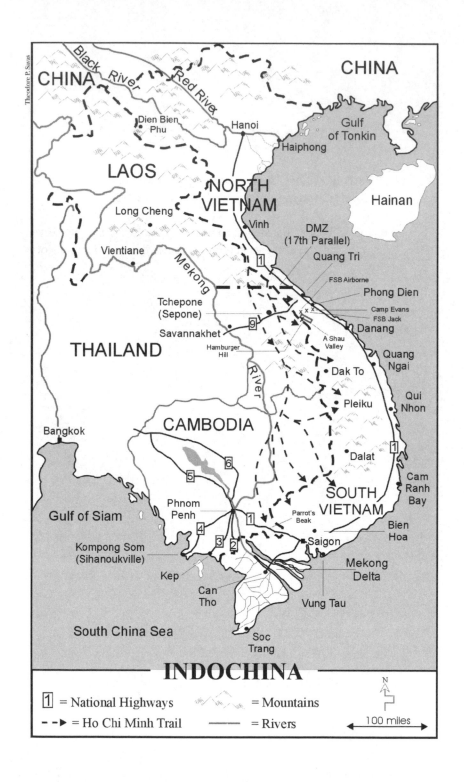

CHINA

Black River

Red River

CHINA

Dien Bien Phu

Hanoi

Gulf of Tonkin

Haiphong

LAOS

Hainan

NORTH VIETNAM

Long Cheng

Vinh

DMZ (17th Parallel)

Quang Tri

Vientiane

Mekong

FSB Airborne

Phong Dien

Tchepone (Sepone)

Camp Evans
FSB Jack

Savannakhet

Danang

Hamburger Hill

A Shau Valley

Quang Ngai

THAILAND

River

Dak To

Pleiku

Qui Nhon

CAMBODIA

Dalat

Bangkok

Cam Ranh Bay

Phnom Penh

Parrot's Beak

SOUTH VIETNAM

Gulf of Siam

Bien Hoa

Kompong Som (Sihanoukville)

Saigon

Mekong Delta

Kep

Can Tho

Vung Tau

South China Sea

Soc Trang

INDOCHINA

1 = National Highways   = Mountains

- - ▶ = Ho Chi Minh Trail   — = Rivers

N

100 miles

Theodore P. Savas

Contents

Contents (continued)

Maps and Illustrations

A photo gallery follows page 130

Youth is the first victim of war: the first fruit of peace. It
takes twenty years or more of peace to make
a man; it takes only twenty seconds of
war to destroy him. —Baudouin I

Preface

This story is about my life in 1969 and 1970 during the height of the Vietnam War. I wrote it to give you a sense of what the average GI endured during this turbulent time in our nation's history. I think it also shows why most young men can go to war and return home without being haunted by their experiences for the rest of their lives, and why some cannot. Although many veterans and their families suffered in different ways, this book does not seek to discredit those killed, wounded, or psychologically affected by the war.

I was drafted into the US Army in 1968 and after extensive stateside training, was sent to Vietnam in 1969 as a non-commissioned officer and infantry squad leader. The military expected me to drop into the middle of the war and, without any experience whatsoever, lead men in combat. I was barely twenty years old. The last thing I wanted was to be fighting an enemy in his jungle on the other side of the world, but there I was, and I was determined to make the best of it. My extra stateside training, discipline, and will to survive instilled within me a resolute goal as a squad leader to finish my tour of duty and go home in one piece—and take as many of my men with me as possible. This usually put me at odds with gung-ho superiors who habitually put the mission ahead of the men.

And so my series of adventures and misadventures began in Vietnam, a country where the bizarre was often the norm. I tried as best I could during my year-long tour of duty to find the humorous side of daily life in Vietnam, where shooting and blowing up other human beings was what you were supposed to do. Finding humor and staying sane in the middle of a war is not an easy thing to do. My occasionally flippant attitude and desire to survive the experience did not always help matters—and certainly did not sit well with my superiors, some of whom were utterly incompetent and dangerous in the field. As a result, I often found myself in outlandish situations, most of my own making.

In addition to trying to survive the war, soldiers had to deal with the unpopularity of the conflict at home, as well as the venom heaped upon us by the anti-war movement, which made it difficult to perform our duties to the fullest. Also, as in all wars, we were forced to endure the ever present specter of human death by gruesome means. Unlike how it is at home, in combat there are no wakes or funerals, and little or no time to grieve. When someone is killed or seriously wounded, we simply acknowledged it and soldiered on. To do anything else would exhibit weakness, something few soldiers were willing to portray.

Nam-Sense is not about heroism and glory, mental breakdowns, or haunting flashbacks; nor does it wallow in self-pity. As you will discover, the vast majority of GIs did not rape, torture, or burn villages. We were not strung out on drugs, and we did not enjoy killing. Although these unfortunate incidents did indeed occur during the war, as they do in every war ever fought, they were not on the grand scale we have been led to believe by people and organizations with different axes to grind. Brutality, violence, and offensive activities are the main ingredients of any war, but they were not the only ingredients of this war. Unfortunately, the media's negative and sensationalized reporting of isolated incidents not only made being a Vietnam veteran an embarrassment, but stereotyped us as well. This book responds to that unfair stereotyped image by revealing the level of courage, principle, kindness, and friendship demonstrated by most GIs. These are the same elements found in every other war Americans have proudly fought in.

This memoir was completed nearly thirty-five years after the fact, and so it was impossible for me to remember the exact name of every person who appears within these pages. A few of the names have been intentionally changed to protect familes, reputations, and memories.

Acknowledgements

As with every book ever written, there are many people to thank. *Nam-Sense* has been "in development" for the better part of three decades. During that time, many people have read bits and pieces of the evolving manuscript, offered their suggestions, and encouraged me to continue. Unfortunately, I cannot now remember everyone who played some role in assisting me. If I have overlooked your contribution to this book, please know it was inadvertent, and that I will forever be in your debt.

First, I would like to thank my Connecticut Local Draft Board #6 for selecting me above so many others for induction into the US military. Thanks are also due to the US Army for sending me to an exotic, dangerous land, riddled by war.

Dennis Silig and Howard Siner, two of the best friends a soldier could ask for, played an important role in my life. They helped to keep me alive and sane. Dennis passed away from cancer some years ago. I miss him.

Bruce Randall edited early versions of *Nam-Sense* and pushed me to keep writing; John Meehan came up with the clever *Nam-Sense* title.

I would also like to thank my publisher David Farnsworth, who directs Casemate Publishing, for believing in this project and accepting it for publication; and Theodore P. "Ted" Savas for rapidly and accurately getting the manuscript into publishable form.

Many people took the time to write letters to me in Vietnam when I needed them the most. I can't thank them enough.

My three daughters supported me along this long road, each in her own way. Sarah never tired of hearing my war stories; whenever I needed to talk, she was there to listen; Kimberly used her skills to prepare the photographs for *Nam-sense* (because her dad is a dinosaur when it comes to technology); when the computer was in her bedroom, Ashley never complained—even when I typed away late into the night with the lights burning bright. My hope is that when each of you read this book you will better understand what so many endured for their country. I love you all, forever.

And finally, my wife Betty-Jane. She spent years typing and re-typing this book on a manual typewriter until we could afford a word processor, and supported me over many years of disappointment and frustration. I could not have done this without her.

Arthur Wiknik, Jr.

"Gentlemen, welcome to
the Republic of South Vietnam."

CHAPTER 1

Vietnam Apprenticeship

The war seemed distant. My tiny New England town had men in the military, but at nineteen years old, I didn't personally know anyone who was serving in Vietnam. Other than the war death of Tommy Shay, a kid I vaguely knew from junior high school, I never had reason to think about the conflict. My free time was spent hanging out with the boys at the hardware store or cruising with my girlfriend in the new Camaro I had recently bought. But in May 1968, my life changed dramatically after I was drafted into the US Army and sent to Fort Polk, Louisiana—"Home of the Combat Infantryman for Vietnam." No longer would I be known as Artie Wiknik . I was now Wiknik, Arthur, US 52725533.

The training at Fort Polk's Tigerland was tough and intense. It had to be. Our training company, with the exception of those men with brothers in Southeast Asia, was Vietnam-bound. I didn't want to go. It's not that I was a coward but I wasn't a hero, either. There was but one honorable escape and even that proved temporary. A five-month NCO (Non-Commissioned Officer) course, taught at Fort Benning, Georgia, was offered to trainees with post high school education who the Lifers felt had leadership potential. After high school I had completed a one-year automotive repair course. It wasn't exactly college, but who was I to argue with military logic?

I accepted the challenge with visions of stalling off the war as long as possible, expecting that the fighting would have ended by the time I had to go. If that illusion didn't hold true, then at least the extra training might increase the chance of survival for the men and myself I would be expected to lead. Unfortunately, my timing could not have been worse, for the war was at its peak.

I completed the NCO course and earned the grade of sergeant without ever setting foot in a war zone. The rank came with the resentment and suspicion of hardcore NCOs who had made the grade over a period of years, rather than months. I was sometimes ridiculed with names like Ninety-Day Wonder, Instant NCO, and Shake-n-Bake Sergeant. Their feelings were understandable, but the Army had given me an opportunity and I grabbed it.

In April 1969, I was sent to Fort Lewis, Washington, a reassignment station for GIs going to or returning from Vietnam. The process of militarily clearing the continental United States was a three-day psychological nightmare. The endless hours of waiting in long lines with extended periods of idleness gave us too much time to think about our destination. As infantrymen, we knew we had the Army's shortest life expectancy position and were being sent to fight in a war that had already claimed 25,000 American lives. It was also a war that was rapidly losing what little public support it had. We felt lonely and miserable knowing our inevitable departure was unnoticed or unpopular with a large segment of the nation.

To make matters worse, our stay coincided with the arrival of several planeloads of happy homeward-bound GIs. When we were in the clothes warehouse being issued jungle fatigues, they were being handed dress greens. The veteran GIs joked, hooted, and slapped each other on the back as they embraced their new freedom. They also shouted cruel obscenities in our direction—not meant to hurt us, but rather mocking the war, the Army, and the world. We did nothing in return except to watch them in awe, hoping that one year from now we too would be alive to experience the same high. The exuberant mood of the veterans left us so depressed that when word finally came to ship out, it was almost a relief.

We were bused to McChord Air Force Base in Washington state, where a waiting McDonnell Douglas DC-8 was fueled up and ready to go. The sun had already gone down when we boarded the plane so we were denied what would be, for many of us, a last look at our homeland. It was the final insult of an already gloomy process.

There were 250 GIs on our flight. We were mostly kids between the ages of eighteen and twenty-two, and hardly any of who knew each other. Only a few spoke or made eye contact. Most of the men sat quietly in a self-imposed daze. The mood was one of alienation and fear that we were flying off to our deaths. Sadly, for some that was true.

The 8,000-mile trip to the Republic of South Vietnam took nearly twenty hours. Our first stop was at Elmendorf Air Force Base just outside of Anchorage, Alaska, where we stayed only long enough to fill the fuel tanks. No one was allowed off the plane and we wondered why. It seemed unlikely anyone would wander off because it was winter there, and the only thing we could see in every direction was wilderness and snow. Once airborne again, our gloominess gave way to casual conversation or short naps. No one really slept because we wanted to savor our last hours of relative safety.

The next morning we landed at Haneda Airport in Tokyo, Japan. We were allowed off the plane for two hours, but only to a restricted area of the airport. As usual, there wasn't much to do but hang around. This was the first time I saw masses of Asians. I supposed the culture shock was an indication of things to come.

We left Tokyo and flew directly to the coastal port of Cam Ranh Bay in South Vietnam. Halfway there, our American greenbacks were exchanged for MPC (Military Payment Certificates), an all paper currency that looked like monopoly money with better pictures. Even the coin denominations were made of paper, just different colors. MPC was used to keep American dollars from flooding the fragile Vietnamese economy. To discourage profiteering on the back market, the MPC script was changed periodically, without notice.

When we left Fort Lewis, no one told us what to expect when we arrived at Cam Ranh Bay. I imagined our plane being shot out of the sky or that the instant we landed we would sprint across the runway to the nearest bunker. The closer we got, the more nervous I became. As we began our descent I looked around, expecting the crew to pass out M-16s for our defense. They didn't.

As we approached the airfield, I glanced out the window at the distant green mountains. Below us were irregular patches of undergrowth, grass huts, and rusting hulks of destroyed vehicles. I thought we were landing in the jungle on the edge of the battlefield. I was wrong again.

We landed without incident on a modern concrete runway. I stepped out of the plane to an unexpected sun-drenched paradise. The initial blast of tropical heat was shocking, but other than that Cam Ranh Bay looked like a scene from a movie. The bay area was a natural harbor with warm white sand stretching from the sparkling ocean water a quarter of a mile inland. Palm and banana trees dotted the landscape, shading picturesque thatch huts. Vietnamese civilians busily scurried in different directions as if they were rehearsing for a tourism advertisement. A war? Here? Impossible.

A deeply tanned staff sergeant led us around the back of the tiny air terminal where several US Air Force shuttle buses were parked.

"Gentlemen," he began in a loud southern drawl, "welcome to the Republic of South Vietnam. Pay no attention to the humidity because it actually gets worse in the summer. You will spend the next twenty-four hours at the 90th Replacement Battalion for orientation. Your paperwork will also be reviewed for errors, omissions, and false statements. While at the 90th, do not speak with, or attempt to make contact with the Vietnamese civilians working there. Now grab your gear and climb aboard the buses."

No one spoke as we timidly looked for seats. I was surprised to see the bus windows covered with chicken-wire screens to keep grenades from being tossed inside. The ten-minute ride took us through a tiny section of the sprawling military port. Along the way we passed huge sandbagged bunkers strategically positioned behind rows of concertina wire. GI guards were posted atop each bunker, but they seemed quite relaxed without their shirts or helmets on.

The 90th Replacement compound was small, consisting of two large open-wall rectangular buildings for processing our paperwork and a dozen smaller structures for housing and supplies. There was no air conditioning or fans. A boardwalk linked each building because the compound was a virtual sand pit.

The replacement process was similar to that at Fort Lewis because both stateside-bound GIs and those unfortunates just starting their tour were at the same location. The only difference was that the GIs going home weren't yet as jubilant as those at Fort Lewis because they were still in Vietnam.

There was, however, a notable contrast in our appearance to that of the veterans. We were "cherries" or FNGs (Fuckin' New Guys), and it was written all over us with our new fatigues, shiny boots, and pale winter complexions. We couldn't help but stare at the rugged-looking soldiers. A few wore clean pressed uniforms, but the majority sported faded fatigues with mud stains like they'd just been plucked from a foxhole.

As the processing continued, there were the usual long delays which the Army took advantage of to complete various work details. There were no septic systems in this area of Vietnam, so the most common chore was the cleaning of the enlisted men's latrine. The latrine was little more than a screened outhouse with partial walls concealing a person from the waist down. Anyone walking past could easily see who was sitting on the throne. The building sat on a cement slab. Inside was a long wooden bench with a row of ten toilet seats and no privacy partitions. Underneath each seat was a 25-gallon barrel shit-tub in which sloshed about varying amounts of human waste.

I was selected to supervise a five-man team tasked with exchanging the full barrels with empty ones. Tubs with only a small amount were dumped into full ones and then replaced under the seats for use while the cleaning was going on. As we played musical chairs with the barrels, a GI came in and defecated on the floor.

"Hey!" I yelled at him. "Can't you see that there's no tub underneath you? You just shit on the floor!"

He casually looked at me saying, "I never check to see where my turd is going to land. Do you?"

Who would argue with that logic? After he finished, one of my helpers shoveled up the mess and tossed it into a tub we had already pulled out.

The next step was to place the full barrels in a row and saturate them with diesel fuel. Then we lit them on fire, stirring each one until all the contents were consumed. The stench was unbelievable. Carrying tubs of shit was bad enough, but burning it was nearly too much.

If anyone had to urinate, they could not use the latrine. Only solids were allowed there. The urine made the tubs too heavy to pick up, and there was always the chance of getting splashed. Besides, piss doesn't burn very well. The only place to urinate was in a piss-tube, an exposed six-inch diameter pipe stuck in the ground at an angle. The tubes are never cleaned or moved to a new location, so before long the surrounding soil becomes saturated and the tubes overflowed. When that happened, most guys just pissed on the ground next to it. The accumulation of urine became so rancid that piss-tubes could be easily found in the dark.

Early the next day, many of us finished processing and were cleared to attend a full week of training at SERTS (Screaming Eagle Replacement Training School) in Bien Hoa, the giant US air base 200 miles west of Cam Ranh Bay. We flew to Bien Hoa in a C-130 Hercules transport, a four-engine turbo-prop aircraft used for airfreight or long distance troop deployment. The plane held forty of us, and we sat or spread out on the bare metal floor because there were no seats. There were no windows either, only two rows of six-inch glass portholes too dirty to see out of. The walls had no cover or insulation. Wires, pipes and framework were exposed. The four engines made such a racket that the only method of communication was by shouting or hand signals. It was like a flying garbage truck. The noise and vibration helped to keep me from thinking about what lay ahead. My immediate concern was whether the plane would get shot down or simply fall out of the sky. We landed without incident.

The SERTS training was to prepare us for permanent assignment into the 101st Airborne Division. Our instruction included classes on the Vietnamese people and their culture, the war and the enemy, and weapons familiarization. At night, we pulled bunker line guard duty. During the day, we performed light physical activities to help get us accustomed to the climate. However, just like all my other stops, I still had to go through the paperwork routine. As I did, the clerk specialist reviewing my file asked a few questions.

"Is there anything in your records you think should be removed?"

"Sure," I answered eagerly. "I've got an Article 15 for being AWOL (Absent Without Leave) from Fort Benning for two days. I was on a three-day pass, but I traveled too far and didn't get back in time."

He flipped through the pages searching for the document.

"Here it is," he said, as he tore it out and crumpled it into a ball. "Is there anything else you don't want in there?"

"How can you do that?" I asked, somewhat surprised.

"We like to give new guys a clean record so they will have no problems when they reach their units."

"How come I'm being placed in an airborne division? I'm infantry!"

"The NCO squad leaders in the 101st have a rather high casualty rate," he said seriously, "so they need you guys pretty bad."

That was comforting.

On the second day of training, a loudmouth infantry specialist named Doyen joined our group. He had been in-country for three months when he got wounded. After spending several weeks in the hospital, Doyen's unit didn't want him returning to the field without first refreshing his military skills. He resented the decision and made life intolerable for the rest of us by constantly complaining and making stupid wisecracks. While we were on a class break, he noticed my sergeant stripes and decided to direct his anger at me.

"You're a Shake-n-Bake, aren't you?" he asked.

"Yes," I answered. "Is that a problem?"

"You better believe it. You Shake-n-Bake's are walking death."

"What do you mean?" I asked, bewildered.

"How do you think I got wounded? A Shake-n-Bake fucked up. When I get back to my unit, I'm gonna fix him good. Ever hear of fragging?"

I had. It was the killing of superiors by their own men, usually by a hand grenade.

"Yeah, what's that got to do with me?"

"Are you kidding?" he laughed. "You better have your GI insurance paid up because you are going to die. Instant NCOs never make it home. You guys come over here, don't know shit about Nam, and then try to take charge of grunts who have survived for months without you. That's why there is such a high casualty rate for squad leaders. They get shot by their own men. So I'm warning you, when the shit hits the fan, you'd better look around to see where the bullets are coming from."

I stared at him for a few seconds in utter disbelief. My easy-going nature always had me looking at the humorous side of things, but his attitude was nothing to laugh about. I didn't know how to respond to such an encounter. Luckily, a first sergeant who overheard the conversation from inside the classroom walked out to lead Doyen away. The sergeant gave him hell for trying to scare the new guys and destroy their confidence. He also threatened to bring charges against Doyen for insubordination to a NCO. Doyen never bothered me again, but he certainly got me thinking about how my future subordinates might receive me when I get to the field.

Upon completion of SERTS training, I was sent to Camp Evans, a permanent duty station 400 miles north of Bien Hoa. There was little comfort in going to a war zone post known as a camp. Especially since this camp was located so close to the enemy's homeland in one of the northernmost regions of South Vietnam.

Transportation to Camp Evans was on another C-130 Hercules that proved to be just as nerve-wracking as the first one, except this flight was much longer. I ignored the plane's unpleasant surroundings and instead fantasized that I was back home with my family. I used to think that my parents were too hard on me, but now I would gladly trade any of their chores or discipline to be free of this situation.

Suddenly, a desperate feeling came over me as I realized just how good I had it at home and how much I missed everyone. Since the Army had taken away nearly everything that was important to me, I wondered how other GIs were able to deal with it. I wanted to cry, but pulled myself together knowing that my extra military training and strong family ties would help guide me.

The C-130 landed safely at Camp Evans, a circular tent city nearly one-half mile across, built on gentle rolling hills and surrounded by open grasslands. The camp is defended by perimeter bunker guards and fenced in with dozens of rows of concertina wire. A dirt road splits the camp down the middle. Trucks and jeeps comprised most of the camp's activity as they traveled back and forth with their tires kicking up red clouds of dust. Countless GIs inhabited the camp but very few carried any weapons.

Camp Evans was named after Lance Corporal Paul Evans, a Marine hero killed in action on December 22, 1966, near the present site of the camp. In 1967, the Navy Seabees built a major portion of the camp for the occupation of the US 1st Marine Division and the Army's 1st Cavalry Division. In October of 1968, the camp became the permanent home of 101st Airborne Division's 3rd Brigade.

Camp Evans was primarily self-sufficient. Besides the airstrip, it had its own fuel depot, motor pool, PX (Post Exchange), post office, ammunition dump, outdoor movie theater and bandstand, a seventy-bed hospital, and a system of gasoline-powered generators to provide electricity. The camp is re-supplied by both truck and air. However, no aircraft were housed there because the remote location made them too inviting of a target for the enemy.

The closest civilians to Camp Evans were from the village of Phong Dien, located about one mile from the main gate. Primitive by American standards, the village had no electricity or running water. The villagers lived in thatch huts clustered on tiny plots surrounded by hundreds of acres of fertile farmland. The farmer's most valuable possession was the domesticated water buffalo, which served as both tractor and transportation. Although the villagers were friendly toward us, the only civilians allowed inside Camp Evans were barbers and tailors.

I was assigned to Company A, 2nd Battalion, 506th Infantry Regiment. But before reporting to my unit, I was officially welcomed into the 101st Airborne Division by the 506th battalion commander. Lieutenant Colonel Brookes was a tall, imposing figure who demanded to be addressed by his radio call-name—Ajax. From inside his huge operations bunker, Ajax stood at a podium reading from notes to me, his audience of one. He gave the customary pep talk I'd heard a dozen times already since I'd been drafted.

"We have accepted the challenge of a very important mission in South Vietnam. Freedom will come at a high cost, sometimes at the supreme sacrifice, but we are willing to fight for justice and humanity. We will win this war. The tide is turning. There is light at the end of the tunnel. The US Army is the most powerful army on earth and we are making this country safe for democracy by squeezing the enemy from his position and destroying him with swift blows."

The colonel rambled on, waving his arms but never making eye contact. I felt as if he was talking to the wall. I started to daydream. Perhaps Ajax fancied himself to be like the Greek warrior of the same name or like the popular laundry detergent so he could clean up Vietnam. Either way, when he finally finished speaking, Ajax shook my hand and directed me to the site that would be my home base for the next year, provided I lived that long.

The 506th battalion area consisted of ten identical buildings referred to as "hooches." Lining both sides of a dirt roadway, the hooches resembled the rudimentary huts of a Boy Scout summer camp with walls that were half wood and half screens. Each hooch was elevated about a foot off the ground and surrounded by a four-foot high wall of sandbags.

The corrugated aluminum roofs were weighted down with several dozen sandbags to prevent strong winds from blowing the aluminum sheets off.

The main hooch was the battalion orderly room and field personnel headquarters. A first sergeant and a company clerk manned it. Two adjacent hooches were used as supply sheds, while three others housed rear echelon staff. The five companies of our battalion alternately used the remaining buildings whenever they came in from the field for rest periods.

Alongside the hooches were two water towers for showers. For toilet facilities, there was an officer's latrine and an enlisted men's latrine. Piss-tubes were also strategically placed for optimum use. Beyond that, nothing was done to make the area appealing. There was no grass or plants. The grounds consisted of oil-soaked red clay. The air was permeated with the odor of diesel, dirt, and urine. It was a dreary site.

I signed in with the company clerk, an unfriendly fellow who wasn't much for small talk.

"You'll be going to the field today sergeant," he said in a monotone rhythm, as if he were reading the words. "The supply room is the second hooch on the left. Someone there will outfit you with the necessary gear. After that, wait for the truck to take you out."

The supply sergeant must have known I was coming. When I walked in, he handed me a rucksack already filled with a three-day supply of C-rations, four canteens of water, four hand grenades, four smoke grenades, 100 rounds of M-60 machine gun ammunition, 24 magazines of M-16 rifle ammunition, a claymore mine, helmet, poncho, and entrenching tool. Then he handed me a brand-new M-16 rifle, serial number 127346. I'd remember the number as well as my name because that weapon would become a part of me. I would eat, sleep, fight and even shit with it, never leaving it more than an arm's length away.

The M-16 is a magnificent lightweight infantry rifle. It has a twenty-round magazine that can be emptied in the semi-automatic mode by firing one round for each pull of the trigger. On full automatic, a burst of twenty rounds could be fired in three seconds. We called that "rock n' roll."

I had an hour to kill before a pickup truck would take me out to my unit. It was too hot to sit in the sun so I waited quietly inside an empty hooch. Camp Evans was nothing like Cam Ranh Bay. Out the door I could see an almost deserted battalion area, where an occasional GI wandered past. On the horizon, the heavily vegetated Annamite Mountain range rose up from the plains before topping out at about 2,000 feet. The dark peaks looked sinister. The rugged territory was where the crafty NVA (North Vietnamese Army) and the persistent VC (Viet Cong) staged their raids. GIs called it "Injun Country."

Sitting alone like that gave me too much time to think. I felt numb. I stared blankly into space, wishing this was all a hideous joke. My trance was broken when a weary Grunt walked in. Unshaven and desperately in need of a bath, he must have just come in from the field. I watched as he carefully placed his gear on a cot. He never looked directly at me. As he headed back out the door, he stopped when he caught a glimpse of my sergeant's stripes. Then he stared at me oddly. Nervously, I stood up and put my hand out to say hello. He exhaled loudly out of the corner of his mouth before spitting on the floor near my feet. I quickly jerked my hand back. He shook his head, mumbled something about a cherry NCO, and walked outside.

"What the hell was that all about?" I wondered. These guys don't know anything about me and already I'm hated. Maybe that screwball Specialist Doyen at SERTS was right. Maybe being an Instant NCO could be a death wish.

Shortly afterward, the truck pulled up and I was on my way. It felt strange to be driven out to the combat zone in the back of a pickup truck because I thought we made an easy target. We drove out the rear gate of Camp Evans past well-tended rice paddies and tea tree gardens. The nearby village gave off a sour odor from the burning of incense and sandalwood. Away from the farmed area, the region abruptly changed to a desolate no-man's land. Known as the flat lands, the rolling grassy hills were similar to the prairies of Nebraska. However, thickets with giant ferns, elephant grass, bamboo hedgerows and other exotic plants made me think it was a prehistoric land.

In less than ten minutes we pulled up to the 2nd platoon's DDP (Daytime Defensive Position). The men were set in a one-acre bamboo thicket only a half-mile from Camp Evans and a half-mile from one of the sparsely populated hamlets that made up Phong Dien. I jumped off the truck as the driver waved to someone and yelled, "Fresh meat!"

The 2nd platoon consisted of more or less thirty soldiers, as GIs came and went to the rear for one reason or another. There were three squads of nine men each. Each squad had an NCO leader and two four-man fire teams. There was also one medic and one RTO (Radio Telephone Operator). A 1st Lieutenant platoon leader was in charge of the platoon with a senior NCO platoon sergeant as his second in command.

No one paid much attention as I made my way into the thicket. It looked like the platoon had been in there for quite a while, because the underbrush was matted down and litter was strewn about. Several guys had their shirts off and no one was wearing a helmet.

"Lieutenant Bruckner," I called out, not sure who he is. "Sergeant Wiknik reporting for duty."

A smiling face greeted me.

"Welcome to the platoon," Bruckner said, firmly shaking my hand. "Toss your gear down so we can get acquainted."

Bruckner looked to be about thirty years old. He spoke in an authoritative but friendly tone. My initial impression was that he's an all right guy, but he had an intense stare that made me feel uneasy.

"This is Sergeant First Class Krol," he said, motioning to the platoon sergeant, "my right hand man."

Krol was much older, probably forty. He was sitting on the ground and made no effort to greet me. I walked over and shook his hand. He didn't get up. When we made eye contact, Krol looked me over as if I carried a curse. I got the feeling he wasn't the friendly type.

"We've been expecting you," Bruckner said, deliberately speaking loud enough for everyone to hear. "I've had an open slot for an NCO for several weeks, but there is no one in the platoon who could step up to the task."

I glanced around to see that the men were all looking at me. I couldn't imagine what they were thinking. But I wondered if they were as bad as Bruckner said, or whether he was purposely trying to start me off at a disadvantage.

"Are there any other NCO graduates in the platoon?" I asked.

"We've got one, Sergeant Wakefield. He's fallen into line quite well. Life out here for Instant NCOs can be simple, if you know your place. Just observe what's going on, then do what you're told, when you're told."

I didn't dare ask what he meant. I could only guess that he expected me to be a yes-man, but I was always taught that respect should be earned, not demanded.

"So Wiknik," Bruckner began again, "did you enlist or were you drafted?"

"Drafted, sir."

"Ah, that's too bad. The Army's always looking for people who want to be here, not who have to be here. But, you never know, you might find a home in the Army. Take me for instance. I used to be a NCO, but I realized there are more money and more glory in being an officer. Remember General Custer, the Indian fighter? He didn't care about money; he only wanted the glory that came from being a hero. Me, I want both. If you've got the same desire, you're going to have to make a bold career move at re-enlistment time."

"Thanks, I'll be sure to think about it."

What a nut. I plan on having a long career all right—but as a civilian, not a soldier. Bruckner had the makings of a good leader because he experienced the Army from two perspectives, but his ambition seemed to be getting in the way.

I soon found out that Sergeant Krol was no better. To his credit, Krol was a veteran of the Korean War, but to everyone's discontent, he was also a fitness buff. Krol loved the Army and the infantry—sort of a Lifer's lifer. His favorite pastime was to show us "kids" how tough he was by taking different squads out and forcing them to hump until someone collapsed. He was a real charmer.

With Bruckner and Krol running the show, this was going to be a tough year. They had their own agenda and it didn't sound like they were going to be flexible. Initially, my encounters with Doyen and the spitting Grunt had me thinking that any personality problems would come from my squad members. But now, I was more concerned about my superiors. For my survival, and that of the platoon's, I'd have to find a way to convince the Grunts that I was on their side.

Lieutenant Bruckner gave me command of the second squad. My fire team leaders were Specialists Stanley Alcon and Freddie Shaw. Alcon was a California beach lover who constantly talked about girls, cars, and drag-racing. However, with jet-black hair and brown eyes, he didn't fit the blond, blue-eyed surfer boy image. Shaw was black and came from the Virginia Bible belt, so he never swore or used foul language. If he had to shit, he called it a rump dump; to piss was a tinkle. His two front teeth were gold capped, each had a pattern cut out of it so the white of the tooth showed through. One pattern was of a cross and the other was a star. Shaw rarely associated with other blacks. He never said why.

Our machine gunner was PFC (Private First Class) Jimmy Smith from Kentucky. Smith was tall, quiet, and spoke with a light Southern accent. PFC William Scoggins, a Texan, was the assistant machine gunner. He was also quiet and liked to stay out of everyone's way. Our pointman was Norman Keoka from Hawaii, who was affectionately nicknamed "Pineapple." The rest of the squad was a mix of average guys, mostly white and and one other black. Each man had combat experience and they all knew I was a Shake-n-Bake with no combat experience. Naturally, I was worried they might hold that against me, maybe even kill me for it. All I could do was speak honestly to the men and explain how I intended to run the squad until I gained experience.

"I'm what a lot of people call an Instant NCO," I began slowly and deliberately. "I didn't want to come to Vietnam. I wanted to stay in the World. That's why I went to NCO school, but you can see how well that worked. I'm not a Lifer, I got drafted. The only thing I want out of this war is to go home in one piece and to help you guys do the same. I don't know shit about Vietnam yet, but I hope you'll correct me anytime you think I'm doing something wrong. I don't want anyone getting fucked-up because of a stupid mistake. We're all in this together with a huge responsibility to one another, so I expect everyone to cover each other's ass."

I thought my little speech was a good icebreaker, but the men gave no reaction at all. They listened and bobbed their heads as if to pacify me. I realized it would take a lot more than talk to gain their respect. I also didn't want to make the mistake of giving the wrong impression with an ego remark like, "Here I am, and I'm in charge!"

During my first week, I wasn't allowed to do much of anything related to the war until I got accustomed to the heat and the platoon's daily routines. However, I didn't like sitting back while others went out on patrol or ambush because I stood out too much as it was. I wanted to blend in so badly that I purposely tripped and fell, hoping to soil my uniform to look like everyone else's. But the weight of my rucksack propelled me to belly flop into the mud. Everyone chuckled as I emerged looking like the victim of a water buffalo attack.

My dirty look paid off, but not with the old-timers. The next day, when a new guy joined my squad, he thought I was a seasoned veteran.

"Hi Sarge," he said, nervously introducing himself, "I'm PFC Howard Siner, but everyone usually calls me Howard. Do you mind being called Sarge?" I thought "Sarge" sounded stupid, but I didn't say anything about it.

"Put your gear over there," I said, pointing to a clump of bamboo. "Where are you from Siner?"

"The Bronx, New York City," he proudly announced, "home of the New York Yankees."

"And Cousin Bruce Morrow on WABC radio," I added.

"That's right!" Siner beamed. "Are you from the city?"

"No, central Connecticut. We don't have any decent radio personalities, so at night we listen to New York stations."

Siner nodded knowingly as he began to feel at ease.

"Boy, it must be rough out here. Look at you Sarge, you're filthy. Were you in a firefight today?"

Everybody laughed.

"No, Siner," I embarrassingly admitted, "I look like this because I fell in the mud. I haven't been here long enough to get sniped at, let alone be in a firefight. I'm just as cherry as you are."

PFC Siner was the tallest man in the platoon, but his size hid his calm demeanor. He had already spent two years in college, where he learned to take a slow methodical approach to situations, a trait many of us would come to admire. I had no way of knowing it at the time, but in the months ahead, Howard Siner would become one of my best and most trusted friends in Vietnam.

If there was anything tolerable about being in the field, it was that there was no military etiquette. We never stood at attention, saluted officers, or had inspections. The only formality we displayed was when we called the Lieutenant "Sir" and Krol "Sergeant." The most intolerable thing about the field was just being there, especially the physical demands.

Each man carried his world on his back. Up to seventy pounds of food, ammunition, and creature comforts were packed into a bulging rucksack. We were so familiar with its contents that we could easily retrieve a toothpick from it on a moonless night. Any personal items, like a wallet, a photograph, matches, or toilet paper were usually carried in our pockets inside tiny plastic bags to protect them from sweat or other moisture.

Mornings started with brushing our teeth from a canteen of rice patty water rendered potable by adding two purification tablets. Some men shaved, many did not, and no one ever used deodorant. Chow consisted of our choice of any one of a dozen equally unappetizing C-ration selections, which we either ate or went hungry. One meal, ham and lima beans, was so bad we called it "Ham and Mother-fuckers." But no meal was more hated than the infamous jellied version of ham and eggs. Even the villagers, who were always looking for a free meal, wouldn't eat it. A heat tablet that sat inside a tiny stove fashioned from a discarded cracker tin warmed the food. Nearly everyone drank coffee or hot chocolate, while a fortunate few made lemonade from powdered mixes sent from home.

Manners meant nothing in the field, even during mealtime. A person might urinate only five feet away, while another is burping, farting, or scratching his nuts. When someone needed to perform their daily constitutional, there was no privacy either. A buddy went along to guard against a VC sniper shooting him in mid-shit.

We rarely bathed. During the hottest part of the day, if we were located near a stream, some men took sponge baths, or jumped in clothes and all. We wore the same sweat-soaked fatigues for weeks at a time. The only way to get a clean or new uniform was if something got torn open. The only reserve clothing we carried was an extra pair of socks and a medium-size bath towel. The towel was issued for shaving and bathing, but it was most often used to wipe the sweat from our brows or draped over the shoulders to keep the rucksack straps from digging in.

April was the dry season, but about every fourth day a brief rain shower soaked us just before dusk, too late for anything to dry out. As hot as it was in the daytime, we were often cold during the night because everything was still wet. The soggy conditions were ideal for developing ugly pus-seeping body sores that never seemed to heal. This skin ailment, known to GIs as jungle rot, thrived in the damp areas of poorly ventilated wet clothing. Not everyone got the sores, but we took no chances either. No one wore under-shorts because crotch rot was a very real and painful blight.

We slept on the ground, usually on a waterproof poncho, sometimes covered by a lightweight poncho liner. As soon as the sun went down, it was as if the dinner bell had rung for the bugs. Mosquitoes that seemed to be as big as birds would carry someone off unless they were doused with the Army issue insect repellent we nicknamed "bug juice." It was a foul, eye-burning chemical strong enough to melt holes through rubber. Some guys developed a rash from the bug juice, so they wore a face net to keep insects from crawling into their eyes and ears.

Our AO (Area of Operations) outside the village of Phong Dien was relatively quiet with rare enemy confrontations. During the daylight hours, when not humping, we stayed concealed in one of the many bamboo thickets, playing cards, writing letters, sleeping, or just hanging around. Other than the mail, our only diversion from the war's activities was an illegal transistor radio each squad took turns passing around. AFVN (American Forces Vietnam Network) was the only American station with broadcasts limited to top forty rock, country western, the news, and some interviews. Otherwise strictly forbidden, the radio was a luxury allowed only during daylight in a considerably safe location.

Each night we moved to an ambush site to wait for an unsuspecting VC to walk by. The routine became boring, and boredom itself became an enemy. We did the same thing every day and every night. Relaxation followed by the extreme tension of waiting for something to happen that never did. After a while, the frustration affected us such that we wanted to fight. One day we blasted a large snake out of existence as it tried to slither past our position. It was a welcome relief just to fire our weapons.

Some of our duty was hard to take seriously, especially our daytime positions around the outskirts of the village. We were supposed to be concealed, but because there was such a maze of footpaths throughout the AO, the villagers would pass by our location and wave hello to us. Sometimes they would even come in looking for food. If we got real lucky, the local boom-boom girl would stop by to offer her services.

There was a dull humor to us hiding in the bushes. Our weapons could wipe out most anything in our way while the peasants walked by with only farm tools as they traveled to work their fields and rice paddies. Night, of course, was a different story. No one dared to venture from the security of the village. Once darkness fell, the area became a free-fire zone, and anyone out there was fair game. It was strictly shoot first, and ask questions later.

"We've got a dead Gook out there!
I can smell him!"

CHAPTER 2

No Career Moves for Me

With the coming of dusk, the mixed character of the local Vietnamese, who were friendly by day, often enemy by night, made relocation of our platoon a first priority for survival. After spending the entire day in a bamboo thicket, we moved at twilight to a nearby position to decoy any VC that may have observed us earlier.

I had been in the field only two weeks, but easily fell into the quiet dusk-assembling routine. There was no talking, and the only noises were the dull thuds of equipment being gathered. With everything collected, we stood motionless in the eerie quiet, darting glances at one another until the point man was given the hand signal to move out. With owl-like eyes I glanced at the men in front of me and observed the surrounding terrain in the fading light. To our left was a series of dark hulks–the village huts. To the right, the distant lights of Camp Evans. Directly ahead, the grass knolls had faded, casting heavy shadows on the low-lying shrubs and bamboo thickets.

Suddenly, the column stopped. The point man signaled us to kneel down as he pointed to the right. On the horizon, we could barely distinguish what appeared to be a squad of VC walking toward us. They moved to within 100 yards until their leader stopped, staring cautiously in our direction, somehow sensing our presence. He motioned his squad to retreat, but the instant they turned, we opened fire. The VC scattered as two M-60s, two M-79s and twenty-six M-16s unleashed an awesome five-minute burst of firepower. I expected the only remains would be tiny chunks of flesh.

As quickly as it had been shattered, the silence returned. Sergeant Krol ordered us to form a line and assault in a wave. Assault? In the dark? My mind raced. I felt I was looking into the face of death. We moved rapidly toward the impact area, listening intently for sounds but hearing only our own heavy breathing and the brush rustling underfoot. I tried to stay beside the man on each side of me, not wanting to neither fall behind nor get ahead. It was the safety in numbers thing; the age-old herd mentality that has not yet been bred out of humans.

The irregular vegetation looked like the perfect hiding place for a wounded VC to wait in the darkness to cut my throat as I passed by. I squeezed every bit of energy to visually penetrate each shrub. Suddenly, a bush in front of me moved! I swung around firing wildly into the shadows. Then I wondered why I was the only person shooting.

"Who fired those rounds?" shouted Lieutenant Bruckner.

"Wiknik, sir," I answered sheepishly.

"Whadya get?"

I closed in on the undergrowth. There was nothing there. I only thought it had moved.

"I shot a bush, sir."

"Nice going, Cherry. Let's hope you killed it," he chided me as a few snickers were heard within the ranks. "I don't want it sneaking up on us in the middle of the night."

We continued combing the area for another ten minutes but found nothing. It was now too dark to see anything, so we decided to abandon the search until first light.

The platoon separated into four-man positions to set up a perimeter guard about one hundred feet across. The Lieutenant, his RTO and the Platoon Sergeant formed a CP (Command Post) in the center.

My position had PFCs Smith and Scoggins, each with nearly six months of experience in the field. They were regular guys who had trained together stateside, arrived together in Vietnam, and had become close friends. They didn't bother anyone, and in return just wanted to be left alone. They never volunteered for anything, but they also never refused to do their part. I felt safe with them.

The other GI in our position was Specialist Harrison, the platoon's longevity man with more than ten months in the field. Eager to return home, he was always pulling some goofy stunt, trying without success, to get sent to the rear. His nasal Kentucky twang and permanent grin sometimes made us think his antics were a sure sign he was a burned-out GI. Standing a scant five and one-half feet tall, three inches shorter than me, he was someone we all looked up to.

Early in his tour, Harrison had taken part in a night ambush of what was believed to be an North Vietnamese squad. Instead, his platoon had engaged the lead element of a company-sized enemy force. The ambush turned into a bloody firefight complete with aerial flares, artillery, and air support. During the battle, Harrison ran out of ammunition and was forced to scavenge M-16 magazines from a dead GI. While trying to reload his weapon, Harrison looked up to see an enemy soldier standing five feet away pointing an AK-47 at his head. When the NVA pulled his trigger, the rifle misfired, giving Harrison the split-second edge he needed to bayonet the soldier to death. The nightmarish event changed Harrison forever.

"Who wants first guard?" asked Smith.

"How about giving it to the bush killer?" offered Harrison.

"Yeah," said Scoggins, "he sure as hell won't crash tonight."

"Okay you guys, so I was nervous. That was my first contact."

"Man, that wasn't shit," chided Harrison. "The only thing we did was scare the crap out of those Gooks. You ain't seen nothin' yet."

"Tell me something," I said curiously, "I've been in the field for two weeks now and still don't know what the hell we're doing patrolling around this village."

"Well, it's like this," said Harrison, "the VC are out here every night trying to get stuff from the villagers like food, clothes, money, recruits, even information. But most of the villagers are friendly toward us and don't want anything to do with the Gooks. So, our job is to ambush the VC and let 'em die for their cause."

"Well, now that we made enemy contact, how come we're not digging in?"

"You kidding? If we dug in every night this place would be so full of holes we'd never be able to move in the dark without breakin' our fuckin' necks."

"What if the VC counter attack in the middle of the night?"

"They don't do that shit anymore. Now they just run around setting up booby traps, hitting us only when it's to their advantage. Besides, we're so close to Camp Evans that we can bring the world down on top of them and they know it."

"Hey," laughed Smith. "Did you guys see that dip shit Halveston firing his M-60 over Evans?"

"Yeah," said Scoggins, "he's so stupid. Those tracers sailed right past the bunker line. I'm surprised they didn't shoot back at us."

"They were probably sleeping," added Harrison. "That bunker line guard duty is really boring."

"Here, Wiknik," said Scoggins. "Take this handful of stones."

"Stones? Stones for what?"

"To throw at Halveston. He's always falling asleep during his guard and he snores so loud that he might give away our position. So we toss stones at him to keep him awake."

"Geez, I can't believe that guy is in the field."

"Neither can we, but so far he's been harmless."

The banter continued until my companions settled down for their turn at sleep. The stillness of the evening surrounded me as I sat alone, contemplating my chances of surviving the year-long tour of duty. It didn't look promising if more nights started out like this one had.

At dawn, we performed our morning routines while waiting for enough light to resume our search. That's when Harrison started up.

"We've got a dead Gook out there! I can smell him!"

"Knock it off, Harrison!" shouted the Lieutenant.

"Hey, man. I can smell him," he growled back, pointing toward an opening in the brush. "Look over there."

Nobody believed him, of course, thinking it was just another one of his acts to convince us he's crazy. Krol took five guys to check it out just in case. After a few minutes one of the men yelled, "Over here! A dead Gook!"

"I told you we got one," Harrison smugly said. We looked at him in amazement, wondering whether he had some magical power or if he was just plain nuts.

I couldn't resist the temptation to check out our kill. Death must have been instantaneous. The body lay face down with arms and legs frozen in a running position. Near the right shoulder blade, the shirt had a tiny bloodstained bullet hole. One of the men prodded the corpse several times before rolling it over. Each person stepped back with the same astonished look on his face. I felt nausea. There was a gaping hole in the shoulder big enough to put a softball in. The mutilated tangle of splintered bones and flesh seemed unreal. The face was contorted with teeth gritted and eyes closed. I squirmed inside as the lifeless form became recognizable. The physique was that of a young woman, maybe in her late teens, about my age. We had killed a girl. During my sheltered civilian life I had never been to a wake or funeral, and now the first dead human I set my eyes upon was a female with her shoulder blown away. It was sickening.

A few of the platoon members came over for a glimpse of the body. The others, not caring, continued eating and talking. I was subconsciously glued to the spot, watching as the Lieutenant searched over the grisly corpse.

"She didn't even have a weapon," I said faintly.

"The Gooks know the rules. Don't get caught after dark."

"Holy fuck!" shouted Stan Alcon as he wandered over. "That's the boom-boom girl I screwed the other day!"

"Are you sure?" asked Lieutenant Bruckner.

"I'm positive. She came around with her pimp about three days ago. Cost me five bucks."

"She was probably a VC, but we won't know until someone from G-2 checks these documents she was carrying."

"See if she's got my five bucks."

"There's no money, you asshole! Only these papers."

I walked back to fill Harrison in. He seemed happy.

"Good," Harrison remarked. "We don't get laid that much, so now them Charlies won't get laid either."

The villagers started coming around then. After all the shooting the night before, they knew something was up, but we wouldn't let any of them near the corpse. An hour later, an Intelligence officer and two GIs drove out in a pickup truck to recover the body. They loaded her into the back like a piece of firewood. As they drove away the villagers chased after them, perhaps to see if they could recognize the remains. When the truck was out of sight, we hiked off in the opposite direction as if shooting women was routine.

Between the ambushes and hiding in thickets, each squad took turns going out on a RIF (Reconnaissance in Force) patrol. A RIF involved sweeping over large areas to make our presence known so the village would be less likely to be threatened by the VC. Except for booby traps, however, there was very little evidence of enemy activity. There weren't a lot of them, but enough to keep us on our toes.

The most common booby trap was a trip-wired hand grenade, usually placed inside a discarded C-ration can or tied to a tree. A thin wire attached to the grenade pin is stretched across a footpath just high enough so anyone walking by would kick the wire, activating the grenade. Our fear of hidden traps forced us to be constantly vigilant for wires or suspicious objects. Whenever a booby trap was located, we hooked onto the trip-wire with a rope then tugged on it from a safe distance to set it off.

The RIFs and booby trap hunts were radical on-the-job training exercises, with very serious consequences. One afternoon, two men were considered lucky to receive only minor wounds when one of them tripped a poorly aimed trip-wired grenade. Also, on two separate occasions, men were evacuated due to heat exhaustion. Losing men to injuries or sickness was an expensive way for our platoon to gain experience. It was obvious we had developed some bad tactical habits. The men bitched about it, but only to each other. No one dared make a formal complaint for fear that Krol would make us hump all the more. That's when I decided it was time for me to speak up. Even though I was the new guy with minimal experience, I figured there was nothing to lose by offering alternatives. Besides, if anything I said was of value, it might contribute to the success of each mission. With that in mind, I confidently went to the CP to discuss my concerns with Bruckner and Krol.

"I've been watching how we operate," I started, "so I thought you might be interested in my observations."

"Go ahead, Wiknik," Lieutenant Bruckner said curiously. "Whatcha got?"

"Well Sir, our AO seems to have its fair share of hand grenade booby traps, so I think we should be crushing our C-ration cans to keep the

Gooks from using them against us. We should also be walking in single file, stepping where the last man did, not sweeping over the terrain like we're trying to find booby traps. I also think we could eliminate the heat exhaustion problem if we humped during the cool of the morning rather than the blazing heat of midday."

Before responding, Lieutenant Bruckner paused to look at Krol who stared back at him with his eyebrows raised. Their silence worried me.

"Sergeant Wiknik," Bruckner began, sounding slightly irritated. "Do you think we don't know what we are doing out here?"

"No sir, that's not it at all. I just think some of the things we do are dangerous and should be done differently."

"I'm going to let you in on a little secret," he said rigidly. "We're in the middle of a fuckin' war here, and war is dangerous. We cannot be expected to win this thing if we sit back playing it safe. However, I'm not an unreasonable man, Sergeant Krol and I will consider your suggestions. But you may want more field experience before you get too many bright ideas. Most old-timers don't like it when Cherries try to change things overnight. You better think about that."

I didn't know if I had done the right thing or not. They looked at me as if I was a malcontent who had just insulted them. Like typical Lifers, they either doubted my ability and training, or felt threatened by it.

Several hours later, Bruckner told me I was correct about the crushing of C-ration cans and also about the way we walked on our patrols, but he sure didn't like admitting it. There was also a price to pay for my speaking out, we still went out on mid-afternoon patrols, and my squad was selected for the honor more than any other.

The everyday RIFs got old real fast, especially when it got so hot that Krol stayed back, sending us out by ourselves. His attitude made me more determined that no one from my squad would get hurt or sick while I was in charge. On my next patrol, we traveled far enough to get out of sight of the platoon then hid in the bushes. I kept calling in different locations on the radio to make it appear as if we were moving.

No one in the squad said a word. In fact, the guys were obviously relieved, not just because we were avoiding booby traps, but also because it was too hot to be humping around. I knew it was no way to fight a war, but because of the extreme heat and no enemy activity, I felt it was the safest way to operate. Besides, there was always a chance that a stupid Gook might stumble onto us, instead of us onto him.

Occasionally we sat watching a squad from one of the other platoons pass in the distance while conducting their RIF. One of those times, a squad from the 3rd Platoon discovered us tucked away. Their leader was Sergeant James Burke who, like myself, was an Instant NCO, but that was all we had in common. Burke had been in Vietnam only two weeks longer than me, but had quickly given in to the Lifer mentality. To him, being a squad leader meant total control over subordinates. As his men approached, they were tired, sweaty, and hot.

"Hi guys," I cheerfully called to them, "come over and sit in the shade for a while."

"You people stay put!" ordered Burke, not allowing his men to get out of the sun.

"Come on Burke," I said sympathetically. "It's too fuckin' hot to be pushing your guys like that."

"Don't worry about my men; at least we're doing our job, not like you hiding in the bushes. I heard you on the radio, this isn't the position you called in, unless you can't read a map."

"We're conserving our energy," I retorted. "You never know when a boom-boom girl will come around and we want to be well rested."

Everybody laughed, even his men. But they abruptly stopped when Burke glared at them.

"You're a real comedian Wiknik. You would be of more use in a USO (United Services Organization) show because it's obvious you're not doing any good out here."

"I'd rather be in a USO show than out here!" I shot back.

"You're setting a poor example for your men. If I were you, I would get back to the job you are being paid for and keep this area clear of VC."

"That is so stupid. The VC knows we've got patrols out and they won't approach the village in broad daylight. The only time they move is after dark."

"Yes," he said with a sly grin, "and their strategy can be rewarding. After all, you did kill a VC girl the other night."

So, he had heard about it. "Yeah, but we don't get off on killing women. Maybe you do, as long as the kill can be used for the body count. We're just here to put our time in and then go home. Man, we don't even get much support from the people back in the World. They're either protesting or running off to Canada. Do you want to die for something like that?"

"You have a bad attitude, Wiknik. You won't be an NCO much longer with all that negativism."

"Look, if we come across the Gooks, we'll fight, but I'm not going to look for trouble unless we have the advantage."

"A Grunt's job is to search out and destroy the enemy, not hide in the bushes from them. You are not doing your job."

I was raised to be tolerant of narrow-minded people, but Burke was so aggravating that I finally lost my cool.

"Burke," I began in a snotty tone, "you are nothing but a gung-ho asshole who's going to get someone killed. I don't know what these poor bastards ever did to deserve someone like you. The Army must have been pretty desperate to make you a NCO. You better lighten up on the Lifer bullshit before you find that the VC isn't your only enemy."

Everyone silently watched as Burke began leading his squad away.

"This doesn't end here Wiknik!" he barked over his shoulder. "There's an unwritten law that forbids NCOs to argue with each other in front of their men. You just violated that law."

"Tell someone who cares!" I yelled back.

I didn't know if Burke would make trouble for me, but I didn't care. The silly smirks on my men's faces told me of their support. I was finally accepted.

Our next RIF found us at the Camp Evans dump located in a large natural depression just outside the bunker line. We were responding to a call that the villagers had been raiding the dump and a few of them were bitten by rats while picking through the garbage. To the destitute peasants, the dump was a goldmine, but that didn't matter to the Army. Our job was to kick them out and keep them out.

This was my first official dealing with the locals, and it was a fiasco. There were about fifteen of them, mostly old women, a couple of young mothers, and the rest kids. After we arrived, it was easy to round them up, probably because we had the guns. But when we told them they had to leave, the only English they seemed to know was "Fuck you, GI."

Talking wasn't going to do it, so we herded the villagers together and chased them away. After a few minutes, they appeared at the far side of the dump. We went after them again but they disappeared over a small hill. By the time we walked across the dump, they were back at the entrance, pointing and laughing at us. The villagers were obviously hard core scroungers with no plans to leave until their picking was done.

When we rousted them for the third time, they taunted us more by yelling, "Fuck you!" and making obscene gestures. That's when we decided enough was enough and that our only remaining option was to shoot tear gas at them. We fired three M-79 gas canisters, which were surprisingly effective. They screamed like banshees and scattered. Our action sure wouldn't win us any friends, but it was still funny to watch.

We hung around for a while, hoping that the villagers had had enough and gone home. But they regrouped and appeared several hundred feet behind us yelling again, so we shot more tear gas at them. Only this time, they didn't run. The gas cloud was suspended in front of them for a moment, and then it drifted back in our direction. We were downwind and had gassed ourselves! The villagers set us up and we fell for it. Luckily, by the time the gas traveled to our position it had weakened enough to be only a minor irritant, but it was pretty embarrassing. We finally consented to let them take what they wanted, but we spot-checked each one as they came out to be sure that they didn't find any live ammunition or something their VC friends could use against us.

As we searched their pickings, I noticed a woman who appeared to have something concealed under her blouse near her chest. We questioned her but she didn't understand us until one of my men pulled his shirt over his head, mimicking what we wanted her to do. She finally got the message.

The woman started to jabber then lifted her blouse exposing her breasts. We almost shit. She had one normal small breast but the other was swollen to the size of a grapefruit. Our jaws dropped and we stood motionless, afraid that the affliction might be contagious. Not wanting to find out, we waved at her to quickly pick up her stuff and go away.

The woman noticed our repulsion and laughed. Then she held the swollen breast with both hands, pointing it at us like a weapon. As we slowly backed off, she squeezed hard and let loose a stream of pus. I ducked from the spray so she took aim at Howard Siner, hitting him in the arm. We ran around like a bunch of kids while she chased us trying to squirt anyone in her range. Even the villagers were laughing at us. When the woman finally ran out of ammunition she calmly collected her pickings and waved good-bye. We saw no reason to check anyone else. How could we? An American patrol had just gassed itself and been defeated by an infected tit. After that, the Army sent a bulldozer out every afternoon to crush and bury the garbage.

*   *   *

Our AO extended only two or three miles from the edge of the village. Although it wasn't far out, I noticed something eerily quiet about the region. There were no songbirds. It was as if they knew there was a war on and the only safe place for them was close to the village. Their absence created a sad environment, increasing my feeling of remoteness from the outside world. Vietnam was far away from America and we were even farther. Grunts were so detached from everything that it felt as if we were on a planet in outer space while everyone forgot where we were. Our common bond was that we endured the same frustrating, unforgiving conditions that had control of us. We saw the infantry as more than just an experience; it was a culture of depending on each other for sanity and survival.

The misery of being in the field didn't start new with each day; it just never ended from the day before. To cope, GIs conceived a favorite saying, "Fuck it. Don't mean nothin.'" No matter how bad things got—the weather, the enemy, or the morale, we focused on a hardened "Fuck it. Don't mean nothin.'" Our only consolation was that the passage of time brought each man closer to his ticket home.

The misery also came at us from the upper ranks of the Army. Colonel Ajax was being replaced by a Lieutenant Colonel who called himself Condor (they must sit up all night thinking of those code names). Ajax wanted to turn over a clean AO, so his last directive was for us to go back to all of our daytime positions to bag any discarded litter and carry the trash to a point where a truck could pick it up. I suggested burying it in a deep hole, but Bruckner said we wouldn't be following orders if we did that. So we carried the garbage, sometimes as far as a half-mile. There is nothing like having a tidy war.

In keeping with Army tradition, it seemed that no matter what we did, someone else didn't like the way it was done or that it was done at all. Such was the case with the cleanup operation. Colonel Condor couldn't care less how spotless the AO was because his philosophy wasn't to have a clean war. He wanted destruction. He ordered us to burn anything that would ignite, except of course, the village. We set fire to bamboo thickets, hedgerows, grassy areas, everything. The burning turned out to be a good idea because after the flames subsided we found booby-trapped artillery rounds that were previously hidden. We burned for several weeks with some of the fires continuing through the night. We loved it.

About every third day we returned to the same bamboo thicket to set up our DDP because it could easily be re-supplied by truck and we would receive a hot meal at the same time. This particular thicket was about one hundred feet in diameter, plenty of room to conceal thirty men. But our available resting area became increasingly smaller at each visit. In basic training, soldiers were taught the field rule of digging a cat hole in which to bury their human waste. Some of the guys must have slept through that class because they would shit almost anywhere, leaving it uncovered for some poor slob to step in. There were few things more disgusting than cleaning someone's turd from the cleats of a jungle boot.

I could put up with the poor toilet training, but it didn't seem like a good idea to come back to the same thicket so often. It was like inviting the Gooks to set up booby traps. I felt there was no other option but to speak with Bruckner about it.

"Lieutenant," I began, hoping he would accept my opinions in the spirit intended, "I think we're taking a chance at returning to this location just to get hot food and mail. The Gooks must know our routine by now, so what's to stop them from booby trapping the area?"

"You don't know when to quit, do you?" he asked, sounding irritated. "Why do you find it necessary to continue questioning my judgment?"

"Well Sir, in practically every infantry class I attended, the instructors harped on how the VC takes advantage of our bad habits to set up their ambushes and booby traps. I'm just trying to keep the men from getting killed or wounded."

"This is not fuckin' NCO school!" he shouted angrily. "This platoon will be run as I see fit, not by some chalkboard pipe dream! If the time ever comes when the men need to know the textbook explanation of a troop deployment, I'll be sure to call on you! Now get back to your position and leave the thinking to me!"

I didn't realize Bruckner was so touchy, or that I was that aggravating. Whatever the case, his attitude convinced me that I should direct my energy toward keeping the men safe. If I ever need my backside protected, they'd be the ones more apt to do it, not Bruckner or Krol."

The next day, our company commander came out to visit the platoon. Captain Hartwell was a distinguished looking individual, about thirty years old. He spoke as if he had a strong educational background. He was a Lifer, but didn't display the typical Lifer mentality I have been experiencing. While reviewing our defenses, he talked briefly with some of the men and seemed genuinely concerned that our basic needs were being met. Hartwell also spent several minutes speaking privately with Bruckner and Krol. When they finished, I was summoned to the CP.

"Sergeant Wiknik," Hartwell began in an accusing tone, "it's been brought to our attention that you were given an assignment and failed to carry it out. Three days ago, Sergeant Burke observed your squad tucked in the bushes when you were supposed to be on a RIF. What have you got to say for yourself?"

His knowing about my encounter with Burke caught me off guard. "It was a very hot day, Sir," I answered, trying to stay as close to the truth without actually telling him the truth, "so we found a shady place to rest. One of my men, Specialist Harrison, felt we were being followed. So I radioed in a distant location so we could watch to see if anyone showed up, but instead, Burke found our lookout spot. He accused me of hiding from the enemy and not being able to read a map. That's when we started to argue."

"If what you're telling me is true, why would Burke make such an accusation?"

"To me, Burke seems obsessed with killing Gooks and he's jealous about us shooting that VC girl last week. Maybe he figured by trailing us, a VC might get flushed his way, but he got caught in his own scheme."

"Both your stories sound like bullshit," replied Hartwell. "But I don't have the time or energy to referee squabbling NCOs. You two are going to have to learn to get along, so work it out between yourselves."

"It won't happen again, Sir."

Only four weeks in Vietnam and already I was on everyone's shit list. What the hell, I still felt my actions were justified under the circumstances. From that day on, I was a marked man. Both Bruckner and Krol kept a watchful eye, waiting for me to screw up. It wasn't long before they caught me.

The next night I was assigned to a two-hour radio watch, but the man I was supposed to relieve failed to wake me up. In turn, I failed to wake up the next guy, which left us for several hours with no radio contact. In the morning, Lieutenant Bruckner charged everyone involved with an Article 15 for sleeping on guard and levied a $50.00 fine on top of it. Krol also added to the punishment in his own brutal way with plenty of extra humping. I believe Bruckner gave us the Article 15 because I was involved, and he wanted to begin building a case against me.

At least the squad backed me up. PFC Scoggins confided that the entire squad was on my side, and added that it was a welcome relief to finally see someone stand up and try to change the arbitrary tactics we were forced to follow. The encouragement of the men fueled my determination to continue fighting the Lifers and the war with as little recklessness as possible.

"That's all the guys want you to do, keep them alive."

CHAPTER 3

The Battle for Hamburger Hill

I had just completed my first month in-country when our company was sent to Eagle Beach, the 101st division rest site, to enjoy a three-day stand down. A stand down was a Grunt's best friend because it was one of the few times that officers and senior NCOs did not have total control over us. They relaxed with their peers, and we relaxed with ours.

Since Eagle Beach was nearly fifty miles from Camp Evans, we thought the Army would fly us there. Instead, we rode in the back of ten large transport trucks. Our convoy rolled out Camp Evans' front gate onto Quoc-Lo 1, the only blacktop route in northern I Corps. Running parallel to the South China Sea, Quoc-Lo 1 connected the region's coastal cities and villages with a steady flow of US and ARVN (Army of the Republic of Vietnam) military vehicles and civilian buses and motor scooters.

As we traveled through the flatlands of Phong Dien, I got to view the inhabitants of the Vietnam I would rarely see: attentive farmers, mostly old men and women, working tiny plots of land to support their meager existence. They lived in poverty yet maintained the traditional work ethic passed down from their ancestors. In the midst of war they labored as if the outcome didn't matter. Whoever the victor was, they simply wanted to keep their land.

Several miles later we began entering the heavily populated streets of Hue, Vietnam's ancient capital. Hue was a city of constant activity. The streets were filled with kamikaze-driven motor scooters and taxicabs. Vietnamese outdoor markets bustled with shoppers while sidewalk vendors sold everything from stolen black market goods to live chickens. The air reeked of exhaust fumes, dried fish, and burning incense. At each major street intersection there was a sandbagged military checkpoint reminding everyone that even the large city of Hue was not immune from the war.

One of the most pleasant sights in Hue was the teenage schoolgirls dressed in the traditional Vietnamese ao dais apparel. The girls looked like travel brochure models as they strolled beneath shade trees. We waved to them but they would not acknowledge us.

An hour later we arrived at Eagle Beach, a military installation so far removed from the war that it looked and felt more like summer camp. We bunked in cabin-style hooches perched a mere two hundred feet from the sandy beaches of the South China Sea. Gone were the drab surroundings of concertina wire, bunkers, and piss-tubes. In their place were asphalt courts for basketball, tennis, and volleyball. We could swim in the ocean or water ski in the nearby bay. Some soldiers caught up on sleep, wrote letters home, or hung around the jukebox listening to the latest tunes from the outside world. Each night there was live entertainment from different Filipino bands followed by a movie. While all this was going on, we had nonstop hot dogs, hamburgers, and traditional barbecue fare, plus all the beer and soda we could handle.

Our only responsibility was that two members from each platoon took turns guarding the weapons and equipment. Since I considered myself a Cherry, and somewhat unworthy of celebrating with old-timers who had seen combat, I frequently volunteered for the guard duty. Although guarding equipment was not an NCOs job, I wasn't going to make my men do anything that I wouldn't do myself. I figured simple acts like this would help the men realize I was on their side.

PFC Howard Siner pulled guard with me a few times. We talked about sports, music, and our common interests from living only one hundred miles apart back in the World. But Siner surprised me when he spoke about what he thought his role should be in the squad.

"You're the Sarge," he said, as if making a profound statement, "and it's my job to protect you."

"What the hell are you talking about?" I asked, thinking he had lost his mind.

"I've been watching you, and I've been watching how the men react to you not being afraid to question stupid tactics. Some of them nicknamed you 'Mugwump' because of your independent thinking. They want you to keep it up. Bruckner and Krol probably hate you, but we think you're doing a good job."

"Listen Siner, I'm flattered by their faith in me, but I haven't been here long enough to take on that kind of pressure. I haven't even been under fire yet. I'm just trying to keep everyone alive."

"That's all the guys want you to do, keep them alive."

I didn't realize things were so bad that the men would start placing their trust in a new guy like me, but it sure felt good to be wanted.

Eagle Beach strengthened our camaraderie but stand downs, like all good things, must come to an end. Before we knew what happened, our three days were up and we were sent back to Camp Evans. Some men returned with cans of beer hidden in their rucksacks so they could stay drunk, but the majority came back with hangovers that were magnified by the bumpy truck ride and the diesel exhaust fumes.

Upon arrival, Captain Hartwell called everyone together to inform us of our new assignment. "Men," he began, sounding quite official, "we have a new AO. We are going into the A Shau Valley. Some of your buddies have run into a problem out there and we're going in to help. Each man will carry a minimum of 300 rounds of M-16 ammo, 100 rounds of M-60 ammo, six frags and six M-79 grenades. I suggest you start getting your shit together because we will be on the chopper pad before dawn."

"Gawd!" Stan Alcon exclaimed. "The Gooks drive trucks in the A Shau. We're going there? No more booby traps and shit like that. Now you're talking ambushes and bayonets."

The situation sounded depressing. Up to this point we had only contended with small infiltrations of VC, but soon we would be facing a fierce opponent who did not hesitate to attack openly and in large numbers. I wondered just what kind of trouble our buddies were facing out there.

The A Shau is a 35-mile fertile valley paralleling the western South Vietnam frontier less than two miles from the Laotian border. As early as 1962, the American and Vietnamese military established bases in the valley to protect the Montagnard inhabitants. In 1966, the NVA had overrun the last of the bases and drove out all the tribesmen. For the next two years, the Communists had unchallenged control of the region.

The close proximity to the Ho Chi Minh trail and Laotian sanctuaries allowed the NVA to develop the valley into a formidable supply and staging area. In 1968, the 1st Calvary Division and the 101st made several successful raids, disrupting enemy supply routes in the valley. Now, the renewed presence of the 101st denied the NVA the use of Highway 548, a major artery of the Ho Chi Minh Trail. The loss of this dirt truck route, which zigzagged along the valley floor, forced the NVA into the new strategy of taking a defensive position and fighting.

We learned that four companies from the 3/187th Infantry had been engaged with the enemy for eight straight days. The action was initiated on May 10 as our troops conducted sweeps of the area. During that first day, they discovered a network of enemy trails, communication wires and cables, spider holes, huts, bunkers, and discarded miscellaneous clothing and equipment. Whenever the GIs neared Dong Ap Bia Mountain (Hill 937 on military maps) they were shot at by snipers with RPGs (Rocket Propelled Grenades) or ambushed by machine gun fire and command detonated claymore mines dangling from bushes and trees.

The first concentrated attempt to take Hill 937 occurred on May 14. Up to that day, most of the action had been on the ridges and in the draws around the base of the hill, making it difficult to pinpoint the location of the main enemy forces. For the next four days, artillery and tactical air strikes pounded away at the hill, pulverizing the terrain, but not enough to soften the enemy so the hill could be taken. Each successive ground assault met fiercer resistance. There was no question the NVA were on the hill in formidable numbers and they had no intention of leaving without a fight. By the time our company arrived several assaults, countless snipers, and dozens of ambushed patrols left an estimated fifty GIs dead, fifteen missing and presumed dead, and almost 300 wounded. Worse yet, four of the dead and 53 of the wounded resulted from three separate incidents of misguided helicopter gunship fire. The fact the

NVA had lost men at ten times our rate was of little comfort to men who watched as Americans accidentally killed Americans.

On Sunday morning, May 18, it was still dark when we assembled on the helipad. The rumble of three giant CH-47 Chinook transport helicopters broke the ominous pre-dawn silence. The choppers drifted in slowly, landing one at a time, staying on the ground just long enough for thirty-five men to climb aboard each ship.

We sat against the fuselage wall, facing each other across the aisle. The Chinook was too noisy for us to talk, so no one bothered. We just looked past each other and out the windows at the shadowy mountains below. During the half-hour flight the morning sun began to shine on the mountaintops. From where we sat, the jungle below looked peaceful; everyone knew differently.

We were taken to a staging area on the A Shau Valley floor where we had to provide our own security while waiting for the next phase of the operation. After the Chinooks roared out of sight the men became unusually quiet as we examined our new surroundings. The valley was less humid than the flatlands, almost comfortable. But that was the only thing that felt good about this eerie place. Just outside our position, ten-foot tall elephant grass had been matted down by the Chinook's powerful rotor wash, leaving nothing to conceal us if we were attacked. Beyond that, steep mountains with sharp ridges walled up the valley where fog and clouds seemed to manifest themselves from the triple canopy jungle. The A Shau Valley was a strange place that seemed not to want us there any more than we wanted to be there.

"Do you think we're being watched?" Freddie Shaw asked, looking up at the ridgeline.

"Are you kidding?" Harrison laughed. "Every fuckin' NVA in the valley knows we're here. If those three Chinooks didn't give our position away, nothing will."

"It looks like the Gooks could easily mortar us from those ridges," added Scoggins. "Or maybe attack us from the other side of that tall grass."

"Knock it off!" shouted Lieutenant Bruckner. "They'll be plenty of time to worry about the NVA when we get to where we're going."

No one said anything else.

After an hour-long wait, sixteen Bell-UH1D slicks arrived to take us to our destination. We piled aboard, six men to a bird, our feet dangling out the open doors. The ships lifted off but didn't go very far. We simply flew above the valley in a huge circle. When I asked the door-gunner why we weren't heading in any direction, he pointed to a desolate mountain, saying that we couldn't land because the LZ (landing zone) was taking small arms fire. Just what I needed to hear—my first helicopter assault would drop us into a hot LZ.

I gazed at the mountain with its oddly brown slopes against the otherwise green backdrop. We circled about a mile away and on each pass I stared at the mountain with its limbless trees standing like twisted telephone poles after a violent storm. As the flight continued, I looked down at hundreds of water-filled bomb craters on the valley floor. None of it looked good. Man how I wished I was back in the flatlands.

Suddenly our chopper dove toward a hillside LZ about a half-mile from the mountain. The co-pilot told us we were not going to touch down because the NVA were still shooting at each aircraft that came in. Instead, we would be given a scant five seconds to jump out. As we approached, the door-gunner fired his M-60 into the jungle while two machine gunners on the ground did the same. We were already standing on the skids when the chopper began hovering, but we didn't get any closer than ten feet above the ground. The door-gunner yelled at us to jump, but I thought ten feet with a full rucksack and extra ammo was too high. I was about to tell him so when my five seconds expired and he shoved me. I landed flat on my face.

As the helicopter sped away, I scrambled to the tree line where Major General Melvin Zais, commander of the 101st Airborne, grinned as he watched our unloading acrobatics. He seemed to get a big kick out of it. I gave him a "What the fuck are you smiling at?" glance, but he looked right past me, still grinning. Then it hit me. A US Army general was way out here? I looked around to see at least 300 other GIs also assembled for action. That was when I realized we were in the middle of something big, and playing for keeps.

We moved a short distance from the LZ and spent the rest of the day digging in and rebuilding damaged bunkers and fighting positions to protect us against mortar or infantry attacks. I thought we would go into battle that day, but we remained in our defensive positions and set up for the night.

"Wow," Freddie Shaw commented, "there are a lot of guys here. I wonder how bad it really is?"

"Pretty bad," answered Alcon. "Look at the shrapnel scars in the trees. I bet the NVA have been mortaring the place."

"Did you guys see that two-star General?" asked Jimmy Smith. "I don't think a guy like that will still be here after dark."

"Do you blame him?" added Scoggins. "I don't even want to be here in the daylight. I can't imagine what it's going to be like at night."

As darkness approached, strange noises were heard from the jungle below us. It sounded like enemy movement, but we later discovered it was only splintered bamboo reacting from previous artillery barrages. High on the hill, the NVA came out of their tunnels and bunkers to light dozens of small cooking fires. They kept them burning through the night as if to taunt us. In response to the fires, our artillery and mortars shelled the side of the hill at random intervals just to let the NVA know we were not going anywhere. Since both sides knew exactly where the other was, the normal discipline of keeping quiet after dark was sometimes ignored. Despite our rival forces positioned so close together, the night passed without incident.

Just after sunrise, a pair of F-4 Phantom jets provided tactical air strikes. They dropped several 250-pound bombs where bunkers had been spotted and in areas that needed to be cleared for the next ground assault. We cheered each explosion, feeling exhilarated when the ground shook as the planes took turns releasing their ordnance. The raid included napalm canisters that crashed to the earth with a giant fireball so intense that, for a moment, we felt the heat where we stood. The savagery of the attacks was awesome.

After the planes left, it was our turn. We loaded ourselves with ammunition and attached bayonets to our rifles. Each man also carried a field bandage and a canteen of water. No food was allowed, but I took a C-ration can of peaches along just the same. Our rucksacks were too clumsy for this mission so they were collected by a rear guard and placed in a big pile. Howard Siner and I hid our packs in the bushes, figuring it would be easier to reclaim them rather than sort them out from among hundreds of others.

We moved out in single file following a ridge trail toward the base of the hill where we would later link up with the 3/187th. The trail was well used and up to five feet wide in some places. Both sides were littered with discarded US Army equipment, half-used machine gun belts, empty M-16 magazines, canteens, ponchos, and web gear. As we rounded a turn, we came upon three body bags lying along the trail's edge, each with a dead American inside. Our column stopped there, so we sat down to wait. From down the line I watched Sergeant Krol moving closer until he reached my position.

"What's the holdup?" he asked officially.

"I don't know. Everyone just stopped."

Krol looked around for a place to sit then casually sat on one of the body bags.

"Hey!" I yelled, "there's a GI in that bag. Don't you care?"

"What's the problem?" Krol asked honestly. "He's dead. He doesn't feel a thing."

"You're a heartless bastard."

"Watch it, Wiknik. Being insubordinate will just get you into a deeper hole."

It was all I could do to keep quiet, but I didn't say anything more to the son-of-a-bitch because no one backed me up. A few minutes later, the column moved again.

Farther along the trail lay the decomposing bodies of two NVA soldiers who had been dead for at least a week. Their lips were receded, exposing the teeth, and their eyes were only shriveled remnants. Insects of every variety were feasting on the flesh. Aside from the bullet holes, their uniforms looked new, quite unlike the black pajamas worn by the VC. We covered our noses and mouths with towels; the stench was stomach-turning.

As we reached the base of the hill, we came upon the men of the 3/187th. It was from this location they had been launching their attacks. The place looked awful. All the ground vegetation was trampled down to the dirt, military equipment was strewn everywhere, and the area stunk of human waste. The GIs were unnaturally quiet as we approached. Most were filthy, unshaven, and exhausted. Some had the thousand-mile stare, the dead, distant gaze many combat soldiers acquire. It was as if they had seen the gates of hell. Looking at them, I felt ashamed of the Army and myself. While this misery was going on, my company should have been here. Instead, we were at Eagle Beach having a picnic and getting drunk.

One of their soldiers focused on me. "Hey, Sergeant," he called, motioning to my shirt sleeves, "unless you rip those stripes off, you'll never see the top of that hill. The Gooks shoot the leaders first. And you better remove the tracers from your machine gun belts because the Gooks can see where the bullets are coming from. Then they shoot at the gunners, too."

I nodded as if we would follow his suggestions, but I didn't know if he was serious. Then he started again, only this time with more emotion.

"None of you will ever see the top of that hill!" he shouted, pointing at us. "Every time we get near the crest, the Gooks pop out of their holes from behind us and shoot us in the back. That's why we call it Hamburger Hill. Because anyone who goes up there gets chewed up. I've got friends still lying out there and we can't even bring their bodies back." Then he began to sob, but there were no tears. "Why can't the Army just let it be and get us the fuck out of here?"

Eventually, one of his buddies came over to lead him away. The other GIs just looked at us with blank expressions because everyone knew the Army was not about to give it up.

We moved out again, this time cutting our own trail along a finger-like ridge. As we slowly advanced, I caught glimpses of the hill through the vegetation. It looked barren, as if no one could possibly be up there.

Suddenly, our lead element opened fire with their M-16s. We hit the dirt but the shooting lasted only seconds. Moments later, word came down that the point had killed an NVA sniper who had tied himself high in a tree. The sniper didn't fall out. Instead, he hung grotesquely like a rag doll with a rope around his waist. As we passed by, dripping blood from the body sprinkled down like raindrops. We had no respect for the dead enemy soldier, and left him hanging as a warning to his buddies.

By the time we got into our attack location it was late afternoon, so there would be no assault that day. We set up a close defensive line of three man positions to prevent any NVA from sneaking between us. In my position were PFC Howard Siner and PFC Lennie Person.

Lennie Person was a black inner-city kid from Ohio who hated being in Vietnam because he was convinced he was going to die. Many of us were vocal about hating Vietnam, but we kept the fear of dying a secret so no one would think less of us.

"Hey Sergeant," Lennie asked. "Remember that GI who told you to take off your stripes and remove the tracers from our machine gun belts?"

"Sure," I answered, "I could never forget him. He was a basket case."

"Well, do you really think the NVA are picking out targets to shoot at? I mean, do you think they want to shoot blacks too?"

"Lennie," I started, unsure of what to really tell him. "They'll be shooting at all of us. But try not to worry about it. We've got them outnumbered and surrounded. Besides, how many can be left up there? This whole thing will be over before noon tomorrow."

Siner looked at me as if I was crazy because he knew that I didn't know what I was talking about. But he also knew I had to make up something to keep Lennie from becoming so scared that he would be useless.

"Lennie," Siner said, trying to console him, "I'm almost twice your size and I can carry lots of ammo. Why don't you stick with me tomorrow? That way we can protect each other."

Lennie was so relieved by Siner's offer that he shook his hand in appreciation. Siner glanced back at me as if to say, "I had to do something." I gave him an affirmative nod because I knew he did the right thing.

We didn't dig in because the ridge was too steep, but we were able to level the ground enough for sleeping. Hardly anyone slept. Throughout the night, distant voices and other noises were heard coming from the hill. Many of us hoped that the NVA were fleeing because of the massive allied buildup of 600 GIs, 200 ARVNs and 300 more GIs in close reserve that formed a circular barrier along the base of the hill stretched out nearly one mile long.

At daybreak, enemy small arms fire cracked over the hillside, telling us at least someone was still up there. In response, air strikes were called in which stopped the shooting. Between the bombing runs, the NVA dropped random mortar rounds near the hill base to harass us as well.

Small arms fire cracked again, but this time it was M-16's as men from my company killed another enemy soldier. Not carrying a weapon, the lone NVA had walked directly to one of our positions, as if to surrender. When he got closer, someone noticed a Chicom grenade in his left hand. The soldier was immediately gunned down. The grenade turned out to be a dud. After that, orders came down that there would be no prisoners taken. Our commanders correctly believed that any NVA fanatical enough to still be in the area would also be willing to fight to the death.

Things got quiet again as we waited for other units to get into their final attack positions. While sitting there, I began to feel hunger pains. I suspect everybody did because we had not eaten for nearly twenty hours.

The problem was the only food close by was my can of peaches. So I had to think of a way to eat them without being seen. It didn't work. As soon as the can was open, everybody glared at me. They all wanted peaches. I couldn't share them with 100 men, so I hunched over and wolfed them down just to get it over with. Nobody said anything, but their sneering sure made me uncomfortable.

Shortly after 9:00 a.m., the hill was bombarded with a final onslaught of our artillery. This prep was the softening needed for us to make what was hoped to be the last assault. The fusillade was so intense that there was hardly a moment without an explosion. All the firebases in the A Shau fired with such incredible accuracy that the rounds impacted every square yard of the battle area for nearly an hour. The mountain was being raked by so much shrapnel that some of it struck the tall trees above us, knocking down branches. When this final barrage ended, Ap Bia Mountain had taken a total of 155 air strikes and 20,000 artillery rounds during the ten-day campaign.

At exactly 10:00 a.m., we were given the command to assault. Everyone moved out from the vegetation cover, forming a long skirmish line. The hill was monstrous and, despite the fact that it was completely denuded from all the bombing, would still be a formidable obstacle to climb. Loose dirt, splintered logs, stumps with exposed roots, and deep bomb craters made the terrain look like the aftermath of a nuclear explosion. The extent of the destruction convinced many of us that there could not possibly be any NVA left to fight. In fact, when the assault began, the only shooting came from GIs when we laid down suppressive fire as a tactical precaution. To our surprise, the NVA were still there. Ten minutes into what was believed to be a one-way assault, distant units on our right met light resistance. We didn't know it at the time but several hundred NVA continued to occupy the hill.

Our advance was slow and deliberate, either crawling or moving diagonally from stump to hole, then waiting for the next person to catch up before moving again. By 10:30 a.m., most of my company had reached the first row of enemy bunkers. Although the bunkers were mostly destroyed and abandoned, we tossed grenades into them to be sure.

As our skirmish line worked past the bunkers, a squad of NVA poured from a trench, attacking an element of the beleaguered 3/187th. Although eight or nine men were initially wounded, all the GIs in that area rallied to wipe out the enemy squad. Directly above the spot more NVA appeared, and a pitched battle of RPGs, hand grenades, and small arms fire began. As if on cue, the knoll in front of my position suddenly erupted as NVA poured out to attack us.

Unaware of these events, I continued evasive action, still assuming the shooting in my area was only coming from our weapons. As I crawled forward the dirt in front and alongside of me spit as if subterranean air bubbles were rising to the surface. I thought I was witnessing a rare geological phenomenon until I realized bullets were hitting the ground and that I was the target! If there was a sporting event for the low-crawl, I set a new speed record crabbing my way to the nearest bomb crater. I looked to find the source of the shooting but the hill had no features left that could possibly hide enemy forces. The NVA must have survived the ten-day pounding by staying inside deep bunkers and spider holes.

The shooting intensified and again the dirt erupted around me, so I decided to strike back. Lying in the crater, I raised my rifle high above my head and let loose a full burst of rock n' roll. I had no specific target, but loaded another magazine and sprayed the hillside once more before moving out to find a deeper hole.

I saw a GI waving his hand so I crawled to his location and rolled behind a stump that offered enough protection for me to peek up the hillside. I saw a lone NVA run from his bunker but before I could draw a bead to shoot, someone else nailed him and he fell dead to the ground. When I turned back to the GI, he was still laying on his back waving his hand in the air.

"What the hell are you doing?" I shouted.

"Trying to get shot in the arm!" he answered firmly.

"Are you nuts?" I screamed back.

"No. I just want to go home, but not in a body bag."

I had to get away from him. Even though I had decent cover, it didn't make sense to hang around someone trying to draw fire to himself. I crawled off to hide alongside a fallen tree. When I got there, splinters of wood flew off as enemy bullets ripped into it. I had no choice but to lay low until the NVA decided to pick on someone else.

As the fighting continued around me, I fired several bursts over the top of the log without even looking to see where I was shooting. It was an ineffective tactic that forced me to stay hidden because every time I was exposed, an NVA shot at me.

While lying there, I felt the need to urinate. Since battlefield body functions were something never discussed during training, I waited for the urge to pass. It didn't. With everything that was going on, I actually paused to consider whether to piss on the ground or in my pants. I chose the ground. Pissing in a prone position was new for me but everything flowed out the same. However, as soon as I started urinating, bullets once again zeroed in on my location, pulverizing the log. The Gooks must be trying to shoot my penis off! I had to finish the job by wetting myself.

Jimmy Smith finally got our machine gun into position and laid down a murderous 500-round burst that sprayed an area the size of a football field. I enjoyed watching him work, but with so much smoke pouring off the gun barrel I worried that it might overheat. The machine gunner's volley gave everyone the chance to advance. I gained almost a hundred feet before crawling into a bomb crater alongside PFC Anderson, from our platoon's 3rd squad.

Lying face to face in the crater, our eyes connected for an instant. We didn't speak. We didn't need to. We looked at each other in the only way that men on the brink of death could. We conveyed a silent message to each that said, "This could be it, but let's try to keep each other alive."

We were close to the NVA now because the crack of AK-47's was distinguishable from the M-16's. The frequency of firing diminished slightly, giving us a chance to see where the shooting was coming from.

"See anything?" I asked, barely peering over the crater's edge.

"Yeah," said Anderson, pointing, "near the crest I can see the dust fly from muzzle blasts."

"I see it too. It looks over a hundred feet away. Too far for a grenade."

"At least it's a target. What should we do?"

"There's no ground cover, so we can't advance. Let's shoot a couple of magazines up there and see what happens. Maybe we'll get lucky and zap the bastard."

Our firing was furious but not deadly. The only thing we accomplished was to draw the NVA's attention. Suppressive enemy fire quickly rained down and forced us to hug the ground.

"That didn't work!" I yelled, as bullets impacted around us. "I think there's more than one Gook in that position! This time, let's take turns firing. I'll go first."

We never got a chance to see if my strategy would work. When we rolled over to return fire, I was suddenly sprayed with water as Anderson let out a painful howl. An enemy bullet had ripped through his leg and into a canteen of water he carried in a side pants pocket, causing it to burst. Like a sequence from an eerie movie, it seemed to happen in slow motion.

"How bad is it? How bad?" he yelled. "I don't want to look!"

"It's nothing," I answered, as if it were nothing. "They just nicked you in the thigh. It's all meat there, no bones to worry about. It's hardly even bleeding." I was lying some, because it looked like a serious wound and there was a fair amount of blood. Still, I saw no reason to scare the guy. I tried to apply my field dressing but he wouldn't lay still. Our fearless medic Doc Meehan, who never carried a weapon, appeared out of the chaos to attend to Anderson.

Now I was scared. A guy right next to me was shot. The Gooks really meant business! I didn't know what to do. Dirt erupted again as more bullets hit the ground around us. I started firing back like a madman, not aiming at anything, just shooting wildly at the massive hill. I knew I had to get away because the three of us made too good of a target.

When the next burst of firing stopped, I got up and ran twenty feet to the next hole. Debris flew as the enemy opened fire again. It seemed the Gooks had singled me out because the bullets followed me wherever I went. Perhaps that emotional GI from the 3/187th was right: the NVA were shooting at me because of my sergeant stripes. I quickly put it out of my mind and wormed up to the edge of the crater. Then, holding my rifle high over my head sprayed two more magazines at the hill. When I peeked above the mound for an escape route, something painful suddenly blinded me. When I reached up to protect my stinging eyes, a bullet slammed into my chest, throwing me backward. I was shot—they got me!

Lying on my back with my eyes and chest in pain, I drifted off. So this is how I'm going to die, I thought, at the bottom of a pit in the middle of nowhere. But aren't the battle sounds supposed to fade away like they do in the movies? I supposed I had to suffer first. The pain in my chest increased. I blinked my eyes a few times, and I could see again! I rubbed them clear enough to examine my chest and saw that my clothes were smoking. Jesus! I was on fire! I instinctively beat out the flames before any ammo caught fire and sent me into orbit. Then I checked my body for bullet holes but found nothing except the burn on my chest. "I'm going to live!" I kept telling myself. Maybe I even said it out loud.

An NVA bullet hitting the ground in front of me had blasted dirt into my eyes. A second slug, apparently a tracer, had lodged in the bandoleers of ammo draped across my chest. The impact knocked me to the ground and the tracer caught my shirt on fire. The Gooks had me cold: I should have been dead. Maybe I was super-GI, but I didn't feel like it. Since that day, the expression, "You've never lived until you've almost died," took on a whole new meaning.

I yanked the destroyed magazine out of the bandoleer and, forgetting that it had saved my life, cast it aside. I tried to decide what to do next but all I could think of was self-preservation. I jumped out of the hole and ran at full speed toward a tree-covered ridge. I held my weapon like a pistol, firing at the hill as enemy bullets nipped at my heels. As I raced past crawling GIs they yelled for me to get down, but my adrenaline drove me to the tree line. I hoped it was a safe place with no shooting. I looked back once yelling, "This way!" figuring that most of the GIs would surely follow me.

The sparse cover thickened as I advanced up the hill, jumping over logs and recklessly pushing bushes aside. I don't know what drove me to move at such a dangerous pace because I could easily have stumbled into an enemy position without knowing it. At the edge of a bombed-out clearing I tripped and then scrambled to a fallen tree to rest. What a view opened up before me! I was on the summit watching the action below. "Below me?" I silently screamed. I had run past the left flank of our attacking force! I turned around to tell the others but no one was there. They hadn't followed me. I was alone. I thought about going back down but realized I would risk our guys shooting me, so I stayed. Besides, exhaustion had suddenly taken command of my body and I could barely move. It became an effort just to turn my head to see if anyone was near, friend or foe.

Thirty paralyzing minutes passed while I watched the assault continue. The GIs made tremendous progress, killing the enemy in their bunkers where many had chosen to stay and die. Scores of other NVA ran off the western slope toward the Laotian border, a mile away. The fleeing enemy could easily be seen from the air where our helicopters directed a wall of artillery, mortars, air strikes, and automatic weapons fire on top of them.

As GIs swept past the front of me, I felt safe enough to stand up and be identified as one of their own. Then someone from behind called me by name, it was Howard Siner. Lennie Person was with him.

"Where's the rest of the platoon?" I asked, looking past them.

"We are the platoon," said Siner. "Nearly everyone was pinned down at the bottom but some of our guys are coming up now."

"Were you two up here long?"

"Maybe fifteen minutes or so. We got separated but just now found each other. We stayed out of sight until more people showed up."

We figured that the three of us were the first ones to the top. We must have been concealed within a hundred feet of each other without knowing it.

"See Lennie," I said, encouraging him with a pat on the shoulder, "you made it to the top without a scratch. Ten years from now you can tell your kids all about this."

"Yeah, right," he responded faintly, then took two steps backward and stared at me. "What the hell happened to you? You look like shit."

After everything that happened to me, I guessed that I probably did look bad. My face resembled a raccoon's from rubbing the dirt out of my eyes. My bandoleers had caught fire and my shirt had a hole burnt in the middle of it. There was a mix of dried mud and urine stains on my pants, and some of Anderson's blood had smeared on me. I had quite a tale to tell, so when more platoon members gathered around, they asked and I told it as dramatically as possible with a slight stretching of the truth. I figured my story would either endear me to them or be my final undoing.

"I look like shit," I began, strutting back and forth and pointing angrily, "because I had to take this side of the hill by myself. Take a good look at me. I got shot in the face, shot in the chest, and I didn't even take time out to piss. When I got into the tree line and called for you guys to follow me, nobody did. I was up here alone until Siner and Person showed up. Thanks for nothing guys. This is the last hill I'll attack by myself."

Everyone was dumbfounded. That little performance turned out to be one of the best things I could have done for myself. When word got around about what happened to me, I was regarded as one of the bravest men in the platoon. This respect may not have been exactly deserved, but as a squad leader it was welcome because the men under my command would be less likely to doubt my abilities and may even adopt my cautious approach to the war.

The fighting had dwindled to sporadic rifle fire and an occasional grenade explosion as our infantry continued swarming over the hill. Cobra gunships roamed the skies firing rockets, mini-guns, and grenades into the remaining enemy positions. The battle was ending. We had won. The final assault had lasted nearly six hours.

Tired, sweaty, and filthy soldiers straggled past us. Sergeant Krol was with them but he wasn't tired. He wasn't even dirty.

"Pork Chop Hill was tougher than this," he said, referring to the famous Korean War fight. "That was a real battle."

We all looked at Krol in disgust. "I'll kill him," grumbled Person.

"No, I'll kill him," I whispered, not sure I didn't really mean it.

"Forget it," said Siner. "He's nothing but an asshole Lifer. He hopes you'll try something. That's his style. Don't let him get to you."

Our company set up positions on the hilltop alongside several huge bomb craters, each deep enough to park a truck in. We were told Lieutenant Bruckner had been wounded and that Krol would take charge of the platoon until a new leader was assigned. It was just what we didn't need; Krol having complete authority over us.

All shooting had ceased by mid-afternoon, but the area remained a flurry of activity. Misplaced GIs criss-crossed the summit trying to locate their units. Cobra gunships and agile Loach helicopters also remained on station to prevent an NVA counter attack. As the regrouping continued, Krol ordered me to help get the walking wounded down the hill for evacuation. Near the bottom was a small LZ from which Loaches flew casualties to firebases for transfer to medevac choppers.

As we headed down through the area were the 3/187th was first hit ten days earlier, I got a good look at the mountain. I estimated the main battlefield covered almost a half of a square mile, more if the draws and ridges were included. There was no trail to follow, just a desolate ridge lined with a dozen body bags, each containing the remains of a slain GI. The dead NVA, and pieces of them, were scattered on either side of the ridge. They were uncovered and some had begun decomposing. The stench of decaying flesh, the shriveled NVA corpses, the silent body bags, and the massive destruction would be my lasting memory of this hellish hill.

With no trees left to shade us, the late afternoon air became unbearably humid. We waited around the LZ just to feel the helicopter rotor wash from each landing and takeoff. After the last of the wounded had safely gone, I began to feel faint. Then, before I could sit down, I blacked out. I was quickly revived by the piercing scent of smelling salts. I looked up as a medic hovering over me joked, "Hey buddy, no one leaves here that easy."

A few minutes later we started up the hill when I remembered the M-16 magazine that had saved my life and decided to go back for it. I found the magazine right where I had tossed it. It was twisted out of shape with a jagged tear across the middle. I knew the magazine was something unique, so I slipped it into my side pants pocket where it stayed for the next three months.

The mountain had become an anthill of soldiers. Everywhere, GIs were digging in. There were also a few souvenir hunters checking over the dead NVA and their bunkers. Interpreters later found evidence of the enemy's determination with commands sewn onto their uniforms reading, "KILL AMERICANS" and "STAY AND FIGHT AND DON'T RUN."

When I got back to the top, there was so much brass stumbling around that it looked like the Pentagon had opened a branch office, everyone wanting to be a part of the action. There was also a square cardboard sign pinned with a bayonet to a blackened tree trunk reading, "HAMBURGER HILL." A weary Grunt trudged over and attached a note to the bottom that read, "Was it worth it?" I stood staring at the sign, contemplating the question, when an officer ran over and tore the note off. "Bastards," I mumbled to myself, thinking that we at least deserved the right to express some feelings.

"Sergeant Wiknik!" Krol yelled, waving me to come over. "Pick three men to go with you to the bottom and bring back some C-rations."

"C-rations at the bottom?" I questioned, as if I didn't hear him right. "If the Brass could be flown up here, why can't our food be flown up too?"

"Our rations are already at the bottom!" he yelled. "So don't argue!"

Everyone within earshot stopped what they were doing and turned their attention on us. I have never hated anyone in my life but at that moment Krol became an exception. His uncaring attitude for sitting on the GI in the body bag and his unwillingness to acknowledge our performance in the battle—especially after his lack of participation in it—was all I could stand.

"I was just down there!" I angrily shouted back at him. "Pick someone else for a change! I'm not going!"

"As your platoon leader, I am giving you a direct order! Now do it!"

The situation turned into a staring contest until Freddie Shaw and two other platoon members appeared between us.

"C'mon Wiknik, we'll go down with you. Let's get them C-rations. Everyone's hungry."

Their action may have saved Krol's life. I had allowed my anger and frustration to get the best of me and was ready to blow him away because he was deliberately harassing me. We turned to go down the hill as a chopper hovering near the top dropped off our rucksacks. I moaned to myself, remembering how Siner and I had hidden our rucksacks in the bushes so they wouldn't get mixed up with all the others. Now there is no worry about them getting mixed up because they'll be hidden there forever.

Again I passed where the body bags had been. The slain GIs were gone now, airlifted to Graves Registration to be prepared for their final journey home. The dead NVA were still lying where they fell and would be left there to rot.

We passed other GIs carrying C-ration cases up the hill, looking more like safari porters than victorious warriors. We went to the same LZ the wounded were flown out of, only now it looked more like a miniature supply depot with stacks of ammunition boxes, dozens of C-ration cases, medical supplies, and water canisters. Hoisting a case onto my shoulder, I gazed at what would be my third trip up the hill, wondering if the day would ever end.

It was nearly dusk when we dropped the C-rations at the platoon CP. When I returned to my position, I was encouraged to find that Siner and Person had finished digging in. They had also leveled a place for me to sleep.

We finally got the chance to talk about the events of the day.

"Man, look at this place," commented Person, "Talk about destruction. How did the Gooks survive such a pounding?"

"They didn't," answered Siner solemnly. "There's body parts all over this hill. I think the NVA decided to make a stand here to prove they weren't afraid to pour their people into it."

"I guess you guys know that Anderson got wounded," I added, "but he should be okay."

"Did you hear how Lieutenant Bruckner got wounded?" Person asked. We hadn't, so he continued. "Apparently he was pinned down behind some rocks, so when he returned fire, he didn't look to see what he was aiming at. The stupid jerk shot into the rocks and one of the bullets ricocheted back into his leg."

"Theoretically," Siner surmised, "Bruckner has a self-inflicted wound. He can get court-martialed for that, maybe even lose his commission."

"And to think the bastard yelled at me for shooting that bush back at Phong Dien," I joked. It was the first time we had laughed all day and it felt good.

I had just begun to relax when a supply chopper began dropping cases of C-rations and canisters of water at our company CP. After all our humping up and down the hill, our supplies were finally brought to us like they should have been in the first place. I didn't react. I couldn't. I was so frustrated that my brain went numb along with the rest of me. I was truly thankful to be alive, but so emotionally drained that I felt closer to dead.

Some positions didn't bother pulling any guard duty that night. With so many GIs crowded on the hill we would have been just guarding each other. However, we were advised to stay in our positions and not move around because it was possible a few NVA could still be alive in tunnels beneath us.

I felt safe with Siner and Person nearby so sleep came easier than expected. During the night I dreamed I had lost my entrenching tool and needed to find it to dig a fighting position. At the same time, Person was having a nightmare that the NVA were coming out of the ground to kill us as we slept. I began fumbling around Person's body, touching him several times until he awoke with a blood-curdling scream. When he grabbed me around the chest, I shrieked too. Neither of us knew what was going on as we tumbled into a bomb crater locked together. The entire hilltop woke up to the clamor. I think Person was on the verge of killing me when Siner jumped in to pull us apart.

At first light, more rucksacks were choppered in. I told the door-gunner where mine and Siner's were hidden and asked if he could have someone find them. Eventually, our rucksacks were located, but as they were being flown back, the helicopter began to take enemy ground-fire. To avoid getting hit, the pilot steered the chopper into a steep bank. That's when our rucksacks slid out the door, disappearing into the jungle. If some lucky Gook finds them, he'll be taking pictures with my camera and reading my letters from home.

At mid morning, our company was airlifted off the hill. As each chopper rose above the disfigured mountain, the survivors glanced down to a nightmare that had come to life. A Presidential Unit Citation for extraordinary heroism was awarded to the twenty-one infantry, medical, artillery, and aviation units that took part in the battle. The entire operation claimed sixty American lives and 480 wounded. Another twenty-five were missing and presumed dead. My company lost one man killed and eight wounded. The 29th NVA Regiment lost an estimated 600 killed. Though we didn't know it at the time, Hill 937 was not regarded as a piece of real estate worth keeping. Within a few days it was deserted by American troops.

The rapid abandonment of such hard-won territory continued to fuel the growing lack of support for the war, which in turn caused President Nixon to accelerate his plans for systematic troop withdrawals from South Vietnam. Ironically, only one month after the battle, NVA forces were reported to be moving back onto Hamburger Hill.

"The A Shau is a very bad place."

CHAPTER 4

The A Shau Valley

US ground troop operations in the A Shau Valley were strengthened by fire support bases strategically located throughout the area. Firebase names like Eagle's Nest, Berchtesgaden, and Currahee evoked connections to the 101st Airborne's storied past during WWII. To us Grunts, the names had little effect in stirring our pride. Instead, the bases were nothing more than tiny safety islands by day and mortar magnets by night. Our assignment after Hamburger Hill was at Firebase Airborne.

Perched high atop a mountain overlooking the valley, Firebase Airborne was about the size of a football field. It was encircled by irregular rows of concertina wire, sandbagged bunkers, trenches, and fighting positions. The firebase housed batteries of 60mm and 81mm mortars, as well as 105mm and 155mm artillery pieces manned by units of the the 211th and 319th Field Artillery. Every fire mission was coordinated through a tactical operations center, which was located in the command bunker. When at maximum strength, 150 men defended

Airborne. There were no comforts there—no bunks, no showers, and no hot food. A rarely used generator provided electricity only to the command bunker when necessary. As with most firebases, Airborne was accessible only by helicopter or foot.

Our arrival at Airborne brought congratulatory handshakes from the artillerymen who monitored and provided some of the fire support for the Hamburger Hill battle. Some said they felt safer knowing we would be guarding them. The battle was a bigger deal than we thought, and several Cherry replacements were in awe of us and what we had done there. Their respect was evident in how they kept their distance, but we didn't want to be treated differently. The real heroes were found in the 3/187th Infantry who suffered through the siege for the entire ten days.

I did delight in the special attention I received when word got around about the M-16 magazine that had saved my life. A group of unknown GIs had sought me out to get a look at it.

"Hey Sergeant," one of them asked. "Can we see that M-16 magazine that everyone's talking about?"

"Sure," I proudly answered, offering it for all to see.

Each man carefully examined the magazine as they passed it around. Then one of them rubbed it over his body as if it were a talisman.

"Will you take fifty bucks for it?" he asked, hesitating to give it back.

"Thanks, but it's not for sale."

"I'll give you a hundred," he insisted.

"No," I sternly answered. "It's a special souvenir I plan to take home. Besides, the power of the magazine can't be bought. It has to be a gift or a blessing."

He looked at me in a funny way, as if I made sense, then handed it back. My guys knew I was kidding, but if a superstitious GI thought he could buy good luck, then he might get careless and put himself in danger.

Shortly after our company settled in, the long arm of the military law caught up with me. The Article 15 I received for sleeping on guard duty when we were in the flatlands needed my signature to make it part of the official record. Captain Hartwell waved the document in my face demanding that I sign the admission of guilt.

"I'm not signing that," I said, glancing away. "No one woke me up so how could I have crashed?"

"Everyone else involved already signed because they knew they were wrong," he scolded me. "If you refuse, I'll personally see that this is elevated to a court-martial."

"But no one woke me up," I pleaded, knowing he only wanted to intimidate me into signing.

"Sleeping on guard duty in a war zone is a serious offense. If you don't want any bad-time, you'd better sign it."

"Bad-time" was the magic word. If I ended up in the stockade, I'd have to make up the time lost to a jail sentence to complete my tour of duty. Not wanting one extra minute in Vietnam, I signed the paper. A few yards away, Sergeant Krol gave me an evil smile, just to let me know how things are done in the Army. I was disgusted with myself for allowing Krol such satisfaction.

Eight days before our arrival at Airborne, a vicious nighttime attack by the NVA there had resulted in the deaths of twelve Americans and thirty-one enemy soldiers. Our job was to repair and protect the base until it was a formidable outpost again. The work began with the construction of stronger bunkers and deeper fighting positions. However, we had to be careful where we dug because after the attack, some of the dead NVA were buried where they fell.

I shared a bunker with Howard Siner, Stanley Alcon, and Freddie Shaw. As luck would have it, our bunker was right on top of a dead NVA. As I dug into the earth, my shovel hit what I thought was a tree root. Instead, what I pulled from the dirt turned out to be a partially decomposed arm. No one was willing to dig deeper, so we ended up with the shallowest of all positions, not much more than a crawl space. The thought of sleeping on top of the NVA, or parts of him, gave us the creeps. So we slept on the roof and spent our free time elsewhere.

After the bunker rebuilding was completed, we worked on the jungle side of the concertina wire removing vegetation for maximum visibility of the terrain. The tree cutting was a revealing experience. Just 200 feet beyond the wire was an enemy observation post built high in a tall tree. The NVA must have used this tiny tree stand to gather information for their attack on the firebase. Before we tore it down, Captain Hartwell made sure everyone saw the observation post to demonstrate how brazen the NVA can be and how lazy our guards had been for not spotting it sooner.

It was during a land clearing detail that I had my final encounter with Sergeant Burke, the NCO who turned me in for hiding in the bushes back at Phong Dien. Our two squads were on a steep slope burning a brush pile. I worked with my men while Burke stood around barking orders at his. I had chopped some branches and was throwing them into the fire when Burke approached.

"Sergeant Wiknik," he began sarcastically, "I see you are still setting a bad example of how an NCO is supposed to act. Your job is to give the orders and your men are expected to carry them out. Rank gives you the privilege of watching your men work." I could not believe what Burke had just said.

"Are you for real?" I shot back, irritated by his attitude. "What makes you think that being an NCO makes you better then your men? No matter what kind of detail we get, I try to make it a team effort so everyone knows who they can depend on. But you can't see that. You've turned into a tyrant on a power trip."

"I told you once before," he answered with a tilted smile. "There's an unwritten law about NCOs arguing in front of their men. If you keep it up, I'll be forced to report you again."

"That's the one thing you're good at Burke; squealing on fellow NCOs." I should have kept quiet and walked away but he was so irritating that I continued. "So tell me Burke, did you turn me in to divert attention away from yourself or was it because you think I'm a threat to you?"

Burke didn't answer. He didn't like me mouthing off in front of his squad, but he obviously enjoyed provoking me. He pushed further.

"If you must work with your subordinates," Burke offered, putting his hand on my shoulder, "at least do the job right. Let me show you the proper method of burning a brush pile."

"Keep your fuckin' paws off me," I shot out through clenched teeth, pushing his hand aside.

Burke's stupid grin showed that he loved every minute of my anger. Then, speaking as if I was a moron, he picked up some branches and threw them into the fire.

"Here's how you do it. You start with small twigs and toss them into the fire. Then you throw bigger sticks on top to pack it down. Little sticks, big sticks. Got it?"

I couldn't stand his idiocy any longer so I turned away, pretending he was no longer there. However, now that everyone's attention was on us, Burke felt he needed to do something dramatic to stay in control of our dispute.

"Oh," Burke continued, speaking to my backside, "I forgot to show you one thing. When the end of a branch burns away like this one. . ." He picked up the burning piece and shook it over my head until hot coals rained down on my bare shoulders.

"Arrrrrhhh!" I screamed, brushing the burning embers away from my scorched flesh. "You fuckin' asshole! What the hell is the matter with you?"

"Oooh, does Sergeant Wiknik have a boo-boo?" he asked, laughing hysterically.

That did it! Burke finally pushed the wrong button and I wanted to retaliate. As I picked up an axe and held it like a baseball bat, everyone backed away, except Burke.

"You've bugged me for the last time!" I shouted at him.

"Temper, temper," he said, mocking me with a wagging finger. "Are you a little 'hot' under the collar?"

"I'll show you how fuckin' hot I am!"

I let out a howling "AAIIEEE!" war whoop and threw the axe at him, barely missing his head. Burke had ducked for the ground just in time. All was silent until the axe landed in the trees far below us. Burke was genuinely terrified as he looked up at me, afraid of what might happen next. I silently glared at him to make sure he got the message then I turned and went back to the firebase perimeter. When I reached the concertina wire, Captain Hartwell was standing there. He had witnessed the entire incident.

"You're lucky you missed him," Hartwell scolded.

I looked back down at Burke and gestured, "He's the one who's lucky."

"Really? Perhaps I should include assault with your Article 15. Or maybe charge you with aiding the enemy."

"Aiding the enemy?" I asked confused. "What are you talking about?"

"Right now, that axe is of more use to the NVA than to us. When you cool off, go back down and find it."

"Yes, sir," I mumbled in return.

Now there was an inspiring example of our priorities. If I had wanted to, I could have killed a man, but the Captain was more concerned about a lost axe. Considering how I felt about Burke, I almost had to agree with Hartwell's wisdom.

Sergeant Burke never spoke to me again. We spent a year in the same company and I only saw him at a distance. I think he was now genuinely afraid that I was crazy enough to kill him.

Our stay at Firebase Airborne was a welcome change from the humping we did around Phong Dien. There was, however, no escape from the typical Army bullshit duties. We were required to perform police calls, latrine duty, and submit to bunker inspections. Our days were spent filling sandbags, pushing the edge of the jungle back, or going out on short patrols. There was little free time. Perhaps the activities were the Army's way of keeping us from thinking about home.

Daytime on the firebase was physically exhausting, and the nights were mentally demanding. The most likely time for an enemy attack was from midnight to dawn, so we rarely got sufficient sleep because Captain Hartwell often put us on 100% alert for up to four hours at a time. When we were allowed to sleep, the artillery battery seemed to have a fire mission at the same time. Rounds might be launched for only one minute, or the mission could drag on for an hour. More often than not, the guns were aimed over our shallow bunker, so every cannon blast shook us from our sleep.

The biggest disadvantage of being on a firebase was that we were sitting ducks for the enemy. Although we weren't directly attacked while I was there, we did get mortared one night. The NVA walked four rounds across the base scoring a direct hit on one of the bunkers, killing three GIs as they slept in a fighting position on the bunker roof. The trio never knew what hit them. The next morning their mangled bodies were found strewn over the sandbagged walls like rag dolls. It was a grim and depressing sight.

We didn't have any body bags, so we loosely wrapped the dead in ponchos. After the bodies were placed on the chopper pad for extraction, I was drawn to the spot where they lay. Their feet were grotesquely tilted in the same direction and the uncovered legs each had an identification tag tied to the right boot. I didn't recognize their names and I couldn't see their faces, which was just as well.

Though the mortar attack deaths were shocking, their impact soon faded as the routine firebase activities resumed. However, Specialist Harrison, the GI who claimed he smelled the VC girl we killed at Phong Dien, went off the deep end. He was mentally unstable and we had not realized it. We watched in amusement as he loaded himself with ammunition and declared, "I'm gonna get me some NVA. Don't you see them watching us from the tree line?"

"Sure Harrison," Freddie Shaw laughed, "they're making faces at us!"

"Take no prisoners!" shouted Stan Alcon. We all laughed. Five seconds later we had stopped laughing and were staring dumbfounded as Harrison leaped over the concertina wire and dashed into the jungle. Once out of sight, he hollered "Geronimo!" then sprayed the jungle with a full magazine burst of M-16 fire, finishing the barrage with several grenades. Two squads scrambled to retrieve Harrison in case the NVA really were out there. When we found him, Harrison complained that the Gooks ran away when they saw him coming. Harrison was clearly a risk to the firebase as well as to himself. The safest thing to do was send him to the rear for psychiatric evaluation or simply keep him busy at Camp Evans until his tour ran out.

"They're sending me to the rear?" he shouted, questioning the move. "Those dirty bastards know damn well I want to be where the action is!"

"Are you crazy?" we scolded him. "Most Grunts only get a couple of days in the rear before going home. You'll have nearly a month."

"They can't fool me," he continued, his eyes open wide as if to better make his point. "They're sending me back to Camp Evans because the

Gooks are digging tunnels under the airstrip and they need me to flush them into the open."

The poor guy had gone crazy. The past eleven months of combat had burned him out. Later that day, a chopper brought out two new guys and prepared to take Harrison back. Most of the men were superstitious about being around a nut case, and so I was one of the few who bothered to say goodbye. Besides, as his squad leader, I felt it my duty to see him off.

Harrison sat in the helicopter looking out at me with a stupid grin. As we shook hands, he pulled me close saying, "Everybody thinks I'm crazy, but I don't give a fuck. I was just crazy enough to get my ass out of the field. Ha, Ha!" His eyes burned into mine.

As the chopper lifted off, I laughed to myself. Harrison wasn't nuts after all. His act fooled everyone, even me. He was just a short timer who had seen so much shit that he pulled something desperate to get out of the field. His scheme worked so well I decided to keep it a secret. Who knows, someday I might need a similar stunt to save myself.

One of the new guys who came out was a platoon leader to replace Lieutenant Bruckner. 2nd Lieutenant Anthony Pizzuto was a baby-faced Italian from a town in Idaho no one had ever heard of. A college graduate who planned on a long military career, Pizzuto wasn't bashful about voicing his belief that serving in Vietnam would provide the necessary grooming for future success. However, I wasn't sure how he planned to accomplish his goal because Pizzuto wasn't interested in meeting the platoon members. Instead, he spent several days in private meetings with Hartwell and Krol.

The other new guy was PFC Dennis Silig. He was a good-looking muscular fellow who didn't act nervous like the average Cherry coming to the field. He was relaxed, friendly, and already talking with some of the men.

"Hello Silig," I said, introducing myself, "I'm Sergeant Wiknik, your squad leader. Where are you from in the World?"

"Lancaster, New York," he answered, shaking my hand and squeezing it hard.

"That's quite a grip. Do you work out?"

"No," he laughed quietly. "In college I played a lot of sports to keep in shape."

"A college man?" I asked puzzled. "What the hell are you doing in the Army? Did you waive your deferment?"

"I couldn't afford my tuition anymore, so I quit. I was just surprised to get drafted so fast."

"Maybe you and Howard Siner should get together," I joked, "he's a New York college dropout, too."

To no one's surprise, Silig and Siner became instant friends. Their kinship of growing up in New York, similar educational background, and enjoyment of professional sports created a natural bond.

The rebuilding work on Firebase Airborne was completed so our next assignment would take us on a month long patrol of the A Shau mountains at the northern tip of the valley. In our absence, each company in our battalion during two-week rotating shifts would defend Airborne.

Our exit from the firebase should have been routine. Instead, it was a fiasco. With no natural clearings big enough to land a helicopter, an LZ had to be cut. The site selected was on a pointed ridge that was visible from the firebase. A five-minute artillery barrage pounded the location to help simplify the tree removal and scare off any lurking NVA. As elements of Echo Company rappelled into the jungle to provide security for a LZ cutting team, Cobra gunships patrolled from the air. With ten GIs already on the ground, everything was going as planned until the third helicopter hovered over the site. Just as the men started down the ropes, hidden NVA soldiers opened fire on the aircraft in an effort to make it crash and block the LZ.

The pilot was shot through both legs. The door-gunners answered back, spraying the jungle with long bursts of machine gun fire. As the co-pilot struggled to take control, a member of Echo Company dropped into an intense firefight on the ground. A second was even less fortunate. He was halfway down the rope when the helicopter suddenly sped skyward, yanking him several hundred feet into the air. The GI dangling fifty feet below the chopper hindered the co-pilot's evasive action, which allowed the NVA to score several hits on the aircraft. When the helicopter began smoking and losing altitude the co-pilot turned back toward the firebase. As the chopper whined its way toward us, we scattered for cover, figuring it could crash anywhere on the tiny outpost. The co-pilot maintained a heading that allowed the dangling GI to hit the ground running and slide free from the rope. It almost worked, but the GI was so terrified when he touched down he forgot to let go. His momentum dragged him headlong over the top of a bunker, depositing him in the concertina wire. He was hospitalized for lacerations, bruises, and shock. The co-pilot's attempt to land on the chopper pad was no more successful. The helicopter landed in a heap on an embankment and rolled over on its side. Miraculously, there was no fire and the crew escaped without additional injuries.

Meanwhile, back at the LZ, the Cobra gunships fired into the jungle and broke up the NVA attack. Three GIs were wounded, but none seriously. There were no enemy dead or wounded left behind. The attacking force was estimated at less than ten men.

Several hours later, the LZ cutting was complete and the operation resumed. We were nervous about going in, but our company landed without incident. After the last of the helicopters flew away the area became eerily quiet.

"The A Shau is a very bad place," observed Tu Huong, a Kit Carson scout we had brought along. "Beaucoup NVA. This is very, very bad." His words made the hair on my neck stand up. Since he was a former VC soldier, Huong was worried about what would happen to him if he was captured by the NVA. His gloomy speculation didn't inspire much confidence in us, either.

Since the NVA knew where we were, it was too dangerous to remain near the LZ because they could easily launch an attack or mortar us. Our only option was to head into the jungle. When our lead element moved out, they came upon a well-used narrow trail along the top of the ridge. Adjacent to the footpath was a set of NVA field telephone communication wires that were severed during the LZ artillery prep. We tapped into the lines, hoping to intercept a message our scout could interpret, but they weren't being used. Rather than wait for a transmission that might never come, we decided to follow the wires.

We quietly advanced about a quarter mile until a full burst of AK-47 rounds sent us scrambling for cover. The bullets struck and badly wounded our point man, PFC Kristoff. He had walked into a well-camouflaged bunker complex where one or two NVA soldiers had been waiting to ambush us. We returned fire, but no more enemy shots were heard and no soldiers were seen. The NVA gave us a taste of their deadly game of hit and run. Kristoff was in bad shape with wounds in both legs and in his lower abdomen. Luckily, the LZ was close enough for us to carry him back for quick evacuation.

A search of the complex revealed twenty bunkers and a command post, enough room to house fifty or more men. We figured the site was used as a rest area, as it offered no military advantages and there were no fighting positions. For many of us, this was the first enemy bunker complex we had seen, and we were impressed with the NVA's ingenuity in developing the site. A small stream flowing through the complex supplied them with drinking water. There were three camp-style cooking locations, each with several small wooden bowls perched on the rocks next to them. The complex had been evacuated while the LZ was being cut. A handful of NVA must have stayed behind to harass the LZ cutters while the main force escaped. The bunkers were five feet deep, each large enough to house three soldiers. Hand woven thatch mats elevated a few inches above the dirt floor provided a moisture barrier for comfortable sleeping. Storage shelves dug in the walls were now empty. Rows of three-inch diameter logs covered with a foot of dirt made the ceiling. Jungle shrubs were planted on the roof to prevent the bunkers from being seen from the air.

The command bunker was much different. It was twice the size of the others, featuring two underground rooms. One room evidently housed the ranking officer and the other his aide. Atop the command bunker was a small thatched hooch that served as a central meeting place. Two hand-made benches and a wooden stool were inside.

The communication wires we had followed ran into the command bunker hooch and hung loosely from a corner post where a field telephone had been. Another set of wires led away from the hooch and down the original trail. We followed the new set for 500 feet to where they were cut. The retreating enemy must have taken the rest of the wire with them.

The NVA had three distinct advantages over us: they knew the terrain, our troop strength, and our approximate location. Not wanting to walk into another ambush, we got off the trail to cut our own route into the jungle. That way, we hoped we could surprise the enemy instead of them surprising us.

To penetrate the undergrowth, our machete-wielding point man slashed at everything in his path. This new route was supposed to conceal us, but the steady chink of the machete advertised our location. To make matters worse, the thick vegetation slowed forward movement to a crawl, forcing us to rotate exhausted point men every fifteen minutes. As we snaked along, we soon realized how clumsy a loosely packed rucksack was. The hanging vines seemed to have claws, which snagged anything protruding from our packs. Canteens were pulled loose, M-60 ammo belts broke free and helmets were knocked off heads. Every so often, a branch let go by the man in front would slap me in the face. By the time I recovered, he had disappeared into the thick jungle and I had to play catch-up.

The foliage eventually became too thick to continue, so we set up for the night where we stood. It was impossible to form a perimeter defense, so we simply squeezed into a twisted line of three-man positions. No one bothered with claymore mines or trip flares because there was no way the enemy could get near us without being detected. The dense jungle proved to be more effective than concertina wire. Darkness came quickly under the thick canopy that obscured the sky. A light breeze kept us comfortable throughout the night. Phosphorescent fungi on the ground emitted an eerie green glow, providing enough scattered light to estimate the lay of the land. It was creepy as hell.

A few hours after we settled in, the men on guard woke everyone because they heard a strange noise in the distance. It sounded like a moronic NVA chanting a garbled "Fuck you," but instead it came out as "Huk Hoo." The shrill outcry became louder as it closed on our location. Did they actually know where we were? Everyone prepared for action. Suddenly, directly alongside us, a foot-long lizard scampered up a tree crying out several high-pitched shrieks: "Huk Hoo! Huk Hoo!" We laughed at our own fears. This peculiar creature sounded human as it scampered its way through the darkness in search of food and companionship. We enjoyed the almost nightly contact with the harmless reptiles, which we nicknamed the "Fuck You Lizards."

The next morning we continued slashing our way until we broke out onto a different NVA trail. From that day on, we followed established trails because they were the easiest, quietest method of travel, though probably not the safest. Besides, in our search for the enemy, we had little other choice. The NVA would be found on or near the trails and paths, not in the middle of tangled undergrowth.

By now, our company traveled far enough from the LZ and deep enough into the jungle to where the NVA could no longer be sure of our location, losing their major advantage over us. That gave us the opportunity to employ our own style of trail warfare. As our main force slowly advanced, alternating squads remained behind for fifteen minutes. These men provided rear protection and early warning in case we were being followed. If we came upon a trail junction or knoll offering good fields of fire, we set up platoon-size ambushes for the day. At dusk, everyone regrouped into our company-size unit. Despite the soundness of these tactics we never saw an NVA soldier, which made us wonder if we really had eluded them.

As we pressed deeper into the jungle, the vegetation thinned and the terrain became more rugged. The trail followed a ridgeline with sides so steep that it was like walking on the peak of a barn roof. That forced us to set up oval-shaped night perimeters directly on the footpath. All our machine guns were placed on the trail to provide maximum firepower at the most likely avenue of enemy approach. Judging by the terrain, it seemed unlikely the enemy would come from any direction other than the trail. But to be safe, we also put out claymore mines and trip flares.

We moved into four-man positions on the steep slope with our heels dug into the ground. Lying practically vertical, we had no idea of how we were going to sleep without tumbling downhill. Noise discipline prevented us from digging in or leveling off the ground. The only thing to do was to brace our rucksacks against the butt of the trees and try to sleep curled around them.

The company CP didn't have to worry about such problems because they set up their position in the center of the trail where the ground was flat and good for sleeping. However, their location had one major drawback. If we were attacked, the CP was most vulnerable to the enemy. Luckily, the nights were uneventful, although uncomfortable.

Each morning, our first task was to retrieve the trip flares and claymores. The devices were placed about fifty feet from the perimeter, so two men at a time went out to collect them. PFC Norman Keoka, a native Hawaiian who, at a glance could pass for a Vietnamese, got the feeling he was being watched. When he looked up, he spotted two armed NVA soldiers seventy-five feet away walking toward him. The Gooks must have thought our guy was on their side. It took Keoka a few seconds to catch on to what was happening because no one ever expects the NVA to walk right up to them. Suddenly, the enemy soldiers realized they were practically on top of a US Army position. The instant the NVA spun around to flee, Keoka opened fire on them. Behind him, a dozen GIs instinctively joined in. The one-sided hail of gunfire was intense but inaccurate. The shooters gave chase for several hundred feet but the enemy soldiers escaped.

Captain Hartwell gathered twenty men and prepared to continue the pursuit. Questioning the wisdom of us going up the trail, I asked our new Lieutenant to recommend a different tactic.

"Lieutenant Pizzuto," I began, "those two Gooks may be the point for a larger enemy force, and since our shooting gave our position away, they're probably expecting us to go looking for them. We could be walking into an ambush."

"What do you suggest?" he asked in an almost uninterested fashion.

"I think the first thing we should do is fire some artillery up there. If not that, the vegetation looks thin enough so a couple of squads could parallel either side of the trail for a thousand feet or so. That way, we might be able to get an idea of what's waiting for us."

"I will not go to the Captain with dumb ideas like those," he said in a snobbish tone. "I've been warned about you and how you feel it's necessary to challenge our tactics. Unlike you, I've got every confidence in the Captain's decision. He knows what he's doing." As the patrol moved out I didn't say anything else, hoping that I was worried about nothing.

A few minutes after the last man left the perimeter there was a huge explosion at the point followed by a heavy exchange of AK-47 and M-16 rifle fire. The rest of the company sat helplessly behind while the short firefight died out. Minutes later, the patrol returned carrying the point man; he had a horrible face and neck wound. I was shocked to recognize him as one of the GIs who rubbed my mangled Hamburger Hill M-16 magazine over himself for good luck. A second GI was shot in the shoulder but could walk on his own.

Before I could tell Pizzuto "I told you so," our platoon was ordered up the trail. We quickly headed out with Howard Siner, Stan Alcon, and myself at the point taking turns sidestepping the trail and ducking behind trees. We reached the ambush site with no resistance. Directly ahead was a small bunker at a trail junction. We cautiously crept forward until suddenly, Siner pulled the pin on a grenade and charged the position. He rolled on the ground and threw the frag into the bunker entrance. Seconds later, smoke and debris belched out of the opening. Then Siner sprayed a burst of rock n' roll into it. Alcon and I rushed to assist Siner, but the bunker was empty. The Gooks had blown their ambush on the first patrol and ran off. An escape route behind the bunker allowed them to retreat unnoticed. There was no telling which way they had gone, so we left a squad behind to watch the trail junction while the rest of us returned to the company perimeter.

A medevac was called for the wounded men, but a thick and low bank of clouds prevented the chopper from locating our position. By the time the helicopter found us, an hour had passed and the point man was dead. As the chopper hovered above, we fired into the jungle to suppress any NVA close enough to take pot shots at it. At the same time, the dead point man and the wounded GI were winched up in a basket. I was so disgusted I took my frustrations out by shooting into a small tree until it fell over.

After the medevac flew away, our company continued up the trail. Our platoon was at the end of the line, so we quietly watched everyone file by. Lieutenant Pizzuto wandered over with a stupid grin on his face. "This is the same type of resistance the 3/187th encountered as they worked toward Hamburger Hill."

"How do you know that?" I asked, unbelieving.

"I read the after-action report before coming out to the field."

"Is that right?" I said in disgust. "Listen, most of us were on that hill, and we're not ready to go through that again. Hell, you weren't even there. You don't know what it was like."

"That doesn't matter. Our job is to find and kill the enemy. If it takes another Hamburger Hill, we'll just do it again." There was no sense reasoning with Pizzuto. He's just as narrow-minded as the rest of the Lifers.

Late that afternoon we set up for the night on a hilltop where three minor footpaths converged onto the main trail. The area was ideal for a defensive position with gentle slopes, sparse brush, and easy foxhole digging. About an hour before dark a soaking rain fell and a thick fog rolled in behind it. Visibility was nearly zero and the heavy rain falling on the leaves made it impossible to detect any movement outside our positions. The weather forced us to stay on 50% alert throughout the night.

The rain and fog continued in the morning. Each man had a poncho, but after a night of steady rain nearly everyone was cold, wet, and miserable. A few men set up poncho tents during the night, but Captain Hartwell made us take them down because the water reflecting on wet rubber could be spotted by the NVA. He also believed we were not on our best guard if we worried too much about keeping dry. However, the anti-tent rules only applied to the perimeter positions. Our superiors erected their own poncho tents, saying they were necessary to keep maps and radios dry. That was probably true, but the obvious double standard was frustrating—especially when Lieutenant Pizzuto and his RTO only ventured into the rain when they absolutely had too. The real clincher was when Krol set up a hammock under his tent so he wouldn't have to lay on the damp ground like the rest of us.

The wet weather also increased the local wildlife activity. Two-inch long blood-sucking leeches were everywhere. The ugly little nocturnal worms are masters at attaching themselves to exposed flesh without being noticed until morning. The only way to get a leech to release its grip was to burn it with a cigarette or douse it with bug juice. Hidden leeches gorged with blood swelled to twice their size before eventually dropping off. The only evidence of their attack was a harmless pea-sized hickey that disappeared in a few days. For protection, shirt and pants legs were tucked in and sleeves were rolled down and buttoned. The funniest leech encounter occurred when one attached itself under Lennie Person's lower lip while he was sleeping. When Lennie found it, he panicked and jumped around trying to pull off the slimy creature. Whenever Lennie yanked on the leech, his lower lip stretched out as far as it would go. It was hysterical to watch, but Lennie was petrified by what he called a "vampire leech." A well-placed squirt of bug juice finally ended the episode.

As wet as it was, we continued to send out patrols two or three times a day. One platoon ambushed three enemy soldiers, killing two and wounding the third. The wounded NVA was shot in the back and could not move his legs. To administer first aid, the medic cut his pants off. When the medic finished, there wasn't enough left of the pants to put back on, so the NVA was left naked from the waist down. The enemy soldier was young, possibly a teenager, and totally helpless. He was scared to death at being surrounded by so many Americans. Our Kit Carson scout interpreter was unable to get any information from him except that he didn't know where he was or why his buddies left him behind. He must not have known his companions were dead. Nervous, wounded, and half-naked, the NVA could have been a candidate for a cruel attack, but no one bothered him. The young soldier was simply a prisoner of war who required a 24-hour guard.

The weather conditions made for long dull hours. When a platoon was out on patrol, the rest of the company just hung around. Everything was wet, so we could not play cards or write letters. Most guys made hot chocolate or coffee and snacked on C-rations. We didn't bother rationing ourselves because we thought the weather would clear in time for the normal three-day re-supply. As the days passed, nearly everyone ran out of food. The first day without a meal wasn't bad, but on the second day the hunger began in earnest. For the first time I realized what a powerful force an empty stomach is. The coffee and chocolate mix were long gone and our cravings were not satisfied by plain water. There were probably edible plants in the area, but no one knew what they were. The need for food reduced us to chewing and swallowing gum, lapping up teaspoon-size packets of sugar and, as a last resort, eating toothpaste. To keep our spirits up, we guessed which toothpaste had the highest nutritional value, the fluoride brand or the mint-flavored brand. After eating half a tube, no one cared if they ever brushed their teeth again. Our hunger problem brought out the worst in some people. One enterprising GI sold his hoarded C-rations to the highest bidder. He made some money, but lost a few friends in the process.

On my platoon's turn to go on patrol, Lieutenant Pizzuto decided to follow one of the small paths that veered off the main trail. The path led to a steep overlook where the NVA could post an observer to watch activity on the next ridge. There was no one at the overlook because it was too foggy to even see the ridge. We followed the path diagonally down the hill until the slope leveled off. As we neared the bottom, we found ourselves on the edge of a small NVA bunker complex. We quickly spread out to search the area when Freddie Shaw found a spilled bowl of rice near a bunker entrance. On the chance an NVA was hiding there, a hand grenade was pitched inside. After the explosion, Shaw checked it out. The bunker was empty.

Each bunker was approached in the same manner: sneak up carefully, toss in a grenade, wait for the explosion, and check it out. There were no NVA. They must have seen or heard us coming and bugged out. We finished examining the area but turned up nothing worth reporting.

We headed back up the path but as the slope got steeper it became impossible to walk. The soaked ground and our foot traffic had turned the path into a slippery mess. Without any traction, everyone kept falling.

The only way to climb the slope was by grabbing onto shrubs and vines and pulling ourselves up.

Dennis Silig, the new guy from New York, took a spill that ripped out the rear of his pants. He was about ten feet ahead of me, but because of the slope, his butt stayed at eye level. Whenever he leaned forward to grab a branch, his testicles swung into view. I thought it was funny and was smirking about it when Silig happened to look back at me. He seemed a little rattled, probably worried that I had been out in the bush too long and was beginning to think his ass looked good to me.

We returned to the company perimeter exhausted, covered with mud, and with our hands wrinkled from the rain. I wondered how the Gooks could stand it out there like this. When I got to my position, Howard Siner pulled me aside.

"Hey Sarge," he whispered, "I think you should know that while we were out there today, Pizzuto had his M-16 set on rock n' roll."

"Are you sure?" I asked in disbelief. "He can't be that stupid."

"Maybe he was scared."

"I don't give a shit. What if he took a header in the mud? Why didn't you tell me this before?"

"I didn't notice until we were almost back."

I went to the platoon CP to check it out. His rifle was leaning against a tree and it was still set on full automatic. Whether he knew the weapon was off safe or not, he had violated everyone's trust, which was just too important to ignore.

"Lieutenant Pizzuto," I said, trying to be diplomatic, "were you aware that your weapon was on full-auto while we were out?"

"Yes," he admitted casually, walking over to switch it back onto safe. "I must have forgotten about it."

"Sir, it was pretty greasy out there and you fell a couple of times. What if your weapon went off? You risked everyone's safety."

I was hoping Pizzuto would say I was right and that he would be more careful in the future. Instead, he glanced at Krol before chastising me.

"Look young man, I know what I'm doing out there."

"Sir," I began, just before he cut me off.

"Shut-up, Wiknik!" he shouted. Krol grinned with approval as Pizzuto continued. "Who are you to question me? I'm in charge of this platoon. I decide the tactics and how they are carried out. And just for your information, I had my weapon on full-auto so I could provide immediate return fire in case we were ambushed."

"Lieutenant," I groaned, "if we were ambushed, you would be needed to assess the situation, organize our defenses, and call in fire support. The men will shoot back."

"NCOs like you are a disgrace," he blurted, steering away from the subject. "If you don't shape up, I'll start proceedings to get you busted down to a Private. You got that?"

"I hear you, sir," I sighed, knowing that if I ever got busted I would not be in any position to help the men.

"Good. Now get back to your squad and don't bother me unless it's for something important."

Pizzuto and Krol were meant for each other. Regular Army all the way, except in their case, the initials R.A. stood for "Real Assholes." With people like Pizzuto around we wouldn't need the enemy attacking us. We could kill our own men just by being stupid and arrogant.

At least something good finally happened. During the night the sky cleared, ending six days of rain and fog. I never thought a star-filled night in Vietnam could be so beautiful. It meant we would soon get re-supplied.

At first light we began cutting an LZ. Usually it takes a team of twelve half a day to do the job, but everyone knew food would be coming, so thirty volunteers completed the task in about two hours. The supply chopper came in at 10:00 a.m. with C-rations, ammo, and mail. Two Cherries also came out to exchange places with two GIs going on R & R. The wounded NVA was carried onto the supply chopper, but he panicked and started hollering when the crew chief strapped him down. It was probably his first helicopter ride and he was afraid of what might happen once they were airborne. I could hardly blame him. I had heard rumors that enemy soldiers who refused to talk sometimes "fell" out the helicopter door. He may have heard the same thing.

When the C-rations were distributed, we gorged ourselves first with the least desirable meals, figuring this would be the only time they would taste good. After our bellies were full and our mail read, we were like contented sheep. No one even balked when word came down that we would continue deeper into the A Shau to resume searching for the enemy.

Two days later, our platoon was on point when the NVA set off a hit and run ambush. We returned fire but it was obvious the enemy escaped unharmed. We had two wounded, PFC Hoag and Specialist Prue. Their wounds were not life threatening, but both required evacuation. After things calmed down and the wounded were patched up, Prue began yelling into the jungle.

"You Gooks fucked up! We're only wounded! We're going home you fuckin' assholes! You have to stay forever! Ha, ha!"

With less than two months left to serve, Prue knew his wounds were a ticket home. He was so happy to be leaving that he started giving his equipment away. By the time the medevac picked him up, he had only his M-16, helmet, and an empty rucksack to take back. It seemed crazy to be happily wounded, but the life of a Grunt was the worst job imaginable and some men were willing to endure anything to get out of it.

We left the ambush site on a footpath that looked like it had not been used for several weeks. The path led down a slope and merged with an NVA high-speed trail. The trail was a miniature roadway with a hard packed dirt surface and drainage ditches. It was wide enough for two-directional bicycle travel and for transporting wheeled armaments. The trail was cleverly concealed from the air by anchoring treetops with vines to form an arched tunnel. The trail appeared to be abandoned. There were no tire tracks or footprints, and it had patches of new sprouts of jungle foliage. The lack of NVA activity on such well-engineered route seemed unusual, so we decided to follow it.

As we moved cautiously forward, the foliage changed to a dull rusty color; the plant life was dying. The farther we traveled, the worse it became. Eventually every stalk of vegetation was stripped of leaves. Huge teak trees that once shaded the jungle floor stood motionless and bleak, like the dormant winter woods back home. The jungle here was dead. The eerie stillness was interrupted only when the wind rustled crumpled leaves.

"It looks like the edge of two different worlds," Alcon lamented. "What the hell caused it?"

"Agent Orange," Lieutenant Pizzuto announced. "It's a defoliant that kills vegetation to deny the NVA natural cover. It makes it easier for us to detect their supply routes, staging areas, and troop movements."

It could not have been good for us to be exposed to the stuff, so we headed back. When we returned to the living jungle, we took a break.

Before long we spotted three low altitude aircraft spraying more defoliant. As the fine mist slowly settled around us, we looked at one another and shrugged. What could we do about it? At the time, we did not know the chemical's terrible side-effects.

Our next resupply point was on a ridge where the jungle was thin enough for supplies to be dropped from a hovering helicopter. From eighty feet high, the first item tossed out the door got stuck on a tree branch. It was our mailbag. To get the bag down, the helicopter crew chief threw twenty-pound C-ration cases at it. We scattered as the cases bounced and tumbled out of the trees. A key hit finally knocked the bag free.

Things got even dumber after that. We were finally going to get the fresh fruit Captain Hartwell had been begging for. To our dismay, two cardboard boxes of apples were thrown out the helicopter door. The first box struck a tree limb, splitting the box wide open. Apples rained down like hailstones as everyone scattered again. Most of those apples disappeared down a hillside. The second box missed the limb but landed on the ground in a heap, smashing them into fruit cobbler. Needless to say, very few apples were eaten. During the next few hours, thousands of insects were attracted to the mashed apples, forcing us to leave the ridge. Captain Hartwell never asked for fresh fruit again.

A week later we returned to Firebase Airborne. It was good to be back. Portable showers were set up for our fourth bath in three months. We were also issued clean clothes and received daily mail, which included a scheduled delivery of newspapers. After humping in the A Shau for two months, the newspapers made us realize how isolated our assignment was.

The battle for Hamburger Hill was front-page news. We were surprised and proud to have taken part in a victory that captured the attention of the entire nation. However, our spirits were quickly dashed when we read Massachusetts Senator Edward M. Kennedy's charge that Hamburger Hill had no strategic value, calling the assault senseless and irresponsible. His assessment may have been correct, but we resented his taking away our hard-won victory.

Stan Alcon received the June 27 issue of *Life Magazine* carrying the special 13-page article, "Vietnam: One Week's Dead." The story contained pictures and names of the 242 Americans killed in Vietnam during the week of May 28 through June 3. Among the list were 35 men from the 101st, including the three killed on Firebase Airborne when the NVA mortar round exploded on top of their bunker. Captain Hartwell took the magazine away because he thought it was anti-war material. We thought it was sobering.

The July 10 news focused on US troop withdrawals from Vietnam as the first of 25,000 GIs stepped onto American soil at McChord Air Force Base in Washington. Every in-country Grunt hoped and prayed he would soon be one of the lucky ones going back to the World. But the Army was selective in determining which units would go home early and which would not. Unfortunately for us, the 101st was not selected for withdrawal.

As the days passed and more newspapers became available, the most amazing news of 1969 was announced. On July 20, Apollo 11 landed on the moon and astronaut Neil Armstrong became the first man to step onto the lunar surface. Men on the moon—how could it be? The thought was both exhilarating and depressing. Our nation had the technology to send humans 200,000 miles into space and return them safely home. Yet, we could not peacefully resolve a war here on Earth. With nothing to gain by debating the issue, the moon landing was soon forgotten. Our primary concern was still keeping our asses from being shot off.

Not all mail brought welcome news. Howard Siner received a startling letter from his younger brother Michael, who had been drafted into the Army four months earlier. Michael proudly boasted about his recent assignment to the US Army's 4th Infantry Division in South Vietnam's central highlands. Although the US military discouraged brothers from being in the war zone at the same time, either a paperwork mix-up or Michael's own doing had allowed it to happen. The news completely depressed Howard because he had promised his worrisome mother that his Vietnam service would protect Michael from having to participate in the war. Now that promise had unraveled. To top it off, our superiors refused to take action in what they considered a done-deal. Although I had no power to resolve the dilemma, I did have a sympathetic ear.

"What am I going to do about my brother?" Siner moaned. "While he was in basic training, I wrote to him describing what a horrible place Vietnam was and that he should do everything to avoid it. Instead, he thinks war is an adventure."

"An adventure!?" I stammered. "Everything about this place sucks. Why would anyone think war is an adventure?"

"I guess that's my fault," Siner sighed. "I wrote about our experiences on Hamburger Hill. Now he thinks I'm a hero and he wants to be like me."

His situation led me to think about my own younger brother who, though he was not old enough yet, could eventually be drafted into the war as well.

"Maybe both of you being in Vietnam can't be changed," I told him, "but I'll bet the company clerk can find a way for you guys to visit each other. Let's write a request and see what happens."

The possibility of seeing his brother raised Howard's spirits. A few days later, the clerk responded with a tentative timetable for the brothers to meet during a stand down. Even better yet, with some creative scheduling Howard and Michael could possibly go on R & R together. Howard was ecstatic. During their concurrent time in Vietnam, Howard and Michael managed to get together on two occasions.

As the days slowly crept by, life on the tiny firebase became a drag. We used what little free time we had writing letters or grabbing short naps. Otherwise, we were tasked with standard make-work projects like building a new latrine, filling the endless supply of sandbags, or stringing another row of concertina wire. Between work projects we went on recon patrols or set up daytime jungle ambushes. At night, we were put on different alert levels or driven practically deaf by artillery fire missions. We endured the same grinding bullshit over and over again.

To ease the monotony of firebase life, pairs of American Red Cross girls, known as Donut Dollies, paid us weekly two-hour visits. Their mission was to bring some close-up cheer to help soldiers forget about the war, if only for a short time. GIs generally liked the Dollies because they were attractive young women fresh out of college and full of high ideals. Their bright blue dresses, ingenuity, and smiling compassion also helped endear them to the men. Lonely GIs gathered around to watch them perform a routine called "the program." The program was a set of audience participation games better suited for adolescents at summer camp than for men in combat. In one game, a Dolly held up a picture of a penny and asked, "Which holiday does this represent?" The answer is Lincoln's Birthday, but the Dollies wanted us to make up titles like

National Coin Day or Annual One-Cent Sale. Some guys got a kick out of it; I thought it was bubble-headed nonsense.

I nicknamed the Donut Dollies the "Biscuit Bitches" to make it easy for me to avoid them. It was nothing personal, and although it was nice to know someone cared, I felt these girls did not belong in the field. The Dollies were round-eyed females casually dangled in front of young men who hadn't seen a woman for months. I thought they were a tease, and they only deepened the lonely remoteness of the war.

To me, the Donut Dollies were no different from other free people who made token visits to the field. Free people like reporters, photographers, politicians, and others had a choice about being in Vietnam and were not bound by a tour of duty. They caught mere glimpses of the war without having to live it or become part of the GI's world. None of them could feel what we felt, and none of them were stuck like us until death or DEROS (Date Eligible for Return from Overseas).

However, one welcome diversion from the war did arrive from the World in the form of packages sent from mothers and girlfriends. A typical package consisted of cookies, fruit cakes, seasonings, powdered juices, and a variety of canned goods. One package from my mother contained several seven-ounce cans of apple juice. It was the first real juice I'd had in more than three months and it was so refreshing I wrote a thank you letter to the manufacturer. In it, I briefly described infantry life in Vietnam and explained how the juice was such a welcome change that I wanted to purchase some to share with my squad. About two weeks later, I received a complimentary case of twenty-four cans. The manufacturer's representative said it was their way of showing support for the troops. As I divided the juice among the men, they were surprised that something good happened to us. After drinking water from rice paddies and rubber bladders for such a long time, the juice gift revitalized our taste buds and restored some lost faith in the folks back home.

The men's enthusiastic reaction sparked an idea. Maybe, with the right kind of letters I could get us more free food. After sifting through the garbage for addresses of hard to get foodstuffs from the World, I tabulated a log of manufacturers and distributors and sent requests to them at one-week intervals. The log was necessary to avoid contacting the same manufacturer twice. Plus, I thought it would be interesting to note who was generous, who was cheap, and who didn't bother to respond.

It didn't take long for the goodies to start rolling in. In the coming months I received peanuts, pretzels, fruit nectar, canned berries, sardines, steak sauce, and more. As a joke, I asked a tobacco distributor for cigar prices and they sent me a box of decent stogies! Everyone was curious about how I got case after case of the provisions, but I just shrugged and told them, "Somebody likes me." If they knew the truth, they might try the same thing, and it wouldn't take long for manufacturers to catch on to the scheme.

Freddie Shaw nicknamed me "Operator" because I reminded him of the Private Sefton character portrayed by William Holden in the 1953 movie "Stalag 17." However, unlike Private Sefton, I shared everything that came my way. It could be said that I took unfair advantage of some generous people back home. But the end result was appreciated. To Boonie Rats stuck with the same twelve meals for a straight year, the products helped make our situation (just) bearable.

We had been back at Firebase Airborne for several weeks where, in our routine security role, we had not fired a single shot in anger. The lack of enemy activity frustrated Lieutenant Pizzuto. During a squad leader meeting he let his feelings be known.

"This is no way to fight a war," he griped, "trapped here playing nursemaid to a bunch of artillery lazies. We're being denied the chance of proving ourselves in combat when there's plenty of Gooks out there just waiting to die for their country. Hell, a token attack on the firebase is the least the NVA could do."

I think I was the only one who thought he was nuts.

"Lieutenant, listen to yourself!" I said, disbelieving his idiotic statements. "You sound as if we're invincible. Every time we've had enemy contact someone dies or gets wounded because it's always been on the NVA terms, not ours. We should be putting more thought into our strategy before wishing for trouble."

"Sergeant Wiknik!" Pizzuto shot back with a cold glare. "I don't remember asking for your opinion. In fact, I don't think anyone here is interested in your opinion. Why would they? You are nothing but a malcontent who wants to destroy the morale of this unit. If I hear one more negative word from you I'll charge you with insubordination so fast it'll make your head spin."

The other squad leaders stared at me shaking their heads with disapproval. They didn't understand that Pizzuto was just an advocate of recklessness. I didn't say anything more.

A few days later, Pizzuto got especially upset when a platoon of elite ARVN Rangers used the firebase as a stepping off point for a raid on a suspected NVA base camp. The ARVNs returned the next day after killing three NVA and capturing a soldier and a female medic. That was all Pizzuto could stand. He begged Captain Hartwell to set up a joint search-and-destroy operation with the ARVNs. The Captain agreed to a one-day mission. The problem was we didn't get the elite rangers. Instead, we got a platoon of ARVN Cherries on their first time out.

GIs were paired off with ARVN soldiers, making for a combined troop strength of forty-five. None of the ARVNs understood English and they only brought one interpreter. When spoken to, they smiled, uttering a goofy, "Okay GI."

Our insertion to an LZ about one mile away was uneventful. From the LZ, we began a zigzag trek back to the firebase. We hiked along a thickly vegetated ridge with my partner clinging to me like a shadow. Sometimes I stopped quickly to see if he would bump into me. He didn't.

Less than half a mile from Airborne we came upon five deserted NVA bunkers. A routine search turned up nothing, so we took a break. While sitting on a stump I noticed a camouflaged bunker previously passed over and decided to check it out. The entrance was jammed with fresh cut branches and there were several footprints nearby. I checked for booby traps before gingerly pulling each branch out of the entrance. When the opening was clear I eased my way inside.

In the bunker were several long wooden boxes. I opened one and found a dozen Chicom SKS assault rifles. An arms cache! I grabbed one of the weapons and scrambled out the door waving it around yelling, "Rifles! This bunker is full of rifles!" Everyone ran over as I went back inside for more to pass around. The ARVNs joined in and immediately went to work removing the weapons. As they did, we conducted a more intensive search of the area.

About thirty feet away we found another bunker with no doorway at all. It looked like a mound of dirt. We dug a hole through the top and broke into a chamber that contained two burlap sacks filled with AK-47 ammunition and several stacks of 82mm mortar rounds.

Figuring there must be more munitions in the area, we expanded the search. Our final discovery was a small thatch hooch built over a four-foot square bamboo bin. The bin contained hundreds of wooden-handled Chicom hand grenades.

The total cache contained sixty-seven SKS assault rifles, 450 mortar rounds, nearly 1,000 hand grenades, and more than 15,000 rounds of small arms ammunition. Everything was airlifted back to Airborne for display and inventory. We were thrilled to take something away from the enemy without firing a shot.

The mission was a double success. Not only did we capture a substantial amount of enemy supplies, but we may have saved American lives as well. The proximity of the cache to Firebase Airborne made it clear that the NVA were planning a major attack.

Since I had found the cache, I figured there would be a medal or citation in it for me. There wasn't. In fact, Lieutenant Pizzuto did not acknowledge my role at all. Instead, his report stated that the credit belonged to the teamwork of the operation. I was disappointed, but at least I was able to keep a rifle for a souvenir.

My cache discovery was all the incentive Lieutenant Pizzuto needed to start making his mark in the war. The very next day he submitted a list of ideas to Captain Hartwell for a series of platoon-sized operations. Unfortunately for us, Pizzuto didn't have to wait long before his volunteering paid off.

Just two days later, Firebase Berchtesgaden, five miles south of Firebase Airborne, was overrun in a pre-dawn attack by an estimated ninety NVA. Nine Americans were killed while the enemy lost thirty-five. The NVA had broken through the wire and swarmed over the compound like ants. Savage hand-to-hand combat and superior firepower eventually repulsed them. Our battalion commander suspected the NVA might try again that night, so Lieutenant Pizzuto was more than eager for us to set up several blocking ambushes on the ridges adjacent to Berchtesgaden.

When we arrived at Berchtesgaden, GIs were stacking the last of the dead NVA into a grotesque pile atop a cargo net. The bodies would be flown to a mass grave. Pizzuto gazed at the enemy remains and was disappointed he had not been there to add to the casualty count. "Ah, we should have been here." None of us shared his enthusiasm.

Our platoon split into four squad-sized ambushes equally spaced on the hills surrounding the firebase. Once in position, we were so convinced the NVA would return that we maintained 100% alert through the night. We sat motionless in the creepy darkness as artillery damaged tree limbs cracked and fell to the ground. Every time a twig snapped we wondered if the cause was natural or man-made. The waiting and watching continued all night, but the enemy never showed.

After returning to Firebase Airborne that morning, we were greeted with the news that the NVA had made several light random attacks and probes of different firebases throughout the valley. To combat the threat, each firebase began a program of sending out an LP (Listening Post) each night. An LP is a four-man night position located 300 to 500 feet outside the firebase near a likely avenue of enemy approach. The LP is not supposed to engage the enemy, but rather provide early warning in the event the NVA probe the bunker line or mass for an attack. Grunt's hated LP because it seemed more like punishment than performing a duty. The position is so vulnerable that strict noise discipline and mental alertness had to be maintained during the entire night.

Communication between the LP and the firebase was performed with non-verbal radio signals, unless there was enemy activity. If enemy activity was confirmed, the LP would radio in the situation and try to get safely back to the firebase. That's when things really got dangerous, because now the enemy was behind them and their own men on the bunker line were armed and waiting in front of them. If the guards weren't forewarned that friendlies were coming in or someone was trigger-happy, the LP risked getting shot returning to their own base. Although our LPs rarely ran into trouble, those nocturnal stake-outs made the already spooky nights seem darker, longer, and more threatening than ever.

On my first LP, an angry mongoose periodically circled our position, hissing and growling because we were located too close to its home. As the night wore on, we were afraid the mongoose's antics might attract any nearby NVA. We couldn't move to a new location because the firebase plotted their harassing artillery fire around us. We couldn't kill the animal because then we would give our position away for sure. The only option was to sit tight. Our position was stationary and although the mongoose wasn't being threatened, it kept coming around. Since wild creatures normally fear humans, any NVA moving in our direction would probably scare the animal away. As it continued to hang around, it dawned on us that its presence was probably a good thing because it meant there were no NVA.

Whether on LP or bunker line guard duty, the night jungle around Firebase Airborne was so quiet that we sometimes welcomed an odd noise just to keep us on our toes. Usually it was the faint explosions of distant artillery barrages, but they often sounded more like a thunderstorm than a fire mission. Sometimes it was the tin cans rattling around our garbage heap outside the perimeter as nighttime animals scavenged for food. The only other sounds came from within the firebase when someone fumbled with his equipment or coughed.

One night we were treated to a B-52 air strike on the Ho Chi Minh Trail, which was only three miles away. From our vantage point the air strike had three distinct features, each more impressive than the last. The strike began with a massive display of bright orange flashes as hundreds of 500-pound bombs detonated. Several seconds later, the sound of the explosions roared past us like a pounding drum roll. The noise lasted for only a minute or so, but it was so intense we could not help snickering at the havoc that must be taking place at the impact area. The last phase was the bouncing vibration of the earth. The ground where we stood trembled like an earthquake, causing loosely stacked sandbags to fall over. In the morning, B-52s struck the same location again. In their wake, a giant dust cloud climbed several thousand feet high and took nearly an hour to dissipate. Witnessing such a display made an artillery fire mission seem insignificant.

A few days later, a task force of eighty armored personnel carriers and thirteen tanks entered the A Shau, marking the first appearance of tracked vehicles in the valley's history. Nine of the tanks and five personnel carriers made their way to the top of Hamburger Hill and criss-crossed the summit at will, proclaiming an uncontested victory.

"Big fucking deal," said a sarcastic Alcon. "We got to the top the hard way; by fighting to it."

"Yeah," added Lennie Person, "nobody gave us a ride. What did those tank guys have to be afraid of? No infantry unit would be stupid enough to stand up against armor anyway."

"I think you guys missed the real issue," remarked Howard Siner. "If tanks could go up Hamburger Hill now, why weren't they used during the battle? I think the Army was looking for a big infantry victory and tanks would have scared the NVA away."

"So what does that mean?" asked Freddie Shaw. "We were expendable?"Afraid to speculate, no one answered his question.

The armor task force encountered little enemy contact but did uncover several large weapons caches. Convinced the NVA would try to defend or remove remaining caches, the top Brass decided it was time to ambush the valley floor. The target was Highway 548, a dirt truck route along which the NVA had driven their vehicles a few months earlier.

When Lieutenant Pizzuto heard about the plan he immediately volunteered our platoon's services. Nice guy. Since I was always skeptical of any plan that sounded too risky, I felt it was my duty to protest.

"Lieutenant Pizzuto," I asked, questioning his sanity but trying to do it in a respectful way. "Why in the world did you volunteer us for such a dangerous mission? The NVA own the valley floor."

"That's exactly why the NVA won't be expecting us," he answered confidently. "It should be easy for us to catch them with their pants down. Besides, if we get into trouble, every firebase in the valley will have their guns ready to support us."

"A mission like this should be a company-size operation," I added, "not platoon-sized."

"It won't even be a platoon, wise guy. It will be two squads, yours and Sergeant Wakefield's. Fifteen men can sneak into an ambush position much easier than thirty can, you should know that. But I'm not going to argue with you on this one Wiknik. This is the opportunity I've been waiting for and even you can't spoil it. Now start getting your squad together." It was obvious Pizzuto was only doing this for the glory, which is why anything that I had to say about thinking a little more cautiously was ignored.

We loaded ourselves with the same firepower we carried for the Hamburger Hill battle. Each rifleman carried 300 rounds of M-16 ammo, two claymore mines, and eight hand grenades. Our two M-60 machine guns were bolstered with 1,500 rounds each. We also brought along two night vision starlight scopes and two radios.

Late in the day we left the security of the firebase. After the last man wormed his way through the opening in the concertina wire, the bunker line guards pulled it shut like a castle gate that would not open until morning. We quickly worked our way into the tree line and onto an abandoned enemy trail leading to the valley floor. The steep descent and the log stairs the NVA had constructed made walking easy. There were no signs of recent enemy activity, but I could not shake the feeling of being watched.

Our ambush location on a small knoll was covered with elephant grass six feet tall. After quietly matting down the grass, we had a clear view of the dirt road in both directions. We didn't expect enemy vehicles, but the chances were good that foot soldiers would be moving after dark. Once into position, everyone set out claymores, determined fields of fire, loosened hand grenade pins, and memorized the landscape.

No one slept nor talked as we stayed on 100% alert all night. Time was passed staring into the darkness and concentrating on the terrain. We were too scared to move around for fear of giving our position away, and no one wanted to be the cause of somebody getting zapped. The valley was so still that the slightest noise or movement from inside our perimeter caught everyone's attention. The most frustrating distraction was the battery-powered starlight scopes. Each time one was used, it gave off a high-pitched whine. Although the sound was barely audible, in our nervous state of mind it may as well have been a siren. Eventually we gave up on the scopes entirely.

As the uneventful night crept by, Lieutenant Pizzuto called for random harassment artillery fire to get the enemy moving around. The NVA never showed. Even the Fuck You Lizards and other night creatures stayed away. We welcomed the lack of enemy activity but being terrified for ten hours was draining. Luckily, the road ambush turned out to be just a routine night in the jungle. Lieutenant Pizzuto thought the valley floor ambush was a total failure, especially since he didn't get to go on the next missions. Teams from other platoons took turns but they all ended the same way: no enemy contact.

A week later, we were surprised to learn that the 101st was withdrawing all divisional units from the A Shau Valley. The pullout coincided with the beginning of the monsoon, a season of persistent drizzle and treacherous fog. The changing weather would minimize the effectiveness of the firebases; air mobility would be reduced and resupply would be nearly impossible, allowing the NVA to bring the war close to the coastal cities. Again, Lieutenant Pizzuto was disappointed, but we didn't care; we were leaving the A Shau.

During the next three days, Firebase Airborne was completely dismantled. Tons of ammunition, artillery pieces, and building supplies were airlifted back to Camp Evans as we stripped the tiny outpost down to a dirt mound.

The final dismantling was finished too late in the day for our company to be choppered out, so three platoons stayed for the night. With no concertina wire or artillery or mortar backup, we protected ourselves from a possible ground attack. Our defense was quite simple. In addition to the weapons we normally carried we had thirty cases of fragmentation hand grenades, giving each man about forty grenades apiece.

We didn't realize it at the time, but the final night on Airborne would turn into a therapy session. After being in the field for four straight months, everyone needed to release his frustrations. Around 10:00 p.m., a couple of bored men bet on who could throw a grenade the farthest. It sounded like fun. Besides, if any NVA were close by, the grenades would give them something to think about. So the pins were pulled and the grenades were tossed.

It was difficult to measure how far an exploding object was thrown in the dark so we estimated distance from the flash. If it looked like a tie the contestants threw again. Before long, grenade-tossing contests were taking place all around the perimeter. Whenever someone got the urge, he threw a grenade. The guys just went wild.

Captain Hartwell was pissed off and ordered us to stop, but we were out of control and proud of it. Lieutenant Pizzuto and Sergeant Krol were going crazy trying to catch someone to punish. Wherever there was an explosion they ran over yelling, "Who threw that grenade?" Before they got an answer, five more would explode on the other side of the hill, causing them to run in that direction to check those out. The more they ran around, the sillier we got. It went on like that for an hour until we stopped on our own because we were running out of grenades. However, an occasional grenade would still explode and we'd all laugh. It was a great night, if ever a night in the jungle can be.

Early the next morning we left Firebase Airborne. I felt a tug of emotion for the twenty American lives that were lost protecting that god-forsaken hilltop. It was ironic that the way we left Airborne was no different than the way we left Hamburger Hill: we just walked away and gave it back to the enemy.

Fuck it. Don't mean nothin'.

CHAPTER 5

The Bamboo Shooters

Our company's nearly four-month stint in the A Shau Valley concluded with a well-deserved overnight stand down at Camp Evans. It was such a relief to be out of the field that we poured into the battalion area hooting and hollering like cowboys finishing a cattle drive.

We assembled in a loose formation for a boring but thankfully short speech by Captain Hartwell on the great job we were doing and that he would be expecting more of the same. Hardly anyone listened as we talked among ourselves, played grab-ass, and generally ignored him. Hartwell's announcement that we were free until 9:00 a.m. the next morning met with cheers and applause. But when he told us that new AOs were assigned and tomorrow we would be back in the field, everyone groaned. At least we would have the night off. Our stand down was the first under a new policy where all weapons and ammunition were stored in heavy metal containers called a conex. These were originally used to hold and transport goods aboard ships. On the last stand down, overzealous revelers drank too much, made threats, and were a general nuisance. The final straw was when they shot holes through the movie screen of the Camp Evans theater while watching a monster film.

After securing our gear, the next order of business was to wash off weeks of caked-on dirt. A temporary shower station erected behind the mess hall had no provision for privacy, so we bathed naked to the world. Since this was only my fifth shower in nearly five months, I didn't care. The old-timer's comment that a bath a month is a luxury rang true. After being grubby for so long, it felt odd being clean; even our laundered fatigues felt strange. Our sense of smell had adapted so well to the jungle that the soft aroma of soap seemed almost overpowering.

With clean bodies and clean clothes, our platoon split into several groups, though we did not go far. Camp Evans was too remote to worry about seeing any of the local sights. The village was off limits as well, so there were no women for us either. With nowhere to go, we hung around the battalion area where men who received mail and packages from home sat quietly reading, answering letters, and munching on their mom's cookies. Others bought beer from the PX for the stand down celebration. A small circle of guys we called "Heads" disappeared into the maze of base camp tents seeking their drug contacts.

Drug abuse in Vietnam had its share of bad publicity, but it was rare in our company. More often than not, it was the rear echelon soldiers who had easy access and more off-duty time to indulge who used drugs. The average Grunt avoided drug use for two reasons: first, no one wanted to be labeled as someone who could not cope; second, no one was willing to risk the safety of their buddies by being unable to function properly. Although there were probably isolated cases, I knew of no one—not even the Heads—who used drugs in the boonies. However, with all the hardships we endured, it's surprising that more soldiers didn't get high to escape the war. Here on stand down, my platoon's escape from the war was different. We didn't need illicit stimulants. We drank.

Case after case of beer and several blocks of chopped ice were placed into a 55-gallon barrel. When the brew was cold, thirsty GIs dove into it like kids grabbing Halloween candy. We were surprised at how the beer stung our throats, unaccustomed to anything so cold, but we got used to it soon enough. The beer buzz was something we had not experienced for what seemed like a lifetime. Nearly everyone indulged except Freddie Shaw who tried to talk us out of drinking.

"Where I come from, any beverage containing alcohol is known as ignorant oil," he scolded us. "We call it that because it makes people stupid."

"How do you come up with such nonsense?" asked Scoggins. "Alcohol should be called 'smart juice' because it stimulates the brain."

"That's right," joked Howard Siner. "Even as we speak, my IQ is starting to rise. Within an hour I'll be a rocket scientist." Everyone laughed as Shaw shook his head and walked away.

As expected, we guzzled the beer as if there would be no tomorrow. In addition, since we were in a war zone and fancied ourselves as tough guys, GIs who over-indulged would sneak off to puke to avoid being laughed at. However, everyone knew what was going on because the GIs who returned were sloppy drunks and usually reeked of vomit.

I looked forward to celebrating freedom from the field, but was apprehensive about how much socializing I should do with the troops. As a Sergeant, it was awkward for me to be friendly with the Privates and Specialists, even those in my squad with whom I was so familiar. I thought it appropriate to distance myself, though the life and death experiences we shared created a bond stronger than any friendship I had known back in the World. Some GIs were reluctant to embrace that friendship because of the high emotional cost should the friend be seriously wounded or killed. That self-imposed defense mechanism is one of the infantryman's greatest dilemmas and most painful burdens. As I contemplated my problem, Siner and Silig called out to me.

"Hey Sergeant Wiknik! What do say we forget about the war for a while and have a few beers?"

Their invitation was such a pleasant surprise that I immediately abandoned my role-playing concerns.

"As long as the brew is cold," I answered, accepting their invitation. "But I've got to warn you, I've been accused of not being able to hold my liquor. Back home my friends nicknamed me Bottle-cap Artie."

"Bottle-cap Artie?" a bewildered Silig asked. "What the hell for?"

"Because I have such a low alcohol tolerance they figured I could get drunk by just sniffing bottle-caps."

"Well, look at your size," Silig announced. "You're one of the smallest men in the platoon. It's no wonder why you get drunk so fast."

"Drink this," Siner commanded, handing me a beer. "You've been working too hard and need to relax. By the time we're through with you, you'll be known as 'Two-beer Artie.'"

As we laughed, I felt a warm rush of friendship. I sensed that our similar personalities would create a stronger bond than just a squad leader and his subordinates. We were equally educated, shared the same sense of humor, and had a driving desire to get everyone home alive. Being close to twenty-one years old, we also had a higher level of maturity than the platoon's mostly eighteen and nineteen year olds. Without saying it, we knew we would be the ones to teach new guys how to survive and to keep their wits about them. I felt fortunate to have Siner and Silig as friends.

Late in the day we walked to the camp's outdoor theater to hear a Filipino band perform popular American songs. They played good music but the singing detracted from the performance.

"Set me fwee why don't joo babe, get out of my wife why don't joo babe."

"What the hell are they trying to sing?" I asked.

"I think it's a Vanilla Fudge song," Silig answered, shaking the butchered words from his head. "But it sounds more like *Elmer Fudge*."

"Oh, you cwazy wabbit," Siner added with a laugh.

The Filipino's tried hard, but we had not been in the field long enough to consider this worthwhile entertainment. The name of the song was "You keep Me Hanging On," originally performed by the Supremes, and later covered by the rock group Vanilla Fudge, whose version became popular with hippie-types in the late 1960s.

We continued walking. It was relaxing just to not have to carry a weapon and rucksack or watch for trip wires and booby traps. We enjoyed simple pleasures not allowed in the field, like smoking after dark, drinking beer, laughing and talking without having to whisper, drinking beer, sitting on a toilet seat instead of a log—and drinking more beer! As the sunlight faded, the drone of generators peaked. Camp Evans was alive with electric lights, radios, and tape decks. It was a different world in the rear and we wandered around in awe of a time and place so contrasting to our familiar jungle life.

Outside our battalion area, an argument between Lennie Person and an unknown GI had escalated into a heated exchange. The GI, who was obviously drunk, threatened the small crowd of onlookers with an M-16 he had taken from the conex. Lennie grabbed at the weapon and a struggle ensued. Suddenly a shot rang out. Lennie jumped back screaming, "You mother-fucker! You shot me!" and fell to the ground clutching the side of his head. A small chunk of his ear was shot off.

The crowd quickly overpowered the GI, holding him until the MPs (Military Police) arrived. In the meantime, we rushed Lennie to the aid station for treatment. He was okay. The MPs locked up the GI for the night. We never found out what the argument was about. Perhaps Freddie Shaw was right: booze is ignorant oil. We decided to return to the battalion area where it was safer because no one had weapons there.

We got back just in time to see the start of a porno movie. With no screen, the film was shown on a bed sheet nailed to the supply room wall. The movie was about an escaped gorilla that was so horny he decided to try his luck with human females (it was obvious that a man was wearing a cheap gorilla suit). As the animal sneaked through a neighborhood, it broke into a girl's apartment and somehow convinced her to go to bed with him. When the gorilla exposed his penis, everyone could see that it belonged to a white male. That's when a black GI sitting behind us got up yelling, "Fake! Fake! That gorilla ain't real! A real gorilla has a black dick just like me! Where did this movie come from?"

He was serious. Up until that moment he had believed it was a real animal! We laughed so hard we had to rewind the movie for the parts we missed. How could anyone be so naive? Damn that ignorant oil.

The movie was so stupid that we ended up throwing beer cans at the sheet every time the gorilla appeared. One GI tried to feel the girl and accidentally pulled the sheet off the wall. No one bothered to put it back up. After that, the guys wandered back to the hooches to sleep.

The night in our hooch was quiet except for heavy breathing and occasional groans. I was almost asleep when two pranksters giggled outside the screen windows.

"What's so funny?" I drowsily asked.

"You'll find out," came their impish reply. Then they tossed a CS (Chemical Substance, a.k.a. tear gas) grenade onto the ground where a gentle breeze brought the gas inside. In an instant, the fumes snapped me out of my stupor. When I screamed, "Gas! Gas!" twenty-five drunks scrambled like disturbed bees in a hive. We clawed at the walls trying to locate an exit but we couldn't see because the lights didn't work. The clever pranksters had shut our power off. Choking and gagging, we smashed through the screens to escape. Once outside, some guys vomited, while others tripped over each other. We must have been quite a sight. Too sick and drunk to get mad, we waited until the air cleared and then stumbled back into the destroyed hooch to sleep. It was a good joke, though I would rather have been one of the pranksters.

Morning came too quickly and, as expected, everyone was dragging ass from their hangovers. But more important, we grumbled over the fact that we were being sent back to the field. No one wanted to go.

The routine of gathering our gear was interrupted when a jeep pulled up with a trailer full of grenades, claymores, and other ammunition. To avoid a mob scene, each squad leader was supposed to collect ammunition for his men. But almost before the jeep stopped, GIs surged up to the trailer, digging into the load. I could not understand the rush, unless they knew of beer or a boom-boom girl hidden under the ordnance. The men pushed and shoved until one GI backed away holding a grenade pin. He shouted "Grenade!" and everyone ran in several directions. We stood about a dozen yards away curiously watching the trailer until the seemingly harmless yellow smoke appeared from a smoke grenade.

"It's just a smoke grenade," someone yelled. "Pull it out!"

"No!" shouted another. "It's too hot, it'll burn ya!"

"You bunch of candy-asses," chided Lieutenant Pizzuto, as he pushed through the crowd. "I'll get it out."

Just as Pizzuto reached in, there was a loud pop. He jumped back, waited a second, and then started forward again. There was another pop. Then another. Then a cloth bandoleer burst into flames. Unsure of what would happen next, Pizzuto quickly retreated. When a grenade exploded, sending hot ammo twenty feet into the air, we all scattered for cover.

Most of us ran about 150 feet and jumped into a ditch while others simply disappeared. It was a dangerous situation as the fire grew higher and the explosions more frequent but it sure looked funny. Shrapnel flew in all directions as the trailer jiggled and spit burning debris. We laughed when illumination flares shot past us like Fourth of July rockets. In less than one minute the explosions had completely obscured the trailer and caught the jeep on fire. Before long, two sleeping hooches were engulfed and the supply room wall began to burn.

Fire trucks with blaring sirens and flashing lights rushed to the scene. The firefighters began unrolling the hoses before realizing the burning jeep was shooting live rounds. They jumped back into the truck and drove off with the hoses dragging behind. The firefighters parked 500 feet away and watched helplessly as the flames slowly devoured our battalion area. We kept our distance too, but continued to laugh at every loud blast.

When the explosions ceased and the firefighters were able to get close enough to extinguish the blaze, there was hardly anything left to save. The supply room and two sleeping hooches had become charcoal pits. Other nearby structures had bullet and shrapnel damage. Even the ten-gallon coffeepot in the mess hall was punctured. The jeep was totally destroyed and the trailer had vaporized. Most of our rucksacks, canteens and web gear had melted into globs. Only our rifles survived because when the fire broke out we had instinctively ran away with them.

The only thing I felt bad about was losing the M-16 magazine that had saved my life on Hamburger Hill. For safekeeping, I had put it in my duffel bag in the supply room. However, after searching the rubble, the magazine was nowhere to be found. To ease my remorse, I submitted a $200 claim for items lost in the fire. Things like a camera, radio, and smoking jacket that I had never owned but was reimbursed for anyway. If I had known the Army would pay so freely, I would have claimed expensive jewelry, too.

Since our gear was destroyed, we had to spend another night at Camp Evans. However, this time we were strictly confined: drinking, gambling, and movies were prohibited. As long as we were out of the field, we didn't care. Most guys obeyed the confinement rule, but Siner, Silig and I pretended it didn't apply to us. We waited until dark and headed to the nearby EM (Enlisted Men's) Club for a few beers.

Being the only Grunts in the place, we thought it best to keep a low profile. Siner and I found a quiet corner table while Silig ordered drinks from the bar. No sooner had we sat down when two of the firefighters who had responded to our jeep fire began giving Silig a hard time.

"Aren't you one of those crazy Grunts who burned down half your company area today?" one of them asked loudly.

"That fire got us another night in the rear," Silig chuckled, thinking the firefighter was joking with him.

"Is that right?" he said in a nasty tone. "That fucking fire almost got us killed! Shrapnel and bullets were flying everywhere while you guys were laughing! Do you have any idea of how dangerous that was?"

"More than you'll ever know," Silig snickered, walking toward us with the beers. "That's what made it so funny."

The other firefighter did not see the humor so he sucker-punched Silig. Siner and I leapt to Silig's defense as a fistfight broke out. Not everyone joined in; most of the patrons backed off, encircling the melee to watch. The bartender yelled something about the MPs being on their way but that didn't slow us down. Broken glass, beer, and popcorn quickly littered the floor. It was like a cheap western movie as the three of us battled our way to the door. As we slipped outside, the firefighters didn't give chase. Instead, they stood in the door shouting obscenities, telling us never to come back.

Silig shut them up when he yelled; "If you assholes ever get to the boonies then you'd find out what real danger is like! Guys are dying out there while you're huddled in base camp like sniveling whiners. You make me sick."

Embarrassed by the truth, the firefighters sheepishly closed the door. Other than a few minor cuts and bruises, we felt great for defending the honor of Grunts with fists and words. The way we saw it, a battle was won against rear echelon complacency.

The next day we were resupplied with a mix of new and used equipment. The Lifers scrutinized our every move to avoid a repeat of the previous day's fireworks. There was hardly anything left to burn down anyway. We were just happy knowing we had cheated the Army out of a day in the boonies.

Late that afternoon we returned to the flatlands outside the village of Phong Dien. I was surprised to find that our new AO was the same area we patrolled when I first arrived in Vietnam. Our platoon's job, as before, was to protect the village by ambushing the VC trails that led to the mountains.

As we made our way past the village huts, an ominous feeling came over me. It was like we were being watched but no one was there. I felt that an unseen force was telling us we were not welcome, to go away and leave the flatlands alone. Perhaps the eerie sensation was the land's way of saying it was tired of war. The Vietnamese believed in ghosts and spirits and I began to think there was some truth in their folklore. Moreover, our ambush site amplified the spooky atmosphere: it was in the local cemetery.

The graveyard had no gates or borders; it was just a series of randomly positioned circular grave mounds. The Vietnamese believe the round design eased the deceased's transition into the next world. Some of the graves had stone monuments, but most were unmarked. There were no fresh graves, which made me wonder where the villagers were burying their dead. That first night back in the flatlands was uneventful, but it took me several days to shake the mysterious anxiety.

During the next three weeks, we settled into a tedious routine of ambush, RIF and ambush. Enemy activity around Phong Dien had all but ceased. We did not even find any booby traps. Lieutenant Pizzuto, who could not stand the monotony, did us all a favor and transferred to Echo Company. He said he wanted to be where the action is. Echo Company was a collection of gung-ho warmongers who got their kicks by going on long-range recon and ambush missions in six-man teams. Their patrols disappeared into the jungle for up to two weeks at a time, rarely moving and laying in wait along VC trails until they made enemy contact or ran out of food. Echo was the Marines of our battalion, usually being the first to land and establish initial lines of defense. If that's the kind of excitement Pizzuto wanted, then more power to him. As long as he was off my back, I did not care where he was.

Our new Lieutenant was a tall, lanky fellow from Kansas named Petry. Unlike Pizzuto, Petry actively sought advice from the old-timers of the platoon. He knew their longevity was a result of field experience that outweighed any classroom training learned back in the World. Even better, Petry seldom listened to Krol because he wisely realized Krol's old Army method of leadership through intimidation was outdated for Vietnam. We finally had an officer on our side and it drove Krol crazy. Lieutenant Petry would work out just fine.

For the next several days we patrolled the flatlands northward along the base of the mountains. We humped up to three miles each day, moving farther from civilization and deeper into VC territory where huge bomb craters pocked the landscape and the grassy plains grew thicker with large clumps of shrubs. We finally came upon an overgrown dirt road that looked as though the last activity it had witnessed was during the 1950s French occupation. We stopped for the night. Since we had not seen action for nearly a month, I got lazy and placed my claymore only ten feet outside the perimeter instead of the usual 50 feet.

It was almost dark as I gazed at the emerging stars, drifting into a dream of home. Suddenly there was a commotion in the bushes on the opposite side of the perimeter. A Viet Cong, thinking we were his comrades, had walked up to one of our positions. He calmly stood next to Hawaiian Norman Keoka, who was rolling out his poncho with his back turned, and tried to strike up a conversation. Since we had no one with us who could speak Vietnamese, Keoka knew something was wrong. As the VC continued to jabber, Keoka leaped for his M-16. At that instant, the enemy soldier realized his mistake, pushed Keoka over and ran onto the roadway.

Not wanting to chance shooting into the perimeter, Keoka fired several shots skyward and yelled, "Gook! Gook!"

Instinctively, I clutched the claymore detonator. As the VC sprinted past, I fired the device. The explosion spewed shrapnel, dirt, rocks, and twigs into the air, covering half the platoon with debris. Someone spit, then yelled, "Who the fuck blew that claymore?" I didn't answer because I knew I had not placed it correctly.

The intruder hotfooted past our last position where Silig stood ready with his machine gun. A burst of four rounds was the only shots fired because when he stood up to hip-shoot, he jerked the weapon, breaking the gun belt off. By the time he got the weapon back together, the lucky VC had vanished.

Our relaxed attitude not only cost us an easy kill but the subsequent ruckus gave our position away. We stayed on 50% alert all night in case the VC came back with his friends. Fortunately, no one showed. At first light we conducted a token search of the area but found nothing; we couldn't even locate any tracks. That VC earned the nickname "Supergook" because his luck made him impossible to kill.

The next morning we were airlifted to the coastal sand dunes between Camp Evans and the South China Sea to join the rest of the company. The dunes were once home for the native fisherman, but the war had driven them inland to the relative safety of larger villages and hamlets. More recently, the dunes region had become a VC refuge where high concentrations of booby traps were discovered. We were sent there to find out why.

The landscape of the region was a mix of large patches of thick underbrush paralleled by the wind blown dunes. Clumps of tall trees grew where the sub-soil could support them. A network of footpaths was the only means of quick travel through each green oasis. There was no sign of civilians; only the scattered remains of destroyed concrete buildings gave testimony to a life that once was. On some of the walls, the VC painted warnings, "DEATH TO AMERICANS" and "VIETNAM WILL CONQUER." We regarded the threats as feeble attempts to scare us off.

My squad took the first point. We traveled less than 200 feet before Howard Siner found a trip-wired hand grenade. We backed away and exploded it with a rope hook in case it was a double booby trap. After that, we doubled the point with one man concentrating on the ground and a second man on his butt with his eye out for VC. As we progressed, the traps became easier to locate. We didn't know if we were being led into something or if the traps were set out to conceal an enemy retreat.

Squads from each platoon broke off to follow minor paths leading into the brush on both sides of the main trail. As we searched the terrain, booby trap locations were plotted on a map to see if a pattern developed. If it did, we didn't spot it. In just over two days our company discovered twenty-six various type and sizes of booby traps. Our only conclusion was that the VC used the area for booby trap training. We never made enemy contact and, miraculously, the traps hurt no one. Captain Hartwell wisely decided there were too may traps for us to safely maneuver and that we should leave the VC to their fun in the dunes.

The company assembled for extraction on a grassy knoll below one of the abandoned buildings. We spread out and relaxed while waiting for the choppers to pick us up. Lennie Person casually walked toward the bushes to get out of the sun when Siner called out.

"Lennie stop! Look at your feet!"

Just inches to his left were the triple trigger pins of an anti-personnel mine sticking out of the ground. Lennie almost turned white, looked skyward, and leaped backward so fast he could have set a record for the reverse broad jump.

"What the hell is that thing?" a shaking Lennie asked.

"It's a Bouncing Betty," Siner said knowingly. "The mine is activated when one of those little prongs is moved. Then a small explosive propels the main charge to a waist-high altitude, sending shrapnel into a killing zone impossible to escape even by diving to the ground. I'm just surprised that a World War II mine like that would be found out here."

As the news of the Bouncing Betty circulated, we were ordered to stay within the borders of the perimeter. If someone had to relieve himself, it was to be done where we stood. Unfortunately, not everyone heeded the warning.

As if part of a slow-motion movie, I watched as a blond-haired GI walked from the perimeter edge toward the destroyed building. He hesitated for a moment, then stepped through the doorway, tripping a booby-trapped artillery round. The entire structure disintegrated in a giant explosion, belching dust, stones, and gore in every direction. A medic rushed up and leaped over what was left of the walls. He turned left, then right, spun around several times then slowly walked away with his head hung low. There was nothing left to save; even the GI's boots were gone. The poor guy had completely vaporized. As we brushed the dust off our clothes, someone nearby vomited while frantically struggling to get his shirt off. We didn't know what was wrong until we discovered that tiny bits of flesh from the disintegrated GI had splattered on us. It was disgusting to pick the pieces off. A distant voice muttered, "Assholes and booby traps. Some people never learn."

The saddest part of this GI's death was the lack of anything to send home except a memory. As we returned to our positions, eyes darted back and forth but no one spoke. Each man felt sullen but in the back of our minds was the same thought, "I'm glad it wasn't me."

We left the dunes for a return to Eagle Beach, though this visit was not for a stand down. This assignment was to guard American construction companies who were expanding the harbor. Our function was to protect their machinery and equipment from possible sabotage by VC sympathizers. A week of guard duty in a relatively secure area sounded like a good assignment and might even be downright enjoyable. It was not.

On the first night, Scoggins and I were assigned to the deck of a dredging ship anchored 1000 feet offshore in Da Nang Bay. We were the only Americans on board along with a dozen Vietnamese crew members who kept the dredge pumps going during the night. If they decided to sabotage something, we could not tell the difference because we had no idea of how a dredge worked.

"Are we supposed to watch out for the crewmen?" I jokingly asked. "Or are we watching for an attack from the ocean?"

"How should I know?" chided Scoggins. "Maybe the VC are expected to swim out here from shore. But if anything does happen we're on our own because we don't have a radio."

"We better get some rest," I suggested. "There's a wooden picnic table around the corner you can stretch out on. I'll take first guard."

As I gazed out at the ocean, the quiet hum of the pumps and the gentle swaying of the ship lulled me into dreaming about home. I had just placed my helmet on the deck when out of no where I felt a gentle tap on my shoulder. Hearing no one approach, I spun around, accidentally kicking the helmet overboard. Standing before me was a Vietnamese worker, clad only in sneakers, shorts, and a silly safari helmet. He smiled as he leaned over the railing to look into the water that had just swallowed my headgear. I was angry and started to walk away. As I moved, he came in close and tried to put his arm around me.

"Cut it out!" I yelled, pushing him away. "Get the fuck away from me!"

The worker ran off, disappearing around a corner. Scoggins woke up and rushed over to see what happened.

"I think the crew is queer," I stammered. "One of them just tried to get a little too friendly with me."

"Maybe they've been on this ship too long, and they consider us fresh meat," joked Scoggins.

"Ugh! Don't even say that! They have each other to play with. I'll just stick with girls if you don't mind." We decided to pull guard together hidden among the ship's shadows. It made for a long night, but we survived without further incident.

In the morning, we went ashore to get some sleep before the next night's guard duty but decided instead to visit the nearby town. The civilian area was supposed to be off-limits, but there were US military personnel in the town; we decided to go, too.

The bay area was densely populated with townspeople living as poorly as the villagers of Phong Dien. Their dirt floor shanty houses, made from discarded packing crates, sat almost on top of each other. There was no plumbing and sewage flowed in an open ditch alongside the pathway. It was a depressing sight and the stench was awful. As we walked along, a young boy standing in a doorway called out to us in Pidgin English.

"Hey GI, come here. I got what you want."

We walked to the front of the shanty.

"You want numba one boom-boom?" he asked. "We got. My sister is a virgin and wants to make love with you."

"A virgin?" Scoggins asked grinning.

"Yes," he continued. "Mama-san very sick, cannot support family. You make love to my sister. Only five dolla MPC."

"Five bucks for both of us?" I asked hopefully.

"What? You crazy?" he answered pointing. "Five dolla for you and five dolla for you."

I pulled Scoggins aside, "What do you think, should we do it?"

"Let's go for it. I have six months to go and if I get killed without getting laid, I'll never forgive myself."

"Okay, but you go first. I've never done anything like this before."

"You never got laid?"

"Sure I did, but not with a prostitute . . . with my girl," I reminisced, "before I left to come over here . . . sex was my going away present."

"That's a good one. Do you think she's gonna wait for you?"

"What makes you think she won't?" I asked, irritated at his insinuation.

"Are you kidding?" he asked in disbelief. "Girls back in the World got better things to do than sit at home waiting for us. They get lonely too, and there's no shortage of horny guys with draft deferments ready to take them out. My girl already quit waiting for me, she sent me a 'Dear John' two months ago. Come on, anything is better than beating your meat."

We paid the fee and Scoggins went first. I waited outside, fantasizing about the sexual delights I would soon experience. Ten minutes ticked by before Scoggins finally came out.

"How was it?" I eagerly asked.

"Okay," he said, running his fingers through his hair and grinning, "but I don't think she's a virgin. She wasn't very shy."

"Did you use a rubber?"

"You bet I did. I ain't gonna get Black VD (venereal disease)."

"Black VD—what's that?" I asked, cringing.

"That's when your balls turn black and your cock falls off."

"Bullshit," I sneered as Scoggins laughed.

The boy came out and pointed at me, "You next GI."

I stepped into the building where a portly middle-aged woman known simply as Mama-san greeted me. I supposed she was the boy's mother. Mama-san did not speak or show emotion. She waved her hands directing me towards an adjoining room separated by a blanket over the doorway. I entered a cubicle and was surprised by the sparseness of the interior. The walls were simply the inside of the packing crates that made up the shanty. Furnishings were skimpy; a small bed, a wooden folding chair, and a braided rug. A foggy plastic sheet serving as a window flapped with the wind. The room smelled.

The girl sat on the chair with her legs crossed, smoking a cigarette and looking at a magazine. She had a large bath towel wrapped loosely around her. I guessed her age to be about eighteen. She was slender, with straight black hair but not especially attractive.

"Take clothes off," she commanded without glancing up from her magazine. "You want rubber?"

"Yeah . . . sure," I answered timidly.

She called out to Mama-san and an arm appearing from behind the hanging blanket handed her a condom. I quietly undressed as she put the magazine down. The girl glanced over just long enough to be sure I was naked. Then she removed the towel and crawled onto the bed. Still smoking, she handed me the condom saying, "No suckie, only fuckie."

That blew my mind. Nothing was happening like I had imagined. Her pimp brother hustled us, her mother in the next room handed her a rubber, and I'm her second trick in less than fifteen minutes. This unprofessional setup so unnerved me that I began fumbling with the condom, unrolling it like it was a toy. She chided me with a sarcastic laugh when she saw that I didn't know what I was doing.

"You not need rubber," she said. "I no got VD."

"Good," I said, pulling the condom off until it snapped in my hand. She shook her head and laughed again, probably realizing I was an amateur. I climbed onto the bed and asked her to put out the cigarette.

"No way, GI," she said firmly. "I smoke, you make love."

I guessed that kissing would be out too. So much for romance.

I satisfied myself but hardly enjoyed it. As soon as I had finished, the girl nudged me aside and pulled a basin of water out from under the bed. She squatted over it, giving herself a hand douche. It should not have struck me as strange after all I had seen from this family run business. I dressed quickly and dashed outside to join Scoggins.

I was too embarrassed to look at him. I felt I had just dishonored my family. I was also afraid that my girlfriend would somehow find out what

I had done. I just wanted to get far away from there. As we were leaving, Mama-san and the boy yelled at me.

"Hey GI, you numba ten!" they shouted. "You owe one dolla for rubber!"

"Bullshit!" I shot back. "I didn't use it."

"No matter. What GI will use it now? You pay!"

"I ain't paying nothing. I never got my five dollars worth. That bitch wouldn't put out her cigarette or kiss me or anything."

"Kiss you?" Scoggins asked, rolling his eyes as if I was nuts. "Are you out of your mind? You don't kiss a prostitute!"

The boy picked up several baseball-sized rocks and motioned as if to throw them at us. I didn't want any trouble so I tossed at dollar at his feet. He scooped it up and ran back to the shack. After that, we decided to stay out of town and stick to our sentry duties on the dredge. We wondered what was worse, being killed by someone in the jungle, queer-raped by a deranged worker on a ship, or attacked by a rock-throwing adolescent pimp who had just sold us his sister.

For each of three nights our platoon members were spread around the bay guarding everything from air conditioners to pipe insulation. Eventually, we rejoined for a platoon-size guard duty at a US Navy fuel depot located on a river channel that snaked through Da Nang. To get to the depot, a US Navy utility ship motored us up the waterway.

On both sides of the channel, homes built on wooden stilts hung out over the water. As we rounded a bend we spotted Vietnamese kids swimming in the river. When they saw us coming, the kids yelled a warning to each other and quickly scampered from the water. I could not understand why they were so afraid. We weren't going fast, the ship was not close to shore, and no one threatened them. I supposed the ship's wake made for difficult swimming. I was wrong. The kids were scared for good reason. The ship's pilot and signalman spotted a slow swimmer and tossed a concussion grenade at him. Concussion grenades are used to stun enemy soldiers without killing them and are most effective in tight quarters like bunkers, tunnels, and underwater.

"What the hell are you doing?!" I yelled at the signalman in disbelief. "Those are just kids! What have they done to deserve that?!"

"Sergeant," the pilot calmly answered, "don't you know that those kids are the future VC? We're just letting them know who's in charge here."

"You guys are sadistic," I shot back. "We're supposed to win the hearts and minds of the people, not turn them against us." They shook their heads as if I was crazy. With attitudes like theirs, we deserved to be hated and I was embarrassed to be a part of it.

A few minutes later the ship dropped us off at the depot. The tiny supply base was about the size of two football fields. A thirty-foot high chain-link fence enclosed three sides. The dockside of the compound had no protective barrier at all, just the channel. One hundred feet beyond the fence, Vietnamese homes were crowded together. It looked like a middle-class neighborhood because the houses were permanent concrete buildings and not the packing crate variety. At night, some of the residents congregated outside the fence beneath huge floodlights until the 10:00 p.m. curfew.

The depot was in a safe area that had not seen a VC or act of sabotage in nearly a year. The area is protected by weekly rotations of infantry platoons that needed a rest but not a vacation. Our guard posts and sleeping quarters were located in eight huge bunkers strategically placed throughout the compound. Each bunker had two fighting positions and accommodations for up to ten men.

The depot itself consisted of three 50,000-gallon fuel tanks and four US Navy buildings; a barracks, an operations center, a supply room and a mess hall. Each night around 8:00 p.m. the mess hall converted into a liquor bar.

On our first night, there was a going-away party for a homeward bound sailor. We were invited for free snacks and drinks but before that, we had to endure boring speeches about a guy we didn't know. Not many of our men were interested, but to be sociable I hung around for a few beers.

At 9:00 p.m. the party quieted down so I went outside to check on the guards. I was surprised to see that most of the bunkers were not occupied. Instead, several men waited in a line near the doorway of the corner bunker.

"What's going on here?" I asked the last man.

"Boom-boom," he said, pointing to the front of the line. "There's a whore inside taking on everyone for five bucks a pop."

"What?" I asked, stunned at his nonchalance. "How did she get in the compound?"

"There's a hole in the fence so the local talent can sneak in and take turns each night."

A hole in the fence? I could not believe it. The Navy had their own rotating supply of boom-boom girls? I thought about joining in, because now I was experienced with Vietnamese prostitutes. Unfortunately, I was nearly broke. When I turned to leave, the line had grown longer behind me. I didn't want to look like a first-timer turned chicken, so I stayed. I thought it might be fun to see what my last two dollars could get me with a five-dollar whore.

After half an hour, it was my turn. I scooted inside to be nauseated by the stench of sweat and stale beer—and worse. The bunker was dimly lit with incense-coated candles that didn't help the odor much. The girl was about twenty with a homely scowl that made her look like she had crawled through the fence one time too many. Her arms and legs had bruises and her neck bore small scars. She stood in the middle of the bunker with a blanket drooped over her shoulders.

"Five dolla," she demanded with an outstretched hand. "You pay now."

"Not so fast," I shot back. "Don't I get to see what I'm paying for?"

"Okay wise guy." She dropped the blanket and struck a pose. "You pay now!"

"Uh . . . turn around for me."

She rotated but would not turn completely around.

"Now turn the other way."

She turned but was getting aggravated.

When I said, "Now bend over," she reached for a baseball bat carried for people like me. As soon as I saw the bat I ran out the door. She charged after me yelling a combination of profanities. She was still naked and stopped just outside the door. The men in line gave her a few catcalls and sent a few in my direction as well. They were afraid that if I got her pissed-off they would not get laid. But she calmed down and went back to work. Since the free show did not cost me anything, I certainly got my money's worth, but I could not understand how anyone would be willing to pay for sloppy sixteenths or seventeenths. Those guys must have been in the field too long. At least when Scoggins and I had our prostitute, I only had to contend with sloppy seconds—and he had worn a condom.

Our platoon stayed at the depot for a week's worth of bunker sex and booze before returning to the flatlands of Phong Dien.

"The Army isn't as heartless as you might think."

CHAPTER 6

The Emotional Gauntlet

Our platoon's next area of operation was about ten miles northwest of Camp Evans. There we came upon a giant old-growth bamboo thicket where the trees grew fifty feet tall and as much as three inches in diameter. The thicket was eerie because the dense canopy prevented the sun's rays from ever reaching the ground. Even in broad daylight the thicket was a shaded twilight world. At night it was so dark that even the night creatures stayed away. The trees grew far enough apart to make for easy movement, but the terrain was littered with dry bamboo leaves that crunched when we walked on them. To maintain noise discipline, we brushed the leaves aside to make a series of quiet walking paths to each perimeter position.

"It's kind of spooky in here," Howard Siner whispered, looking cautiously around, "it reminds me of an eclipse of the sun."

"It reminds me of the enchanted forest in the movie The Wizard of Oz," I said. "The only thing missing is the flying monkeys."

"The bamboo is as big as drain pipes," Dennis Silig added. "I just hope the VC are afraid of places like this, because I sure don't like it."

"What the hell are you guys worried about?" chided Stan Alcon. "I don't mind this bamboo because we can hear anybody coming a thousand feet away. Besides, as bad as you think this is, anything is better than being in the A Shau Valley." We all nodded in agreement.

Each morning, two six-man teams went on a daylong ambush at a trail junction bordering the thicket. No one ever showed. At sunset, the platoon retreated into the bamboo to ambush any VC who tried walking through it in the dark. No one ever showed up there, either.

On our third night, a frantic radio call came from battalion headquarters ordering us to move to the nearest LZ and prepare for immediate extraction. The entire company was regrouping to intercept a platoon of VC spotted on the outskirts of a village hamlet.

The quickest route to a natural LZ was directly through the thicket and out the other side a half-mile away. Our toughest obstacle was the inky blackness of the bamboo forest. In order for us to proceed without losing anyone, each man held onto the web gear of the man in front of him, forming a human chain. This linked procession voided all noise discipline, so every fifty feet we stopped to listen for sounds other than ours. There were none.

Our advance was too slow to suit Sergeant Krol, so he fired a flare skyward to illuminate the route. It shot through the bamboo canopy and we never saw it again. Krol then fired a second flare parallel to the ground, which provided an instant sight line, but the luminous trail ended abruptly where the flare smacked into a tree. The flare exploded on impact and ignited the dry leaves on fire, providing adequate light to see by. The problem was that if there were any VC around, now they knew our position, and as the fire quickly spread, the smoke rose only a short distance because most of it could not escape through the canopy. To keep from choking on the fumes, we rushed to get out. Just a few hundred feet outside the bamboo was a large natural clearing we could use for an LZ.

After a brief wait, hand-held strobe lights guided five helicopters to our position. The pilots were reluctant to land because from the air they didn't know what to make of the fire glow under the nearby bamboo. After we convinced the pilots that the situation was under control, all five choppers descended at once. When the helicopters neared the ground, powerful landing lights were turned on, obliterating our night vision. As each slick touched down, we stumbled aboard.

This was our first night ride and we couldn't see anything until our eyes readjusted to the dark. I wondered how the pilots saw where they were going. I couldn't even distinguish the bodies of the helicopters flying beside us; I only saw their forward green light and a flashing red taillight. Inside our chopper, the glowing instrument panel cast a pale reflection on our silent faces as we exchanged worried glances over what lay ahead.

When our five helicopters met the choppers carrying the rest of the company, an unseen US Air Force Douglas AC-47 gunship dropped huge parachuted flares to illuminate our synchronized landings. The Air Force gunship, nicknamed "Spooky" or "Puff-The-Magic-Dragon," is a slow-moving transport plane armed with three multi-barrel electric-driven 7.62mm machine guns, each capable of firing 6,000 rounds per minute. Since every fifth bullet is a tracer, when Spooky is shooting, the plane looks like it is attached to an orange column of fire.

Our descent was quick and the landings were completed without incident. We found ourselves in grassy flatlands dotted with patches of short brush and irregular hedgerows. We promptly formed an assault line nearly a half-mile long with each man ten to twenty feet apart. As many as ten flares were in the air simultaneously, lighting the night skies and our surroundings with a bright amber glow. The flares drifting slowly earthward, causing the shadows to dance about. That made it difficult to determine whether enemy soldiers were lurking out in front of us.

As Spooky lit the way, our assault line moved toward the area where the VC were last seen. We pushed forward at a fast pace, stimulated by the magnitude of the operation and the firepower waiting to be unleashed. If our tactics were successful, the VC would be flushed into the open where they would get cut down by Spooky's guns.

During the first hour, nervous Cherries fired occasional shots into the shadows though no enemy was sighted. By the time the second hour passed, the operation was obviously a bust. We finally gave up. The helicopters and flares must have scattered the Gooks in so many directions they would never be found.

As the last of the flares died out, the company broke down into platoons, each securing a knoll for the remainder of the night. We tried to pull 50% guard duty, but with all the earlier excitement we were now exhausted, and hardly anyone could stay awake. Besides, since every VC within ten miles already knew where we were, there was little concern that any of them would be stupid enough to try sneaking past our positions. As a result, most guys slept through an uneventful night.

When I awoke at first light, I discovered that of the entire platoon, only two other men were awake. Rather than going around waking everyone, I decided to make enough noise so they would get up on their own. As I dug into my rucksack I noticed movement behind a hedgerow about one hundred feet away. I studied the area and caught glimpses of a Vietnamese man walking toward our position. I was confused by his blatant approach so I crawled over and woke up Krol.

"Sergeant Krol," I whispered. "There's a Gook just outside the perimeter and he's coming this way."

"He's probably a farmer," Krol said, rubbing the sleep from his face. "Go see what he wants."

"But it's too early for them to be way out here. The sun isn't up yet and we're not that close to the village."

"Just go see what he wants."

That sounded nuts to me, so I returned to my position and patted two sleeping men on the shoulder. "Gook," I said in a quiet urgency. "Wake up."

With my rifle at the ready position, I watched as the man materialized from behind a bush less than fifty feet away. When I saw an AK-47 rifle slung across his chest, I realized he was a Viet Cong. I froze at that moment of recognition, unsure of why he was being so bold. He glanced casually in my direction, then said something in Vietnamese.

"Chieu Hoi!" I yelled back at him.

He laughed and continued closer, apparently thinking I was one of his comrades making a joke. As several GIs quickly gathered behind me I thought he was coming in to give himself up. When Freddie Shaw yelled, "He's got a weapon!" the VC halted.

For a split second, the enemy soldier and I made sharp eye contact, both of us realizing that our thinking was wrong. His expression instantly changed from bewilderment to defeat, but rather than be taken prisoner the VC turned to flee. I could not let him escape, so I quickly reeled off a dozen rounds as five men behind me simultaneously opened fire. Even before the VC hit the ground, rifle and machine gun bursts had cut him to ribbons. As his legs gave out, he managed to shoot a volley of six rounds at us. Our maniacal firing continued until somebody threw a hand grenade, engulfing the VC in an explosion of dust and debris. When the shooting stopped, Dennis Silig joked, "Do you think we got him?"

We looked around to make sure none of us had been hit. Everyone was okay. That's when we spotted Krol crouched behind his rucksack.

"Sergeant Krol," I called, shocked to see he was hiding from the action. "What are you doing behind your rucksack?"

"He shot at me!"

"He shot at you?" I asked, amazed Krol thought he was in more danger than us. "He shot at all of us. Are you hit?"

"I'm not hit, but there could be more of them!"

"He was alone . . . you can come out now."

We were stunned. Had Sergeant Krol turned chicken or was he always a coward finally exposed by this incident. No one dwelled on his behavior. Instead, we rushed to examine our kill. We surrounded the riddled body and silently watched a reflex twitch and a labored last breath. The VC was dead.

"That was the third time in two months an enemy soldier walked up to one of our positions," Siner remarked.

"Maybe the VC draft requirements have been lowered," joked Silig. "They're either stupid, need glasses, or both."

"The VC aren't stupid." I said, knowingly. "We've just been lucky that none of us have been blown away. Let's make a quick patrol of the area to make sure none of his friends are hanging around."

Finding nothing, we returned to the perimeter where Krol and Lieutenant Petry were searching the body. They found a pouch with documents and maps and a wallet with 800 piasters, which Krol pocketed.

"What about us," Silig protested. "That money should be split among the shooters."

"Negative," Krol answered, shaking his head. "Rank has its privileges. This is one of them."

Nothing else was said, but now Krol's complete character had been exposed. He was a coward without a conscience and to the men who realized it, Krol would no longer be trusted or respected. With the excitement over, we returned to our positions for morning chow.

The dead VC was about thirty feet from my position. I looked at the lifeless form, wondering why it didn't repulse me. I remembered when I could not eat for two days after we killed a VC girl early in my tour. And now there I was, eating while looking at a corpse that wasn't even stiff yet. My attitude change had been so gradual it went unnoticed. The violence of the war, no longer shocking, had turned me into a hard-core veteran.

We left the VC to rot and humped two miles to a daytime ambush position. In the meantime, the villagers complained to us that the body could not be left where it was because their farmland would be cursed. Late that afternoon we were ordered back to bury the VC. Since my squad did the killing, we were chosen to do the burying.

By the time we returned to the scene the body had bloated from lying under the hot sun all day. Dozens of buzzing and crawling insects magnified the disgusting image. We didn't want to stay any longer than necessary so we quickly dug a shallow grave, which later turned out to be too small. When the VC was rolled into the hole his feet stuck out. We knew the grave should be deeper and longer but no one wanted to touch the body again. We finished the job with everything buried except his feet. The next morning we received an angry radio call from battalion headquarters about our sloppy burial of the VC. The villagers now complained that his feet sticking out of the ground not only scared the shit out of the local kids, but was an insult to the land.

We returned to the grave site once more. This time we dug up the corpse, which stunk so bad I almost vomited. We slipped the Gook into a body bag. Handling the dead VC for a second time made me feel like death had embedded itself into my hands. It was difficult to shake the sensation. A short time later, a pickup truck arrived to take the body to a more suitable location, probably a mass grave. The entire episode confused me. I thought our job was to kill the enemy, not to conduct burial services for them.

Our next assignment was one of our best ever. We were sent to guard a US Navy Seabee construction site on the banks of the Bo River between Hue City and Camp Evans. The Seabees were rebuilding a two hundred-foot span of railroad bridge that was destroyed six months earlier by VC sappers. It was the kind of guard duty Grunts dream of: hot meals each day, swimming whenever we wanted, and plenty of time to catch up on lost sleep. The rest of our duty was spent lazily watching the local fishermen and other boat traffic on the river. If there were no boats, we turned our attention to the villager's constant procession along a timeworn path connecting two nearby hamlets.

The Seabee compound was no bigger than a suburban house lot, which made it easy to defend. It had the familiar bunkers and concertina wire, but it also had a forty-foot tall concrete railroad tower. The tower provided such a commanding view of the terrain that a two-man team perched within it was the only daytime defense the compound needed. The only drawback was that we had to send out a daily RIF so any nearby VC knew we were actively patrolling the area.

On one RIF, we were walking in a four-foot deep gully when a sniper shot at us from a nearby hedgerow. The bullet zipped over our heads. We figured the sniper was either on his first mission or just plain stupid, because he pinned us down in a location that offered protection and maneuverability. Lieutenant Petry radioed in the situation as we positioned ourselves for an attack. Just when we were ready to shoot back, Petry told us to hold our fire. It turned out that a squad of ARVNs had mistaken us for a group of enemy soldiers they thought were preparing to launch a daring daylight attack on the village. What assholes. We couldn't imagine how the ARVNs had confused us with the VC. After that, we returned to the Seabee compound and never sent out another RIF.

A few days later, Siner and I were on guard in the railroad tower. The view of the distant hedgerows and thickets was picturesque, but being on that lookout all day was a drag. To amuse ourselves, we spied on Sergeant Krol, who spent most of the day relaxing in a hammock under a shade tree.

"Just look at that lazy bastard," I said to Siner. "The only time he gets out of that hammock is to take a leak or fetch something to read."

"I noticed him twice going to the compound gate," remarked Siner. "Both times he spoke with a young village boy. I wonder what he's up to?"

"Probably making a drug deal," I joked. "Either that, or he's a VC sympathizer selling secrets to the enemy."

"Naw, I'll bet he's just trying to buy some beer."

About an hour later, Krol nervously left the compound carrying only his rifle and a bandoleer of ammunition. He walked out to the villager's trail and waited under a shade tree a few hundred feet away. We wondered aloud what that was all about.

Guessing that Krol was up to no good, I radioed Lieutenant Petry and asked him to come up and see for himself. Just as Petry joined us, a motor scooter carrying a well-dressed Vietnamese man and young woman stopped alongside Krol. They spoke briefly and the woman took a rolled blanket from the scooter and led Krol into the bushes. The man stayed behind to smoke a cigarette. We laughed when we realized Krol's clandestine meeting was with a pimp and a prostitute.

"Don't you guys know it isn't polite to watch someone have sex?" asked Petry.

"But Lieutenant," I moaned, "Krol is such a jerk that he doesn't deserve privacy."

"Not only that," added Siner, "Krol's nothing but a hypocrite. He is always preaching to us about avoiding the field whores because they could be working for the VC or have venereal disease. Now he's going to get laid with one of them."

"Forget about Krol," I said excitedly, "I don't care to see his hairy ass. I want a peek at the girl."

After the woman spread the blanket out, both her and Krol stripped naked. The three of us fought over the binoculars for a look at the woman, but Krol quickly mounted her, obscuring our view. Less than a minute later, he rolled off.

"Boy that was quick," commented a laughing Petry. "He dropped his load faster than a B-52."

We laughed and fought over the binoculars again, but the woman dressed herself in an instant. She was a real pro. Krol watched as she walked away and then got dressed himself. When he stood up to look around, his gaze settled upon the tower—and our reflecting binoculars. It took him a few moments to realize what was happening. His chin dropped when we yelled and waved at him. Krol rushed back to the compound where Lieutenant Petry promptly scolded him. Siner and I added to Krol's humiliation by telling everyone what we saw, causing snickers, finger pointing, and a further weakening of his already damaged credibility.

Krol's escapade provided a welcome respite from the war, but the best diversion was always letters from home. GIs depended on the mail because it was our only contact with the outside world. A letter from home temporarily distracted us from our miseries. But sometimes the news was bad, delivering problems impossible to deal with over the great distance and through the military bureaucracy. Problems that I felt immune from until my mail turned nightmarish.

It all started innocently. My sister Diane gave birth to a baby girl, making me an uncle for the first time. But no sooner did I become an uncle, when I lost one. My Uncle Jack was only 57 years old when he died in his sleep. Feeling a little sorry for myself because I was unable to say hello to my niece or good-bye to my uncle, I received worse news. Jimmy Manning, a hometown classmate who was also serving in Vietnam, had been killed by enemy gunfire. It was events like those, coupled with the craziness around me that helped produce an emotional numbness. However, that was just the beginning.

A hometown friend and anti-war activist corresponded with me about twice a month. Most of his letters made for interesting reading, but they were nothing to get excited about. However, after attending the Woodstock Music Festival, which boasted peace, love, and hallucinogenic drugs, he wrote to me for the last time. His letter included a distressing verse from a protest song performed at Woodstock about packing boys off for Vietnam so "your boy could come home in a box." He followed the song with a skull and crossbones sketch. Then splattered red ink over the paper to look like bloodstains. His letter ended with; "The blood on this paper symbolizes the murders committed by the American war machine for which you work. Anyone who willingly participates in an illegal war that kills women and children will also die."

What a pal. It seems that he got caught up in the protest movement and decided to lay a ton of guilt on me in hopes of somehow ending the war sooner, as if that was supposed to work. I simply could not understand his attitude because I had often written to him describing how much I despised the war. I just wished he directed his anger at the US government instead of me. I never wrote to him again.

About the same time, the two or three letters each week from my girlfriend Mary suddenly stopped. I knew there was no problem with the mail service because I continued to receive letters from my family. Something else had to be wrong. With no mail from my sweetheart I became discouraged and listless.

After waiting several agonizing weeks with no mail, a letter finally arrived. I hesitated before opening it, fearing a "Dear John." It was even worse. Mary wrote a shocking account of her experimentation with drugs—uppers to get high and downers to come back to earth. She gave no reason for her behavior, but instead declared how the drugs riddled her with so much guilt that she wanted to end it all with an overdose.

I was angry and confused. How could this be happening? How rough could life be back in the World to entice a healthy, attractive eighteen-year-old girl to get involved with drugs? Mary knew I loved her and needed her support for my survival. I wondered what I could have done to deserve such treatment. Ever since the Army drafted me, Mary and I were separated for months at a time but managed to keep our romance alive. Now that I was in the midst of a full-year Vietnam tour, the long separation had probably overwhelmed her. I didn't know how to handle the situation, so I requested our battalion chaplain to come out and have a talk with me.

A pious looking individual with thick dark eyebrows and a warm smile, Major Barnes gave the impression he was an understanding clergyman. However, after I told him my story, he acted more like a suspicious high school principal.

"Does your girlfriend have a sense of humor?" he asked pointedly. "Could this be her attempt at a joke?"

"A joke?" I asked in disbelief. "This is my first letter from her in more than three weeks. Before that, I got mail all the time. This is no joke."

"Let me see some of her previous letters. Maybe there was a warning sign that you ignored."

"We don't save our letters. After the mail has been read it's burned so the Gooks can't get the home addresses."

"You burned them?" he asked, incredulously. "Aren't you afraid that you'll give your platoon's position away by starting fires in the jungle?" I could not believe what I was being asked and began to wonder if Barnes was a real chaplain.

"Major, please," I begged. "Help me find a way to figure out what's going on with Mary so I can get her to stop taking those pills."

"I hate to disappoint you," he said, looking me in the eye, "but a scheme like this won't get you home any sooner. Who helped you cook it up?"

"Scheme?" I protested, not realizing he was probably testing me. "Do you think this was made up? Mary could be dead right now. Why won't you help me?"

"Now calm down, we'll get this thing resolved. Give me Mary's address and phone number and I'll have someone contact her."

"That's it? That's your plan? How do you think she'll react when some stranger calls her to ask if she's been popping pills and considering suicide?"

"We're a little more subtle than that," he said, changing to a more sympathetic attitude. "The Army isn't as heartless as you might think. We'll have a trained person check it out. You'll just have to trust us."

I knew I could never trust the Army with this issue, especially with someone like Barnes running the show. To be on the safe side, I wrote a letter to my mother, who was a head nurse in a state mental hospital, asking her to look into the problem. She works with several substance abuse psychologists who could offer advice or perhaps speak with Mary.

During the next several weeks I was miserable and lonely. I never realized how much I needed Mary's letters and how important it was to have someone waiting for me. As the days dragged by without any word or explanation I began to wonder if I was being told everything that was going on back home. Now I could understand why it was difficult for some GIs to concentrate on staying alive when they felt they were forgotten.

Eventually, someone got through to Mary because her letters resumed, almost as frequently as before. Except now they read differently. The words were mechanical, as if just filling up space. Her passion was gone. She was slipping away and my absence only added to the helplessness of a depressing situation.

God how I wanted to go home.

"You want numba one boom-boom?
We got it here! Nice girls, no waiting!"

CHAPTER 7

Ghosting in the Rear

Grunts would try anything to get out of the field. A week or even a day in the relative safety of the rear put a GI that much closer to DEROS without having to endure the dangers and miseries of front line duty. The problem was, the Army always found a way to keep us out there. If a GI had a personal problem, the Chaplain was summoned to deal with it. If someone developed a bad attitude, he carried the machine gun for punishment. If a GI contracted gonorrhea, the medic carried penicillin to cure it. If someone got diarrhea, the medic had a pill with enough pucker power to keep a Grunt's ass tight for a week. There was no escape. I needed a break, but to get unscheduled vacation time I had to come up with something new. The answer to my dilemma lay in the soggy swamps and water-filled rice paddies of the flatlands.

We often took time out to dry our boots and socks to prevent immersion foot, a fungal disease caused by the frequent immersion of our feet in stagnant water. I purposely neglected the foot maintenance, hoping for an infection that would require medical attention in the rear.

Within a week my right foot developed an inflammation that worsened as the days went by. When the itch became unbearable, I removed my boot to find that the sock had become stiff from the dirt and moisture and smelled like rotten food. Beyond the sock was a water-wrinkled foot with an oozing sore between two toes. It did not hurt to walk but rather than risk permanent damage, I figured it was time to tell Doc Meehan. However, I never got the chance. While re-lacing my boot, Lieutenant Petry stopped by.

"Sergeant Wiknik," he said with a smile, "how would you like to go to Vung Tau for a couple of days?"

"Vung Tau?" I stammered. "The in-country R & R city?"

"That's the one."

"Why me? We've had guys in the field longer than me."

"If it wasn't for you, we would never have gotten that kill last week. And the body count has been pretty hard to come by lately."

"I'm not going to argue with you," I beamed. "When do I leave?"

"Hot chow will be brought out this afternoon. When the truck goes back to Camp Evans, be on it."

It was a dream come true. With a legitimate opportunity for freedom from the boonies I didn't need an infected foot after all. With excitement running high, my toes were quickly forgotten. But they continued to deteriorate as I failed to pay attention to them.

My first time at Camp Evans without the rest of the platoon felt strange, even lonely. Solitary Grunts in base camp were an oddity, our dirty sweat crusted fatigues usually caused rear echelon soldiers to stare, but I paid no attention to them. I was out of the field!

I reported to our company clerk, Specialist Simmons, who was much friendlier than the clerk who signed me in when I first came to Company A. Simmons was short and stocky with a receding hairline and honest warmth magnified by his distinctive Mississippi drawl.

"Hey there Sergeant Wiknik," he smiled. "Let's get your gear stowed away so you can take a shower and get into some clean fatigues. We can't have you going on R & R looking like you just crawled out of a sewer pipe."

"Thanks," I nodded, feeling welcome by his remarks. "Where do I sleep?"

"Hooch number four is for transient GIs. Just pick out a cot that looks good. If you're hungry, the mess hall is open until 1800 hours. After dark, there's a science fiction movie about women from Mars who plan to take over the Earth. I've already seen it, but I'm going to watch it again because it's the only time we'll see any round-eyed women at Camp Evans."

"There better be some women where I'm going," I quipped.

"Don't worry about that," he said, raising his eyebrows, "I've heard that Vung Tau is loaded with all kinds of women. Now get yourself squared away and I'll check back with you."

After I settled in, Simmons returned to ask about the men. He wanted to know if they had enough writing paper, cigarettes, clean socks, whether their clothes and equipment were in good condition, and if the mail arrived regularly. Simmons was genuinely concerned about the creature comforts that meant so much to us in the field. If there was something we were lacking, he promised to get it. I wished there were more people like Simmons.

I stayed awake late that night catching up on neglected letters and reading magazines. It was so relaxing to feel safe and have a roof over my head that I slept through morning roll call. Simmons must have had other Grunts oversleep because after roll call, he woke me with an understanding grin, waving a set of R & R orders in my face. I skipped breakfast and stumbled down to the chopper pad, where I caught a ride on a Chinook that shuttled GIs to LZ Sally, fifteen miles south of Camp Evans.

Located on Quoc-Lo 1, LZ Sally is a tiny processing and supply station for US military travelers. A circular drive in front is used for motor vehicle access while a rear chopper pad handled the helicopters. The compound consisted of six hooches arranged in a semi-circle. The main hooch is an office for clearing paperwork, three hooches are sleeping quarters for transient GIs, another is a supply shed and the last, a tiny EM club serving cold beer and soda and hot C-rations for snacks.

After clearing through the paperwork, I waited for transportation in the EM Club. When I walked through the door, everyone's eyes focused on me, perhaps because most NCOs stayed out of EM clubs. Initially I felt unwelcome, but moments later everyone went back to what they were doing. Three GIs sat quietly sipping cokes, two more were looking at a magazine, and another was at the jukebox playing the latest music from the World.

Of all the anti-war songs that were popular during this time, one in particular captured the mood of the war with a driving beat: Creedence Clearwater Revival's "Bad Moon Rising." Although it was a very catchy tune, it also was very depressing—if you listened closely to the lyrics. I had my "shit" together, all right, but I was not, as the song asked, "quite prepared to die." I also knew how dangerous the nights were, as alluded to in the lyrics. Whoever wrote that song really knew how to strike a nerve. It was haunting, eery, and depressing. After listening to it, I decided to wait outside.

Eventually, a canvas-covered truck took me and four other R & R traveler's five miles down Quoc-Lo 1 to the Hue-Phu Bai Airport. However, before setting foot in the airport terminal, GIs had to work their way around several Vietnamese shoeshine boys who hustled them for a dollar boot shine. If a soldier made eye contact with one of those kids, that was regarded as the go-ahead signal. Before a GI knew what was happening, polish was smeared onto his boot and he owed a dollar. If a soldier did not want a shine, he had to shake the boy loose or physically push him aside. The rejected entrepreneurs responded with the familiar, "Fuck you, GI." The inside of the terminal was off-limits to the kids, so as soon as GIs were out of reach, the boys moved back and waited for other unsuspecting soldiers to arrive.

The terminal itself was nothing more than a large wood-frame shelter divided into two sections. US military personnel used one side while upper-class Vietnamese nationals used the other. The cooperative segregation was based on cultural differences as well as mode of travel. The Vietnamese flew on domestic airlines while GIs were limited to transport planes. Military air transportation was free to GIs, but proof of travel authorization, such as R & R orders, were required for assignment to the flight manifest. A GI without travel papers could still obtain a ride on standby to anywhere in-country, but ran the risk of getting bumped at the last minute if the manifest was filled.

After a short wait, a US Air Force C-130 transport plane taxied to the terminal. With the engines still running, an Air Force Loadmaster opened a side door and waved us aboard. Inside the plane were twenty-five GIs sitting on the floor alongside four large cargo pallets. As soon as everyone was seated, the Loadmaster closed the door and briefed us on ditching procedures. I don't know why he bothered to explain anything, as none of us had a seat belt, so if the plane ditched the cargo would crush us.

Our destination was the giant Bien Hoa airbase where I first joined the 101st as a Cherry replacement. As the plane rumbled down the runway and lifted off, I suddenly realized that I had to urinate. I knew I wouldn't be able to hold it for the two-hour flight, so after the plane leveled off I waded through the men to ask the Loadmaster where the latrine was, unaware that there was no latrine. He casually pointed to a funnel next to the emergency door. I looked through the opening to the ground far below. To be sure that was where the Loadmaster meant, I glanced back to him for approval.

"Go ahead!" he yelled, loud enough for everyone to hear. "Piss in there and you can piss all over Vietnam!"

Some of the men watched to see what I would do. I really had to go, so I gave Vietnam my own shot of Agent Orange, actually more like Agent Yellow. The plane's air speed created a siphon so I didn't spill a drop. After we landed, I checked the side of the plane and found urine stains streaking from the funnel hole all the way to the tail. It was obvious that plenty of other GIs had been using the hole long before I did.

My arrival at Bien Hoa stirred vague memories. It was only five months since I was there last, and yet it seemed like five years. Bien Hoa should have looked familiar but it did not. I wondered if the war had aged my mind faster than the calendar. After a short layover, those of us going on R & R boarded a different C-130 for the flight to Vung Tau. In less than thirty minutes we landed at a tiny one-runway airstrip with a control tower; there was no terminal. When the plane stopped we got out and traded places with a group of GIs who were leaving Vung Tau. A few minutes later, a shuttle bus arrived to take us to the R & R center.

Vung Tau is a coastal city fifty miles southeast of Saigon located on a narrow peninsula separating the South China Sea from the Saigon River delta. An old city situated in a non-military region of South Vietnam, Vung Tau was well preserved and much cleaner than I expected. The main thoroughfare was lined with souvenir and pawn shops, clothing stores, two and three-story apartment buildings, and the everyday Vietnamese street vendors. The air was filled with the familiar odor of exhaust fumes and burning sandalwood.

Vung Tau's streets were alive with motor scooters, bicycles, and three-wheel Lambretta taxi cabs. Their frantic driver's disregarded every imaginable traffic rule as they zigzagged around pedestrians with reckless abandon. The Vietnamese traffic police, nicknamed "White Mice" for their white gloves and headgear, did little to control the situation. As long as traffic moved in the same direction, they simply watched. Our shuttle bus was one of the largest and most formidable vehicles on Vung Tau's streets, so we were given a wide berth.

The R & R center was an old two-story hotel that had been converted into a fancy barracks. The R & R administrators occupied the top floor, while we bunked on the ground floor. Our sleeping area accommodated up to fifty GIs in four-man dormitory-style cubicles. Each cubicle had two bunk beds, four wall lockers, and a few pieces of simple furniture. The showers and toilets were typically military: one large room used by everyone. A frugal GI could stay at the center without spending any money because the Army was treating us to two buffet meals a day, chambermaid and laundry service, hot showers, a nightly movie, and more. We were also pleased to learn that no officers or senior NCOs would be sharing our R & R. Vung Tau was exclusively for enlisted men recovering from a hardship or those serving an extremely hazardous tour of duty. I didn't think I met either requirement, but I was not about to complain.

It was mandatory for all arriving R & R personnel to attend a conduct lecture before going out on the town. Even though Vung Tau was a wide open city, weapons, drugs, drunkenness, or barroom brawls would not be tolerated. Our travel was restricted to the city limits and everyone had to be back at the hotel by 10:00 p.m. for a head count and lights out. The R & R officials promised not to watch us too closely, but warned that at the first sign of trouble, offenders would be immediately returned to their units.

We were also cautioned against abusive behavior toward the civilians. Unfortunately, some GIs felt that most Vietnamese were beggars, thieves, and whores, and treated them as such. On the other hand, the Vietnamese people, many of whom were forced by the war into unpleasant lives and work, saw the worst side of many Americans as well.

Vung Tau has no factories or heavy industry. Money was pumped into the local economy by the steady stream of free-spending GIs. The most lucrative businesses were barrooms and bordellos. The thriving red-light district, which bristled with neon lights and blaring music, offered scantily clad Vietnamese bar girls who adorned the doorways of each saloon. Like the sirens of Greek mythology they lured GIs inside to buy them drinks. Once inside, an unwary GI could easily spend all his money on the vixens. Only a few bars had bad reputations but we were warned to keep on our toes and to buddy-up with another GI to avoid being taken advantage of.

I did not know any GIs in Vung Tau, but when I noticed a mustached sergeant without a partner I introduced myself.

"Hi," I said, shaking his hand. "I'm Artie Wiknik. I'm not paired up with anyone. How about you?"

"No, not yet," he answered, looking at me long and hard. "I'm Mortimer Moriarity. I hate my name, so if we're going to hang around together, don't call me anything other than Mort."

"That's fine with me," I nodded, trying not to laugh as I wondered how his parents could be so cruel as to give such a name to their son.

"And another thing, I'm an Instant NCO squad leader. So the first time you bust my balls about it . . . I'm gone."

"No sweat, Mort, I'm a Shake-n-Bake myself."

"Really?" he said, pleasantly surprised. "Then I guess we'll have plenty of leadership war stories to discuss."

Mort admitted that he endured the same unwelcome reception I had when he first arrived in Vietnam. As a new squad leader, his subordinates doubted his unproven abilities until a VC ambush wounded their Lieutenant and thrust Mort into the leadership role. While under intense enemy fire, Mort remained calm and accurately called in artillery fire to break off the attack. Mort was never doubted after that. Since our experiences were somewhat similar, it was easy for us to become friends and hang around together.

Not knowing what to do first, we did some limited soul searching and quickly agreed that our first priority was to locate female companionship. Instead of wasting time searching the bars, we opted for a house of ill-repute. The problem was we didn't know what we were looking for. We realized we were not likely to find a flashing sign offering sex, so we walked a couple of blocks taking in the sights when a gaudily dressed Vietnamese man beckoned us from the doorway of a three-story concrete house.

"Hey GIs!" he yelled, waving to us. "You want numba one boom-boom? We got it here! Nice girls, no waiting!"

"Let's check it out," whispered Mort, poking me as he grinned. "I'm in the mood for love, aren't you?"

We entered a parlor area that looked like it was furnished with items bought at a rummage sale. "Please sit down," the man smiled. "I am Phuc, your host. Please wait here." Phuc quickly returned with two girls for our inspection. "You like?" he asked enthusiastically. "Only twenty-five dolla for girl and a room."

"Twenty-five dollars!" I howled. "Are you crazy?"

"Me not crazy. Twenty-five dolla for all night long. You can make love all the time. These girls are very horny."

We both snickered at his bizarre salesmanship because the girls were not very attractive. However, Mort must have thought anyone else he brought out would not be any better, so he grabbed what he thought was the best looking of the pair. The other flirted with me, but she was just too homely to spend that kind of money and time on. I politely requested another selection.

Phuc hustled her away and quickly returned with a surprisingly attractive girl with soft features and short jet-black hair. I wondered why she wasn't brought out earlier. Perhaps the plain ones were offered first in hopes that someone like Mort came along.

I accepted the second girl and paid the fee. She quietly led me to a modestly furnished room on the second floor. The room was unexpectedly homey and neatly arranged. It reminded me of an efficiency apartment without a kitchen area. "Do you want to make love now?" she asked in a businesslike manner.

"In a few minutes," I said, taken back by her boldness. "Since we'll be together all night, we should at least get to know each other. What's your name?"

She walked to the window and slowly pulled down the shade. "My name is Tina."

"My name is Artie . . . Artie Wiknik."

"You are Sergeant Wiknik," she announced, pointing at my stripes. "Now we make love, then rest."

I agreed but we sure did not make love. Tina was less than enthusiastic and seemed determined that I was not going to enjoy it either. After we finished, she rolled over and ordered me to sleep. Her repulsive attitude made me wonder why I had so readily committed to the arrangement. I supposed that the more I was exposed to war, the more trivial moral and social values seemed. Besides, after the anguish my girlfriend put me through with her drug letter, I felt I deserved a weekend of shameless behavior. I put it out of my mind as I drifted off to sleep thinking how comforting it was to lie in a warm bed next to a woman rather than on the cold ground next to a GI.

Sometime during the night we were awakened by a loud commotion at the front door which quickly spread into the parlor area. The military police were searching for GIs who missed the 10:00 p.m. curfew. I was among them. Tina leaped from the bed and helped me gather my belongings so she could hide me on the roof. However, her concern was not for me. If the house got caught with GIs sleeping overnight, it would probably get shut down. I crawled through a hatchway and onto the roof where I met up with Mort, who was already hiding there. We both had a good laugh over the situation. The search netted one unlucky GI. Mort and I figured we were already in trouble for missing the head count, so we stayed for the rest of the night.

In the morning, Mort and I returned to the R & R center to face our punishment. We overheard other GIs talking about the military police waking them up, so we knew we were not the only ones. To our surprise, nothing was said about anyone missing the curfew. We supposed that the late night rousting was a formality to keep the Vietnamese in line. We quickly ate breakfast and then went back to the girls. The first thing I wanted to do was have sex, but Tina did not share my eagerness. She complained that I didn't care about her feelings and never asked what she wanted to do. Since I was paying her to be with me, I didn't think it mattered. However, to keep Tina happy, I agreed to take her out to see the sights. That was a big mistake. Before I realized it, I was buying her all sorts of food and trinkets. I felt like a sucker.

As we walked along, a young boy driving a horse and carriage pulled up. He offered to drive us through the city for two dollars. I didn't want to go because my money was running low. Tina suggested that after the carriage ride, we would go back to the room and make love. We went for the ride. As we rode along Tina held her head high, as if the carriage ride symbolized a form of dignity. Yet, at the same time she looked sad.

"What was Vietnam like before the war?" I asked, trying to make small talk.

"I don't know," she answered, somewhat bewildered by the question. "As long as I can remember, Vietnam has always been at war."

"What about your family, do they live around here?"

"I have not seen my family for a very long time. The work I do is not honorable, so I must stay away from them."

I almost felt sorry for her, which is probably what she wanted. But as a paying customer, slowly getting bled dry, I was not overly interested in her tough life.

When the carriage ride ended, our adolescent driver demanded four dollars, claiming that his fee was two dollars per rider. I refused to pay any extra and an argument broke out. When the kid threatened me with his horsewhip, Tina called a nearby White Mouse to settle the dispute. That only made things worse. The three of them yelled at each other in their native Vietnamese, then the cop and the kid both started yelling at me. As a crowd of civilians began gathering around us. I could not figure out what was going on because they began yelling, too. Finally, I paid the four dollars just to shut everyone up. I figured the little thief planned to embarrass me into paying the extra all along. It worked.

Tina and I returned to the room for our last intimate encounter. After we had sex I told her that I did not have enough money to pay for another night. That was not what she wanted to hear. As soon as we cleaned up, Tina cast me aside like I never existed. It was just as well. After staying with her I found myself questioning the character of some of the Vietnamese people I had met. Of course, GIs like me were not much better since our selfish behavior contributed to their lifestyle.

On my way back to the R & R center a religious library caught my eye. Inside was a reference room where a dozen GIs sat talking, reading, and writing letters. They looked like holy rollers on vacation. An elderly American couple trying to provide an alternative to the shameless behavior around them ran the library. The wife approached to tell me about the fleshy evils so prevalent in Vung Tau.

"Fornication is everywhere," she inflected, "but God will give you the strength to resist if you put your faith in Him."

"Thanks," I said coolly, "but I just stepped in to look around."

"Then look at the soldiers," she whispered, pointing around the room. "They came here to wash the sinful dirt from their souls. Will you also accept the Lord's cleansing power?"

"I suppose I should," I said, somewhat embarrassed. "I haven't exactly been a model citizen since I came to Vung Tau."

"That's more like it, admission is half the battle."

She comforted me with a gentle hand while guiding me across the room to an altar. As we passed the reading GIs, they smiled and nodded as if something wonderful was about to happen. I felt silly but smiled back anyway.

"The first thing you need to do," she said authoritatively, "is relinquish the instrument that allows this wickedness to occur."

"I have to give up something? What?"

"Don't you know?" she smiled, while pointing to an empty collection plate. "You brought money to Vung Tau to spend on harlots and alcohol. That money is better spent to help spread the Word."

She probably was right, but the scenario was unfolding too fast and I felt uncomfortable.

"I don't mind giving you a donation, but I'm not giving all my cash."

"It must be all or nothing, otherwise you'll continue to sin."

She was right again. I guess the love of money is the root of all evil. The old couple supported a good cause, but my lust for fun was stronger than my morality.

"Some other time," I said, turning my back on her message. I left the library more confused about my conduct than before. I wandered the streets for several hours trying to sort things out. I finally gave up and returned to the R & R center to find Mort asleep on his bunk.

"Hey Mort," I called, shaking him awake. "What happened to your girl?"

"I didn't have enough money for another night," he groggily answered. "What about you?"

"Same with me. I blew most of it trying to keep her happy but it turned out she was using me more than I was using her."

"Well let's not hang around here," Mort declared. "Why don't we pool our cash and go bar hopping?"

"Sounds good. We're leaving tomorrow anyway and I'm not going to need money out in the boonies."

We visited several barrooms, staying long enough at each to drink one beer apiece. We tried the famous Vietnamese Ba Muoi Ba beer, but finding it too tart we stuck with American brands. We also chose canned beer because there were rumors that unscrupulous bar owners opened bottled beer and diluted it with water. The tampered bottles were then served to drunk GIs who rarely knew the difference.

Young attractive bar girls were fixtures at every barroom and as soon as we walked in a pair would rush over to coax us into buying them drinks. We only bought for ourselves, so they called us "Cheap Charlies." Since we planned to spend our money on ourselves, we didn't care what they said. Besides, by not buying them drinks we had just as much fun watching them hustle other GIs, and they were very successful. Each time a girl made a sale, the bartender slipped her a poker chip to be traded in for wages at the end of the shift.

We witnessed the same routine over and over until we entered a bar called the Angel Saloon. There, the girls didn't pester us as soon as we walked through the door. Instead, they gave us time to sit down and order a drink before approaching. After the beer was served, a beautiful Eurasian girl strolled over to our table and asked to join us. Her French-Vietnamese lineage made for the most enchanting female I had seen in months. I felt aroused just being in her presence, although all the beer I had been drinking helped to make her even more attractive. I motioned her to sit down and she gracefully positioned herself close to me. When she reached over and put her hand on my thigh, I flinched in delight.

"My name is Kim," she purred. "Will you buy me a Saigon Tea?"

"Sure," I drooled. "What's Saigon Tea?"

"Numba one bar drink that makes me crazy."

How could I refuse? I nodded to the bartender and he brought the tiny dark drink to our table. I gave him a dollar and he gave Kim a poker chip. She slowly took a sip as she caressed my leg. I was so excited that I thought I might wet myself. Mort knew I was captivated by Kim so he wandered off to the jukebox to give us some privacy.

Kim and I chatted as she continued rubbing my leg. After a few minutes, the bartender brought her another Saigon Tea. I didn't remember ordering the drink but thought nothing of it as I handed him another dollar. Ten minutes later, he was back with a third Saigon Tea. That's when I realized they were taking advantage of me.

"Who ordered that drink?!" I demanded of the bartender.

"Her glass was empty," he replied, casually shrugging his shoulders.

"What's the matter with you people? Is money so important that you can't even wait for an order?"

"No sweat, GI," he said, raising his hands upward. "I'll take it back."

"My name is not GI!" I shouted while rising. "I'm just sick and tired of people trying to cheat me." Kim tugged on my arm to sit me back down.

"I'm sorry you feel that way," she said softly.

"Me too," I answered. Looking around the room, I realizing everyone was staring at us. Even Mort looked at me like I was nuts. I had embarrassed both of us, so we knew it was time to leave. I didn't want to just walk away from Kim, though she was probably in on the drink scam.

"Can we meet after you get off?"

"Why?" she smiled warmly. "Do you want to make love to me?"

"Well . . . yes," I answered, surprised by her directness. "But we don't have to if you're not that kind of girl."

"Girls always need money to buy nice things. Meet me across the street at nine o'clock. I want ten dolla for short-time."

"How much for long time?" I asked, knowing I didn't even have enough for short-time.

"I'm only a short-time girl. If we do boom-boom all night, I'll get sore."

I agreed to her terms, though ten dollars was double the average price for a short-time prostitute. I had only four dollars, but I figured Mort would lend me the rest.

"Don't look at me," Mort shrugged as we left. "If my money is going to get someone laid, it's going to be me."

"I don't blame you," I lamented, "but Kim is the closest thing to a round-eye I'll ever see here. I've got to get the extra money somehow."

"Why don't you bum it off the guys at the R & R center?" he joked. "Just tell them the truth; you need it for sex."

As crazy as Mort's idea sounded, mooching was my only hope. I hit the streets and began pestering GIs. Mort wanted no part of my panhandling, so he watched from a distance. I told each GI the same story about a terrible financial bind I was in and that if I didn't get some cash real soon, someone was going to beat the shit out of me. Surprisingly, I collected three dollars, though I lost my dignity in the process. Several GIs simply told me to get lost, while others called me a deadbeat. I was still three dollars short when Mort, who was tired of watching, finally offered to make up the difference.

We went to the Angel Saloon at the appointed time and waited across the street. When the place closed, Kim never showed. I was mad at myself for letting a bar girl make a fool of me. But it wasn't a total loss since I made a few dollars.

As we headed back to the R & R center the streets were empty and quiet. Vietnamese music played softly in the distance. We passed through the city square and a female mute confronted us. She looked like a diseased beggar. Ragged clothes hung loosely on her scrawny frame and her affliction twisted her face into a haunting stare. We tried to walk around her but she blocked our path, grunting as she pointed at Mort's crotch. Then she stuck her finger in her mouth and sucked on it suggesting oral sex. Her proposition was disgusting. This pitiful woman was so destitute that her source of income was from giving blow jobs.

"No! Number ten!" Mort yelled, nudging her aside. "Go away!"

"Numba one," she said with a hollow moan. "Uggerrah. Numba one."

When we turned away, the woman fell to the ground and latched onto Mort's leg like a toddler clinging to a parent. Mort tried to break free but ended up dragging her along.

"One dolla," she cried. "One dolla. Uggerrah. Numba one."

I didn't know what to do. It was the most pathetic display I had ever witnessed.

"Here," I said, reaching into my pocket. "If you need money that bad, take this. I'm not going to need it."

When I handed her the cash, she must have thought I wanted her services. She pushed me against a tree and groped for my pants zipper. I yelled to Mort for help but he was laughing too hard to even move. I quickly wrestled myself free and convinced her that the money was a gift with no obligations. Mort felt the same pity and gave her his money, too. The woman was ecstatic. We did our good deed for the day and felt better than if we had gotten what we paid for, especially if it was from her!

In the morning, our R & R stay ended and we parted company to return to the war. I never saw Mort again. Our brief friendship was typical of the Army life we had come to know. Soldiers with common interests and mutual trust become friends only to have the military separate them forever. I knew I would miss him.

I left Vung Tau anxious to check in at the Camp Evans aid station. While on R & R, I had neglected my infected foot, allowing it to deteriorate to the point where I began limping from the pain. I got as far north as LZ Sally only to find that the Chinook shuttle would not be

Author Art Wiknik in the A Shau Valley. This photo was taken a short time after the Hamburger Hill battle. His platoon has just established a Daytime Defensive Position (DDP).

A stunning aerial view of Hamburger Hill two months after the battle of May 20, 1969. Wiknik and his comrades attacked up the hillside visible in the upper right portion of this image.

101st Airborne Division troops wounded during the 11th and final assault on Dong Ap Bia on the western edge of the A Shau Valley are treated at a small command post waiting helicopter evacuation.

A paratrooper wounded during an assault against 3,000-foot Dong Ap Bia, the mountain dubbed "Hamburger Hill" by GIs, grimaces in pain as he awaits evacuation at base camp in the A Shau Valley near the Laos border.

A chilling scene from hell. Soldiers survey the battlefield after the final assault on Hamburger Hill.

A medevac lands in the midst of destruction atop Hamburger Hill to evacuate the wounded.

In the aftermath the Hamburger Hill battle, soldiers from the 101st Airborne Division try to make sense of what they had just experienced.

High on a mountaintop in the A Shau Valley, FSB Airborne begins to be rebuilt after being overrun only two weeks earlier.

The 155mm gun position at Firebase Airborne in the A Shau Valley.

101st Airborne troops arriving in a Bell-UH1D "slick" helicopter on Firebase Airborne in the A Shau Valley.

A view of the A Shau Valley over a Bell-UH1D helicopter door gunner's M60 machine gun.

Fire mission for artillery battery of 105mm howitzers on
FSB Airborne.

The author poses with NVA weapons cache he
discovered just outside FSB Airborne as ARVN soldiers
and GIs look on.

William Scoggins (left), Tu Huong (center), and Jimmy Smith (right), enjoy a beer at Camp Evans.

On FSB Airborne, Stanley Alcon admires a nude centerfold while fellow soldiers lean in for a closer look.

Camp Evans mess hall: Jimmy Smith (left), William Scoggins (center) and author (right) read and write letters home during an overnight stand down.

Dennis Silig on a hillside near the DMZ. Previous aerial bombing has all but eliminated the jungle.

At the DMZ, the author poses with an NVA soldier's helmet and bones.

Unidentified elements of the 101st Airborne Division discuss tactics during a sweep of the area around the firebase protecting the Montagnard village of Mai Loc near the DMZ.

Howard Siner and author enjoy cigars on Christmas Day outside the Camp Evans aid station.

Christmas Day at Camp Evans. The author is standing where the supply room and two hooches burned to the ground when a jeep and ammunition trailer caught fire.

Outside the rear gate at Camp Evans, unidentified GIs
chide the author for his cheesy moustache.

The author's squad works its way across an area
recently blasted by 105mm artillery in the Annamite
jungle mountains five miles northwest of Camp Evans.

(above) A member of the platoon glances behind him as we carefully investigate an enemy trail in the Annamite jungle mountains five miles northwest of Camp Evans.

The author (right) poses with an M-60 machine gun on his last day in the field, two days after Howard Siner and Dennis Silig were wounded.

Recovering from his head wound, Howard Siner (right) and the author (below) stand outside the 95th Evacuation Hospital in Da Nang. The barbed wire fence was the only thing that separated the hospital from the ocean.

Just days before going home and recently promoted to Staff Sergeant, author poses with SKS rifle at the Camp Evans company area.

After coming home nine days early, my family hastily made this banner and attached it to our house for all to see. It remained in place for another two weeks.

Arthur Wiknik, Jr., December 2004.

flying until the next day. The quickest way back to Camp Evans would be by hitchhiking. Since Quoc-Lo 1 was just outside LZ Sally's front gate, I patiently thumbed for a lift.

Hitchhiking in Vietnam was an adventure. Although it was officially discouraged, thumbing was an acceptable means of travel. The difficulty was in getting a ride. The Vietnamese would not stop for an American unless money was waved at them, and GIs on the road without a weapon were considered fair game for cowboy ARVN trucker's to swerve their vehicles at. As a result, only GIs picked up other GIs.

I eventually hitched a ride on a cargo truck going north to Quang Tri. When the truck arrived at the Camp Evans front gate, I asked the driver to bring me the one-half mile to the battalion aid station but he refused. I eventually hobbled the distance on my own.

The aid station medics examining my foot couldn't believe what they saw. The big toe was pale yellow with a pus-oozing quarter-inch hole on the side. "This is was one of the most advanced cases of immersion foot we have ever seen," one medic sternly announced.

"We might have to report you for letting it get so bad," commented the other. "This looks like a self-inflicted injury."

"I didn't have the foot treated when I came in from the field because I was afraid that I wouldn't be allowed to go to Vung Tau," I said, trying to earn their sympathy.

"That's bullshit," the first one scolded. "As soon as we get your treatment started, we're going to contact your platoon leader to find out what kind of soldier you really are."

Lucky for me, Doc Meehan was in camp for a first aid refresher course. After I explained the situation to Doc, he got me off the hook by telling to the medics that I was a dedicated Boonie Rat who never complained and always maintained good personal hygiene. Thanks Doc!

I spent the next two weeks at Camp Evans in semi-convalescence. Each morning for an hour, I soaked my foot in a nasty solution that ate away the infection and healed the damaged skin tissues. The toes needed fresh air so I wasn't allowed to wear boots, which relieved me from work details.

My foot recovery routine included walking a minimum of two miles each day within the confines of Camp Evans. I easily exceeded that requirement to avoid being noticed hanging around the battalion area and giving anyone the idea of putting me to work. At night, I watched movies, played cards, or drank beer at the EM Club. Passing time that way was the dream of everyone in the field.

Grunts coined a name for people in my position: Ghoster. A Ghoster was an infantryman who schemed his way to the rear when he should be in the field. Time spent in the rear was still "good time" and thus counted toward a soldier's year-long tour of duty. I liked being away from the field, so in the coming months I planned to make ghosting my trademark.

While on the recuperative hikes, I avoided the mud and road dust by cutting between buildings and tents. In so doing, I often discovered hidden details about Camp Evans. Two-hundred feet behind the 18th Surgical Mobile Hospital I encountered a sign reading "Graves Registration: Off Limits." Graves Registration was the military unit that deals with the processing and embalming of dead American soldiers. The tiny facility was tucked away for good reason: seeing dead comrades was disastrous for troop morale. However, my curiosity drew me in for a closer look. I wish it had not.

The doors were open to a large refrigerated compartment where body bags containing dead GIs lay on racks. They were being kept cold to slow the decomposing process before preparing them for the final journey home. It was depressing to see so many silent body bags in a place with the words "Meat Locker" sloppily painted on the doorway. I stared inside until an Army mortician walked around the corner.

"Hey buddy!" he shouted. "Get out of here! This area is off limits!"

Heading his advice, I turned to leave.

"Not that way!" he shouted again, trying to divert me.

It was too late. At my feet was a dead GI. I surmised he had been alive only a few hours ago. A bloodstained towel covered his face, but the real horror was a gigantic chest wound that completely disemboweled the body. The exposed rib cage was splintered, with each rib grotesquely arching skyward. Only the soldier's spine held the upper and lower torso together. The mortician, sympathetic to my shock, told me that the GI had taken an RPG to the mid-section.

Looking at a dead Gook did not bother me, but this poor bastard was so mutilated I almost gagged. I supposed his parents did not know yet their son was dead. I thought about my own parents as I softly said, "I'm glad it wasn't me." The mortician didn't respond. He simply motioned for me to leave. I never hiked in that area again.

During my stay at Camp Evans no Grunts came in from the field, so I seldom had anyone to talk to unless it was with the rear echelon soldiers. But the men who worked in the base camp were far different from the Boonie Rats. Grunts called them Rear Echelon Mother Fuckers, or REMF for short. REMFs had logistical jobs such as a cook, trucker, mechanic, or clerk, which kept them from ever having to set foot in the field. They also had access to cold beer and soda, hot meals, showers, laundry, transportation, off-duty hours, radios, and more. A REMF tour was easy compared to that of a Grunt, yet REMFs often complained about how rough and dangerous it was to be in Vietnam, going so far as to retell overheard war stories to raise a level of self-importance to those around him. As near as I could tell, the only danger a REMF faced was from catching gonorrhea or being run down by a drunken truck driver. And the biggest hardship a REMF contended with was when a generator broke down and their beer got warm or there was no movie that night. It was my opinion that the danger a REMF experienced was limited to reading about it in newspapers.

REMFs always steered clear of Boonie Rats. Some did it out of respect because they knew we often dealt with more adversity in a single day than they saw in a year. Others acted out of fear, believing we were gun-toting crazies. Grunts, in turn, avoided REMFs because we thought they were whiners and war hero wannabes who had no idea of the struggles endured in the jungle. As a result, REMFs and Grunts were totally incompatible.

My low opinion of the REMF was confirmed one day as I soaked my foot at the aid station chopper pad. A Chinook set down a cargo net containing the bodies of twenty dead Viet Cong. When the Chinook flew off to refuel, the rotor wash blasted me with a sickening death stench. The dead VC were mostly naked, lying in a gruesome heap with arms and legs protruding through the net. Some bodies were torn apart by shrapnel. Small arms and machine gun fire had killed the others. A few had bullet wounds to the head, which probably meant there were no prisoners taken that day. A ribbon of fluids that oozed from the pile magnified the nauseating image. A few minutes later, three REMFs ran out to the chopper pad with a camera. I watched in disbelief as they took turns climbing atop the grotesque heap to pose for photographs. It was a morbid scene. The trio probably gave no thought as to how many GIs lost their lives for these and other body counts. As they ridiculed the dead with their ghoulish behavior, I wondered how our values could have sunk so low.

The longer I stayed in the rear, the more I became aware of a volatile situation that was beginning to plague the military. It was the growing resentment among some black American soldiers who were not willing to fight in what they called a "white man's war." Blacks believed that a disproportionate number of them were being drafted and sent to Vietnam. They also believed that even if they survived Vietnam, it meant facing an on-going war of racial unrest when they get home. Initially, the military dismissed their bitterness and frustration, labeling it the whining of malcontents. That is, until there was a riot at the Long Binh Jail, the in-country prison for US military criminals. During this revolt blacks took over part of the stockade. The result was the death of several GIs. There was also an incident at Da Nang's China Beach that almost resulted in a shoot-out between blacks and whites. These events forced an immediate reassessment of US military policy. As a result, Afro haircuts, Black Power paraphernalia, and more soul music were allowed. Some bases even offered black awareness classes, but this wasn't always enough.

Tensions mounted as militant black infantrymen were sent in from the field to face disciplinary action for refusing to fight or obey orders. As a show of solidarity, blacks banded together to form the Camp Evans Black Coalition. The coalition claimed it was not opposed to the war, just to fighting in it. I was especially disappointed to learn that while I was away on R & R, my friend Lennie Person had joined them. I had to ask him why.

"What are you doing with these guys? You don't belong with them; you're a Grunt; you're one of us."

"Not anymore," he announced defiantly. "I refused to put my life on the line by walking point and I refused to carry extra ammo for the machine gun. I'm not going to help the white military establishment win the war with my blood. So now the Army has threatened to court martial me."

"Well, what did you expect?" I asked in disbelief. "Everyone takes turn walking point, even me. And we all carry M-60 ammo for extra firepower. Out in the field everyone's supposed to be on the same team."

"Yeah, the white man's team," he sneered. "You must have forgot that I'm black."

"Man, your color means nothing to me. Just look at the things we've been through, like Hamburger Hill and the A Shau Valley. We did them together and we helped each other stay alive. But now, I don't know you. You've allowed yourself to be brainwashed."

"This problem is bigger than you and me. If the Army wants to court martial us because we're taking a stand against years of white oppression, then let them. But everyday there's going to be more Blacks rebelling and they can't lock us all up."

"Lennie, I may not feel the same things you do, but this way isn't right. The Army is going to lock you up for disobeying orders, not for your political beliefs or your skin color."

Lennie did not waiver. Instead, he tried a different approach. "Why don't you meet some of my new friends? They're not as bad as you might think."

He took me to the coalition's all-black hooch. I was speechless upon walking through the door. A black light illuminated glowing tapestries adorning the walls and ceilings. Several read "Black Power" and "Black Is Beautiful," while another read "Violence If Necessary, Peace If Possible." Some tapestries had images of Martin Luther King, Jr., Malcolm X, and members of the Black Panthers. On a bunk, two black GIs practiced the attention getting "dap" greeting, involving a complex routine of hand slapping, gripping, and fist contact. Many blacks claimed the dap was a display of recognition and unity rather than a gesture of defiance. But when I walked into the hooch, the dap abruptly stopped as one of them raised a clenched fist.

"Power to the people!" he shouted. Others quickly muttered, "Right on Brother." That's when I knew it was time to leave. I walked out, leaving them to their self-imposed isolation. I had little sympathy for their position, especially knowing that our company had more blacks in the rear than in the field. As a result, I felt a renewed respect for blacks like Freddie Shaw who stayed in the boonies and refused to blame whites for the problems of society. Those men should be especially proud of their military service.

* * *

When my case of immersion foot finally healed I returned to the field. It was almost a relief to be back with my friends and away from the nonsense in the rear. When the supply chopper brought me out, Siner announced my return.

"Hey everybody, look who's back!" he yelled with a big grin. "It's Sergeant Wiknik, the only Grunt who can stretch a three-day R & R into three weeks!"

"Alright, alright," I said, defending myself against his playful ribbing. "If you must know, the Army kept me in the rear to see if a Grunt could handle becoming a REMF. I failed."

"You'd make a great REMF," added Silig. "If you could drink more than two beers in one sitting. So why did you come back, did you get tired of watching the same movies?"

"Very funny. I came back because I miss the thrill of getting shot at."

"I hate to disappoint you," Stan Alcon chimed in, "but it's been pretty quiet while you were gone. No enemy contact and very few booby traps. The only thing we've been doing is ambushing VC trails, but nobody ever shows up!"

"Cut the reunion chi-chat!" barked Sergeant Krol. "We're moving out in five minutes!"

All conversation abruptly stopped as the men dejectedly glanced at each other. It was obvious that Krol had not eased up while I was gone. We put our gear together and moved out, following a trail until it eventually intersected with another. Krol and Lieutenant Petry decided it made for a perfect ambush site because the surrounding thick brush would funnel any VC traffic into an escape-proof ground zero.

One trail led north past an abandoned French fort, where Krol positioned his ambush team behind a natural berm. The other trail crossed a shallow slow-moving stream where a second team positioned themselves. A third team retreated two hundred feet back on the route we walked in from in case we were followed. Krol placed my team where the trail crossed the stream, making us the hub position of the other teams. It seemed like an odd location because the only way the VC could get near us was if they walked past or shot their way through one of the other teams. We were also in a dangerous position if any of the ambushes were sprung because friendly fire could be shot in our direction. I didn't like the set up, but since there had been no enemy activity for several weeks, I didn't question anything.

The first line of defense for any ambush was claymore mines, but on this ambush the thick vegetation limited placement of the mines. As a result, my team put out only two. One claymore faced the trail junction and the other was on the trail across the stream. Both mines were less than half the usual fifty feet from our position.

At 3:00 a.m. it was my turn for guard duty. I did not think I would need my M-16 in this weird ambush, so I leaned it against a bush an arm's length away. I checked the claymore detonators and wires to make sure they weren't mixed up. With everything in place I sat still for my two-hour shift. I got tired of eye-straining into the overcast night, so I passed the time fantasizing about home and being with my girlfriend.

My trance ended abruptly when only twenty feet away I saw movement. The misty form slowly materialized into that of a man cautiously moving toward me. When I recognized the silhouetted pork pie hat, I realized he was a VC who must have spotted the reflection of my face in the dark. He came closer, to within fifteen feet, looking long and hard. Another VC came up behind him. Both men stood silently, holding their rifles at the ready position. I didn't dare reach for my M-16 because if they could see my face, they would surely see my hands move and probably open fire. Unsure what to do, I sat stone still, trying not to even breathe. At the same time, I cursed myself for being so stupid for leaning my rifle against that bush.

After what seemed like an eternity the first VC began to slowly retreat. Maybe he was not sure of who, or what, he was staring at. Or maybe he did know but wasn't willing to test our strength. Whatever the reason, he motioned to his partner that they were leaving. I figured as soon as they got twenty-five feet away I could safely reach for my rifle and open fire. But before that happened, one of my men rolled over and rattled some equipment. The first VC heard the noise and in a panic ran toward the stream. I grabbed the claymore detonators and as soon as he splashed in the water, I blew the claymore. The deafening explosion shattered the eerie silence as the second VC ran off in the opposite direction. I estimated the time for him to reach the second claymore and detonated that one, too. Both blasts occurred within seconds, which caused an extra dose of mud and debris to rain down on our position.

"Two Gooks!" I yelled. "They ran off in both directions!"

Before I finished getting the words out of my mouth, the men began spraying gunfire up and down the trail. We ended the two-minute barrage with several hand grenades. Silence. We waited, and waited. And waited. We listened for sounds: rustling brush, groans, anything. There was nothing. I began to wonder if I really saw the VC. This was my first night back in the field and now I began to think it could have been just my imagination. If I gave our position away like a bone-headed Cherry because a night bird or wild animal spooked me, I would be a laughing stock. Finally, much to my relief, Silig's position opened fire with a one-minute salvo. Whether we had a kill or not, at least the Gooks were real. The night fell silent again, but now all our ambush positions remained on 100% alert until we knew how large an enemy force we had engaged or whether the Gooks were coming back. The anxious hours before daybreak dragged slowly by. When it was finally light enough to see, the ambush team from across the stream cautiously approached our position.

"What the hell were you guys shooting at last night?" asked Stan Alcon, knowing any VC near my position must have somehow gotten by his.

"Gooks, what else?" I answered. "Two of them walked right up to me. Didn't you find a body over there?"

"There ain't nothing over here. The way you guys were blasting away, we had to make love to the ground. The bushes all around us were falling down. Anyone could have run past us."

"Well, that's all right," I said confidently. "Silig's position opened fire after we did. They must have a kill."

They didn't. After I blew the claymores, Silig alerted his team. One of the VC, either wounded or shook up from the claymore, hobbled up the trail to within fifty feet when Silig opened fire. At that range, even in the dark, they could not have missed. But in the morning there was no body, no blood, and no tracks. It looked like we were visited by Supergooks.

Allowing the VC to escape was bad enough, but when the shooting started, Petry hastily called battalion headquarters to request artillery support because he thought we were engaged in a regular battle. The problem was our new battalion commander, Colonel Dynamo, overheard the call and got so excited about the potential body count he decided to come out at first light to view the enemy remains. When the Colonel arrived we had nothing to show. Petry tried to explain the ambush scenario, but the Colonel became furious.

"Lieutenant Petry!" he shouted, for everyone to hear. "What the hell were your people doing out here last night? You had VC walking into your ambush positions, practically begging to get shot, and your men blew the opportunity!"

"Colonel," Petry nervously began, "it was an overcast night, making it especially hard to detect movement, the scrub brush . . ."

"I don't want to hear any goddamn excuses!" the Colonel yelled, cutting Petry off. "Based on what I've seen here, your people couldn't shoot a one-legged grandmother in a wheelchair. But if you're so sure you hit something last night, then I want your men to re-search the entire area. Except this time have them look under every bush, in every ditch and under every rock. And I don't care if it takes all day."

We thought the Colonel was overdoing it because no one ever went through such detailed interrogation over a bungled ambush. The body count must have been getting more attention than we thought. We searched area for several hours and found nothing. The Colonel questioned each ambush team in greater detail to determine how things had gone wrong. Somehow, the finger of incompetence was pointed at me.

"Sergeant Wiknik," the Colonel began patronizingly, "you just came back from three weeks of convalescence in the rear, and on your first night back initiated an ambush that yielded nothing. I would say that you had lost your edge. You were not combat ready."

"Sir," I explained, "when I saw the Gooks, they took off in different directions, so I had to choose my targets carefully. When I figured they were close to the claymores, I detonated them."

"Why didn't you fire your M-16 at them?"

"Because I didn't know how many there were and I didn't want to give my position away," I sheepishly answered, not daring to tell him my rifle was leaning against a bush

"Well Sergeant," he said, pointing at the hole in the ground left by the claymore. "It's obvious that your claymore was located too close to the trail. When the VC ran past you, he must have knocked it over. When you detonated it, the blast simply went into the mud."

"Possibly sir, but the other claymore did some damage because Silig's position saw a VC hobbling toward them."

"For all we know, that hobbling VC had a birth defect," the Colonel sneered, looking back at Petry and Krol. "I don't know who laid out this ambush, but the only way the VC got anywhere near Sergeant Wiknik was because they walked past one of the other positions. That means you had people who were not alert, maybe even asleep. Anyone want to confess?"

No one denied or admitted anything.

In retribution for our ineptitude, Colonel Dynamo decided to shake up the platoon with several personnel changes. Sergeant Krol, who we hated and were glad to see go, was transferred to Echo Company to be with his buddy Lieutenant Pizzuto. Sergeant Wakefield, who had been groomed by Krol and Pizzuto, was promoted to Platoon Sergeant. Lieutenant Petry, the first officer who actually listened to us old-timers, would be sent to another platoon as soon as a replacement officer became available.

My heart sunk, however, when the Colonel offered Howard Siner a job in the rear writing articles for the brigade newspaper. Howard was no dummy, and he accepted without hesitation.

Siner was the only one I missed. Besides being the most common sense guy we had, he had also become my best friend, as well as Silig's. Silig and I knew we would have no problem relying on each other, but without Siner's cool head, things would surely be different.

PFC Brian Thompson, a redheaded, freckle-faced GI from Indiana, replaced Howard Siner. Unlike the typical Cherry who came to us scared out of his wits and afraid to speak with anyone, Thompson was quite personable, inquisitive, and learned fast. I felt fortunate to have a Grunt with such potential in my squad. It took several weeks for Thompson's mail to catch up with him. When it did, his letters were addressed to SSG Brian Thompson, not PFC Brian Thompson.

"Hey Thompson, you've got mail but it's addressed to a Staff Sergeant. They sure move you new guys up fast," I joked, treating it as a mistake.

"Uh . . . yes," he answered nervously. "I told some of my friends that I was a sergeant so they would think I was a bad-ass hero. It's only a joke. Heh, heh."

"Well, I don't know if the Army will laugh. They've got regulations against just about everything else, so there's probably one against this. You better tell your friends the truth before you get into trouble."

Thompson didn't answer. He just nodded as he noticed the guys staring at him, wondering why he would tell his hometown friends he was something other than a PFC. As the weeks went by, more mail came addressed to SSG Thompson. One day I jokingly yelled, "Mail for

Sergeant Thompson!" and he quickly came forward, as if comfortable with the title.

Lieutenant Petry became suspicious and placed a call to battalion headquarters inquiring about "Private" Thompson. The next day we received word that Thompson was indeed a Staff Sergeant. When confronted with the truth, Thompson admitted to the masquerade, explaining his bizarre behavior.

"I graduated from NCO school with high marks, earning a promotion to Staff Sergeant. During the second phase of my schooling at an advanced infantry training unit, a jealous Vietnam Veteran who made NCO the hard way threatened me. He claimed to know which unit in Vietnam I would be assigned to, and vowed to have his buddies kill me. I believed him because I had heard rumors about Instant NCOs having a short life expectancy, often dying at the hands of their own men. I got scared. So to increase my chances of survival, I passed myself off as a PFC, hoping to gain some combat experience before I was discovered."

Everyone stared at Thompson with a feeling of shock and anger. Though his disguise was understandable, what he did was wrong. He was specially trained and paid as a Staff Sergeant but was performing the work of a Private and the men resented him for it. Even I toughed it out as a Cherry NCO, so there was no reason for him not to have done so as well.

Lieutenant Petry recognizing right off that it would be a long time before Thompson would earn the respect of our platoon. He wisely had him transferred to another unit. We never saw Thompson again, but the episode left us with a permanent reminder of how monumental the task of being accepted was.

Our next assignment took us to the mountains near the A Shau Valley to provide roving security for a firebase that was being dismantled by Army engineers. Our entire company would saturate the surrounding jungle in ten-man ambush teams to keep the NVA from taking pot shots at the construction crew. Although this would be a short mission of one to two weeks duration, no one wanted any part of the A Shau because the NVA were still a dangerous force in the area.

While waiting for our assignments, one GI, who vowed to never enter the A Shau again, was so desperate to get out he shot himself. Using an M-16 at point blank range, he fired a single round into his lower leg muscle. As carefully a placed shot as it was, the slug left a gaping void, removing a large chunk of flesh. As he writhed in agony, no one other than a medic rushed to his aid. As the medic went to work, GIs turned their backs on the soldier because we did not feel sorry for him. We were scared of the A Shau too, but only cowards stooped so low. The GI would surely get out of the field and probably the Army as well. But the price was too great to pay. The stigma of a self-inflicted wound would haunt him forever.

My ambush team was assigned the task of guarding a section of the American-built Route 547, a winding dirt road linking Camp Eagle, our division base camp, with the A Shau. The roadside terrain was a mix of bulldozed slopes and thick hilltop jungle patches. We spent most of our time tucked in the bushes playing cards, writing letters, and catching up on sleep. Although we were taking it easy, we didn't want to give the NVA a chance to sneak up on us by being too relaxed, so we stayed hidden by maintaining a 24-hour guard duty and noise control.

Our vigilance soon paid off when Alcon alerted us to some noise from deep in the jungle. We instinctively dropped everything and positioned ourselves behind rocks and logs in preparation for battle. After a ten-minute wait with no activity, everyone relaxed and started to return to their original positions.

"Stay put!" Alcon commanded. "They're still moving in our direction." No one else had heard any noise, but we waited just the same.

Living in the field for extended periods under life-threatening situations made everyone survival oriented. Some GIs, extra conscious of the changing environment, developed the fantastic ability to sense danger by becoming totally absorbed with their surroundings. Alcon possessed this keen sensitivity. Soon everyone heard the noise: twigs snapping and leaves rustling. As the commotion moved toward our position, each man silently clicked his the safety off readied their hand grenades. Only two hundred feet away, we could now see bushes and small trees wiggle.

"It's finally our turn to surprise the NVA," someone whispered. "They're going to run right into us."

Suddenly Silig stood up with his arms stretched skyward. "Monkeys!" he groaned. "Goddamn monkeys! We just got aped!"

We were in the path of a horde of three-feet-tall rock apes foraging through the jungle. They spotted us and retreated to the tall trees faster than they had come. If the enemy really had been out there, only Alcon was paying close attention. After that incident, we took guard duty more seriously.

*   *   *

On September 3, 1969, after a period of declining health, seventy-nine-year-old North Vietnamese political leader Ho Chi Minh succumbed to heart failure. American foreign policy makers hoped the Communist war machine would crumble without him. But the revolutionary spirit and memory of Uncle Ho instead became a rallying point to inspire the North Vietnamese into a more determined effort to win the war.

CHAPTER 8

The Bamboo Blues

On October 15, 1969, the American anti-war movement reached historic proportions in what became known as Vietnam Moratorium Day. This nationwide protest attracted hundreds of thousands of people who advocated the total and immediate withdrawal of all US forces from Indochina. It was a day of bell ringing and anti-war speeches followed by an evening of candlelight services. Although this was the largest expression of public dissent ever in the US, opponents of the protest movement cited that the activists in attendance represented only a fraction of the American population as proof that war protesters were a small, yet vocal, minority.

Regardless of this skepticism, the GIs' alliance was mixed. Some sided with the protesters, encouraged by any effort aimed at ending the war; others believed that opposition to the war was demoralizing. The North Vietnamese government in Hanoi joined in the event by sending a letter of encouragement, which was hailed by the moratorium organizers. The letter had many Americans questioning whose side the protesters were on. This widening gap of national commitment made developing a purpose or pride in our involvement difficult. Perhaps it was the organizers' intent to end the war even if it meant destroying America from within. Whatever the case, up to that day 39,000 American troops had the dubious honor of dying in Vietnam. Despite the moratorium, the war continued.

At the end of the French-Indochina War in 1954, the Geneva Agreements left North and South Vietnam divided at a five-mile wide, forty-mile long demarcation line along the 17th parallel. The NVA violated the agreement by repeatedly crossing through the DMZ (Demilitarized Zone). However, sustained heavy US bombing in the aftermath of the 1968 siege on the US Marine base at Khe Sanh and the highly developed Ho Chi Minh trail in nearby Laos left the DMZ nearly free of any organized NVA presence. Therefore, the region was ideal for initiating President Nixon's Vietnamization program by withdrawing the US 3rd Marine Division and assigning the South Vietnamese 1st ARVN Division. To assist in the transition, elements of the 101st were called on to secure suspected enemy infiltration routes and provide reconnaissance patrols. Mai Loc, one of the northernmost villages of South Vietnam, would be our battalion's temporary forward command post.

The native people inhabiting this remote mountain area are the Montagnard tribesmen. A unique aboriginal group, referred to as savages by other Vietnamese, the Montagnards lived simple semi-nomadic lives, hunting animals with handmade weapons such as crossbows. As the war escalated and more American Special Forces advisors supported them, the capable Montagnards became proficient with all types of small arms weapons and explosives. Perhaps this allowed the natives to live so close to the NVA without being wiped out by them. However, the Montagnards avoided taking sides in the war and chose not to be involved with the Vietnamization program.

We flew to the Mai Loc base camp crammed aboard a de-Havilland C-7A Caribou aircraft because the tiny airstrip could not handle the larger C-130 transports. While waiting at Mai Loc for choppers to bring us to our new AO, we were able to casually observe the Montagnards. The women wore colorful sarongs with tight blouses and carefully wrapped shawls on their heads. They also adorned themselves with a clutter of silver and brass arm bracelets. The men had a few bracelets, but for clothing wore nothing more than a loincloth. To the American base camp soldiers, the Montagnards seemed to be honest, loyal, and friendly, making them easy to like. However, we would never get the chance to find out if that was true because before we knew it, dozens of choppers swarmed in to take us on the next leg of our journey.

The helicopter ride afforded us a distant view of North Vietnam, which was just ten miles away. The enemy country appeared to be a restored green jungle while the area of South Vietnam below us remained filthy, scarred, and brown with only scattered patches of green. The most noticeable feature of the region was a 700-foot tall pyramid-shaped rock mass known as The Rockpile. This seemingly out of place centerpiece dominated the otherwise flat and open area of the Cam Lo River basin. The area was once considered a critical piece of military real estate because it contained a maze of natural caves ideal for hiding enemy soldiers and supplies. However, our AO was beyond The Rockpile in the mountain area between Mai Loc and the abandoned US Marine base camp at Khe Sanh.

We landed in an area pulverized the previous year by B-52 bombings. The remnants of this once lush jungle had become a patchwork of scarred trees, bomb craters, and new-growth ground cover. The new plant life benefitted from the monsoon season, now at full strength with constant rain showers and infrequent sunshine. We hated the idea of being wet for long periods but willingly traded our comfort for the positive side of the monsoon: the lack of insects.

Our job at the DMZ was no different than anyplace else we had been: seek out and destroy the enemy through daily patrols and nighttime ambushes. One afternoon, while slashing through elephant grass, our point man found the skeleton of an NVA soldier. The flesh had been picked clean by animals and insects leaving behind bones, a helmet, belt, and boots. We guessed the soldier had been dead for about six months, but still radioed in the location so the remains could be used for the body count.

This was the first time many of us had seen a human skeleton, so we propped the bones against a stump and took turns posing for pictures. When we left the area, one of the men put the skull on a stick and carried it with him. At first we considered the skull a good luck charm to keep the NVA away, but waking up to it every morning eventually gave us the creeps. Besides, we knew we would not want our head separated from our body no matter how long we'd been dead. We decided to leave the skull behind. Someone placed it high on a large boulder so it would have a commanding view of a lush valley.

In the five days since we had arrived at the DMZ we did not spot a single enemy soldier. But we were not without problems. Our food supply dwindled because the poor weather prohibited re-supply. To avoid surviving on toothpaste and roots like we had in the A Shau Valley, a strict rationing program was put into place. To compound matters, several of us were plagued with diarrhea. My condition not only included the GI shits, but also a mysterious case of sore testicles. Eventually, the pain became intolerable and I decided to tell Doc Meehan about it.

"When was the last time you got laid?" he asked, quite seriously.

"More than a month ago," I answered honestly, wondering what kind of medical problem he thought I had. "What's that got to do with it?"

"That means it's not gonorrhea. It sounds more like you have testicular tension."

That didn't sound good. "What?" I gasped.

"The only cure is sex, but out here you'll have to settle for masturbation. Do it tonight. Nothing fancy, just get the job done. You'll feel better in the morning and your balls will get back to normal."

Was he pulling my leg? "I don't know Doc," I winced, "that sounds pretty bizarre."

I was waiting for him to break into laughter, but he didn't. "Don't worry, I've heard about this before," he answered in all seriousness. "You're the only one who can get yourself back on track."

The discomfort was so bad I was willing to try his prescription for relief, but I had to be careful. Grunts had an unspoken code of conduct about masturbation. Everyone was aware of it and often joked as if masturbating was a common practice. Getting caught, however, was more than just embarrassing and many GIs were shunned because of it.

When the time seemed right that night, I mentally prepared myself for the task. "Doctor's orders" I thought, almost laughing. If masturbating would relieve my problem, I may as well enjoy it. I did the deed as fast as I could, but pleasure was nowhere to be found. Instead, at the moment of ejaculation a sharp pain stabbed deep in my abdomen. In the morning I didn't mention anything to Doc because I figured the discomfort was normal for such therapy. However, while sitting down for morning chow my scrotum felt oddly uncomfortable. Without looking, I instinctively scratched at it and continued eating. A few seconds later, I scratched again but when I brought my hand up, the fingers were red. I jumped up to find my crotch was wet with blood, so I immediately I dropped my pants. Horrified onlookers started to back away at the sight of blood pumping from my pecker with each heartbeat. I fell to my knees, as if to beg for help, but no words came out. My voice was weak and garbled as I began slipping into shock.

Doc Meehan called for a medevac and went to work to stop the bleeding. With no wound to patch, he started to wrap gauze around my penis. I vaguely remember him asking for someone to "hold it" while he wrapped, but instead of help he got remarks like "not me" and "I'm not gonna touch that thing."

Doc finished rolling the bandage to a lemon-sized wad. When the flow finally stopped, the wad had soaked up so much blood it felt like a lead weight was attached to me. Doc attached a medical tag to my shirt that boldly read: PROFUSE BLEEDING FROM THE PENIS.

Not knowing what kind of bizarre affliction I had, the tag could have just as well read: "One hour left to live."

When the medevac came in I was in such a daze that two men had to guide me to the LZ. Some of the guys patted me on the back to say what they thought would be a final good-bye, figuring that in my condition I might not be seen or heard from again. I certainly liked getting out of the field—but not this way.

I stumbled onto the medevac and it quickly lifted off. I sat paralyzed, feeling as if my life was draining away through my penis. One of the door-gunner's, curious about my lack of visible wounds, leaned over to read the medical tag to see what was wrong. He studied the tag as if it made no sense, but when he noticed the blood stains on my pants, he knew the condition was real. Rather than being sympathetic he radioed the pilots, figuring they would get a kick out of my ailment. They did, and everyone had a good laugh. I became angry. "I have an advanced case of genital leprosy," I said in all seriousness, leaving the impression it was terribly contagious. Whether they believed me or not I don't know, but they kept their distance and stopped snickering.

Ten minutes later we landed at the Mai Loc aid station, where a team of doctors was waiting to treat me. As I undressed they began to smirk and joke about the condition.

"Boy, that's some case of the clap you've got there," said the first one. They all laughed. "What were you trying to do?" asked the second doctor. "Mummify your pecker?" More laughter.

"Maybe he's the first man to have a menstrual cycle," added the third.

Looking back, they were probably just relieved at the break from treating a steady flow of combat wounds, but at the time I did not see any humor in their remarks. Worried about what kind of treatment these three clowns would give me, I nervously laid down on an examination table.

One of them carefully unwrapped the gauze. The bleeding had stopped.

"I think a leech crawled inside the penis and attached itself to the urethra," proclaimed the first doctor, as the others nodded in agreement. "We'll have to use a probe to pull it out."

"There's no leech in there!" I shouted. "You're not sticking anything in me!"

"Now take it easy," said the second doctor, as an orderly appeared with the instrument. "The probe might be uncomfortable, but it won't hurt."

"Bullshit!" I protested. "You guys are just guessing about the leech. I got this problem from masturbating."

They laughed at my announcement, giving me just enough time to leap from the table and run off. Two orderlies chased me as far as I dared run without my pants. I was captured behind the mess tent and returned to the doctors.

After explaining the masturbation circumstances, the doctors had second thoughts about their leech diagnosis. Figuring I had other problems, they decided to send me to the nearest hospital. To prevent further bleeding, they re-wrapped the penis but got carried away with cotton balls and over ten feet of gauze.

"We are the penis protectors," one of them mused. At least they stopped short of using a splint.

I was medevaced to the 18th Surgical Mobile Hospital at Quang Tri where a sign greeted me that read: 90% OF THE PATIENTS THAT ENTER THIS UNIT HAVE SUFFERED INJURIES CAUSED BY WEAPONS. PLEASE LEAVE YOUR'S OUTSIDE.

A supply sergeant locked my M-16, rucksack, and equipment in a conex for safekeeping. From there, I was directed to the outpatient clinic where a dozen REMFs were on sick call for everything from hangnails to paper cuts. I thought I was in worse shape than any of them, so I asked the desk clerk to get me moved to the front of the line.

"I've got a problem," I said, holding up the medical tag for his inspection.

"Everyone has a problem," he replied without looking. "Get in line and wait your turn."

"But I'm really sick, look at this tag."

"Yeah," he said, reading it but not showing any emotion. "Is it bleeding now?"

"I don't know, it's all bandaged up."

"Get in line; you'll be taken care of."

I was too discouraged to argue so I sat on the bench with the rest of the sick call. After a few minutes, the guy next to me leaned forward to read the tag. Then he looked at my blood stained pants and cautiously edged away. I felt like I was lost in a continuing saga where everyone laughed, ignored me, or kept their distance. It was just a good thing I had mobility or I would really be in trouble.

About fifteen minutes passed when an emergency brought doctors and nurses rushing out to the hospital entrance. A mud covered Grunt, laying face down on a gurney, was wheeled in. The staff prepared him for surgery right in front of us. As the GI's clothing was removed, he let out several tortured moans. With the staff crowded around him I couldn't see what the injury was, but the harsh odor of human waste left little doubt it was an open abdominal wound. After the GI was prepped and wheeled toward the operating room, I saw it. A two-foot long bamboo splinter protruded from his rectum like a spear. The hapless GI had slipped and fallen in the mud, jamming the stick up his ass. The splinter sliced open his intestines causing a loss of bodily functions. And I thought I had problems.

The REMF on the bench who had earlier moved away from me felt no sympathy for the injured Grunt as he joked with another soldier.

"Man, what kind of hospital is this?" he whispered, motioning toward me. "We've got a bleeding pecker over here and a GI on a stick over there. I just hope my infected tattoo will get looked at."

As they laughed at our misfortunes, I lost my cool.

"Mother-fucking REMFs!" I shouted at them. "You guys have no idea what it's like out in the bush! What's the biggest problem you have to face here in the rear—seeing the same movie two nights in a row?" Embarrassed, they got the message and kept quiet.

The patient line kept moving until I finally got to see a doctor. He didn't bother with an examination and he didn't want to hear my story. Instead, he handed me a specimen cup for a urine sample. I wanted to fill the cup in his office, but he had other patients and sent me outside.

I was not ready to unwrap ten feet of gauze at a piss-tube with the whole world watching so I went into the closest latrine. It was a four-seater occupied with two soldiers. Since I wanted privacy I paced the floor while shooting glares at them to leave. They quickly finished and left, but not before mumbling something about a "latrine queen." After they were gone I began unwrapping, worried at the thought of pissing blood into a cup. As the gauze piled up on the floor, a hospital orderly walked in. Startled, I quickly gathered the strips together and turned away.

"Is something wrong?" he curiously asked.

"Y . . . Yes," I answered, spinning around. "Would you mind giving me a hand?"

The orderly flinched and took a step backward. "What do you want me to do?" he asked, unsure of whether to stay or run.

"I have to give a urine sample but I'm too nervous to get these bandages off. Would you help me?"

"All right," he said, slowly kneeling to the floor and looking outside. "Just warn me if anyone comes this way. I don't want anyone thinking we're in love."

As he finished I felt uneasy recalling that, up to now, at least three different men had handled my penis. I shuddered at the thought of any of them enjoying it.

"Thanks for the help," I sighed. "Now would you leave me alone?"

"Are you kidding? I just removed a pound of gauze from a penis that's about to give a urine sample. I have got to see this."

I agreed to let him stay, figuring it might be good to have him standing by in case something went wrong. I held the cup in one hand and my penis in the other then took a deep breath and let out a squirt. There was no pain and it was pure urine. I felt so relieved I continued filling the cup as several tiny blood clots mixed in. Since the hemorrhaging had apparently ceased, I didn't bother to re-wrap.

"I guess you're all set," the orderly said with a nod.

"Not really, now I have to take a crap."

"You mean they want a stool sample too?"

"No . . . I've got diarrhea!"

"In that case, I'm leaving."

I brought the urine sample back to the doctor, but he wouldn't let me stay while it was analyzed. He did allow me to remove that stupid medical tag. While waiting, I searched for a clean pair of pants but none were available. The only jungle fatigues on the premises were shredded, having been cut from wounded GIs. After a few minutes I was called back to the doctor's office.

"Well Doc," I asked, prepared for the worst, "what have I got?"

"Blood in your urine," he shrugged. "I don't know what caused it, so I'm sending you to the 95th Evacuation Hospital in Da Nang for more tests. A C-130 is flying down there shortly. I'll have a clerk arrange a seat for you."

The uncertainty of my condition had me worried, but at least he wasn't jumping to conclusions like the doctors at the Mai Loc aid station.

There was no airport terminal at the hospital, so I just walked out the back door and across the runway to the waiting airplane. I stepped through the doorway into one of the most depressing places I had ever seen. The C-130 was a fully staffed airborne ambulance loaded with GIs on stretchers and in wheelchairs. Some were amputees, others had limbs in a cast or were wrapped with heavy bandages. Many were hooked to an intravenous solution. I tried to sit out of the way, ashamed to occupy the same space as men wounded in combat. I just hoped my masturbating wound would never be revealed to them.

We landed at the giant Da Nang airbase and were taken by bus ambulance to the 350-bed 95th Evacuation Hospital. I was assigned a doctor and told him the entire story about the diarrhea, the testicular tension, Doc Meehan's masturbation prescription, and the leech theory.

"Only an idiot would give masturbation advice, and only a moron would follow it," grumbled the doctor while glaring at me like I was a fool. "Masturbation and leeches will not cause a hemorrhaging penis. It sounds more like a possible bladder tumor. We'll give you a flagging test to determine where the hemorrhage originated."

The flagging test began with me lying on a cold marble table while a radioactive dye was injected into the femoral artery. As the dye pumps into the bloodstream, the flow is scanned by X-ray and displayed on a screen. Any abnormality in the path is most likely the area where the bleeding occurred. However, my test revealed nothing to suggest an abnormal blood flow.

The next test was a manual probe of the lower intestinal track through my rectum. I had told the doctor about my diarrhea so he put on an arm's length rubber glove while attempting a joke about not being able to use his shit-shield because it was at the cleaners. I didn't laugh. When the doctor was ready I closed my eyes, spread open my buttocks and bent over. The entry felt as if he shoved his whole fist up my ass. As I adjusted to the uncomfortable poking and prying, he touched something tender. I howled from the pain and lunged forward out of his reach.

"Sorry about that," he sympathized. "But I found your problem."

"What is it?" I grunted, trying to pucker my ass back down to normal size.

"You have prostatitis. It's an infection of the prostrate gland, something that is common in elderly men. Apparently your diarrhea and continued urination was dehydrating your system, complicating the condition. The pain you experienced from masturbating was coincidental to an internal rupture."

This could be good news! "Am I going home?" I asked hopefully.

"No, not for what you have," he laughed. "But you'll be out of the field for a couple of weeks to heal the prostate and get your system back to normal. There's no medication but you cannot perform any strenuous activity. You also need to drink lots of fluids like milk, juice and water. Absolutely no tea, coffee, soda, or beer." No beer. What a bummer.

The next day I returned to Camp Evans. News from the DMZ came in that our company had seized a huge enemy food cache without firing a shot. The cache consisted of more than a ton of dried fish, nearly two tons of rice, and several hundred cans of meats and vegetables. It seemed strange that the NVA would leave such a giant food supply unattended. G-2 suspected a mass enemy troop build-up was being planned, but the NVA must have forgotten where they left the food or else their guards were scared off. If I were out there, I would be worried that if the troop build-up took place, the NVA would be pissed off about their food stash missing and go after whoever took it. But I stopped myself from being overly concerned about the problems in the field. After all, I had two weeks of ghosting to worry about.

I spent most of my convalescence with Howard Siner, who was now assigned to our battalion headquarters at Camp Evans. Each evening we got together to have a few beers and live the life of a REMF. Of course, after serving nearly six months in the field, Siner was no REMF, but I noticed that he was not his normal confident self.

"I've been hanging around with you for two days," I began, "and all the while you've been acting weird, like you're depressed. What's with you?"

"Sarge," he answered slowly, "you're not going to believe this, but ever since you came back, I realized that I miss my friends. I want to go back to the field."

"Are you c-crazy?!" I stuttered in disbelief. "Or are you just stupid?! Hell, I would do anything to stay in the rear."

"Yes, I believe you would," he said glancing toward the mountains, "but only for short periods of time. After a few weeks, you would need to get back to the boonies to be with the guys who really count, the Grunts." At first I thought Siner was losing his mind, but as he continued I began to understand. "Most of the REMFs I work with are as despicable as we've always imagined. They regard their Vietnam duty as a bothersome nine-to-five routine. They'll spend every night getting drunk, playing cards, and then complain how miserable life is. They have no idea how lucky they are to be back here where it's safe. Whenever I tell them about the real miseries in the jungle, they don't want to hear about it. Grunts are bonded by the danger and suffering we share. REMFs are only bonded by the beer they share."

Perhaps Siner was just stuck with a bad group. Whatever the case, his comments were depressing. As the days went by, Siner continued talking about giving up his job and returning to the boonies. I still thought the idea was nutty, but I would love to have him back with us again.

To occupy myself while Siner working, I decided to register a Chicom SKS rifle from the weapons cache I discovered in the A Shau Valley. For four months the rifles had been locked in a conex, but when Specialist Simmons, the company clerk, opened the door I was stunned to find only eight of the original 67 weapons remained.

"Where the fuck are all the rifles?!" I hollered.

Simmons was almost too ashamed to tell me. "The chopper pilots who flew the cache back to Camp Evans kept half for themselves and the battalion commander gave anyone going home, whether infantry or not, permission to take one as a war souvenir."

"Those rifles were supposed to be saved for the men out in the boonies!" I howled. "How could you let this happen? You're supposed to be the one person back here that would protect our interests!"

"I really tried," Simmons moaned, "but I can't stop the brass by myself."

Siner was right; REMFs don't give a damn about us Grunts. I was not only pissed-off but hurt as well.

"I guess if I'm going to have a war trophy I'd better grab one before the bartender at the EM Club gets it," I told him sarcastically while selecting an SKS. "Now go hide the rest of these rifles and only give them to Grunts from my platoon. We were the ones who found them." Simmons agreed, hanging his head in embarrassment.

That afternoon I hitched a ride to Camp Eagle, where war trophies are registered with the Provost Marshal, the head of the region's military police. Before I entered the Provos' office, a REMF truck driver approached, asking about the SKS.

"Hey there, Sergeant, I'll give you a $100 for that rifle."

"No thanks," I sneered, still angry over our rifles that were given away. "I found it; I'm going to keep it."

"C'mon Sergeant, you're in the infantry, you can always get another one. I'm going home in a few days and I'd sure like to bring something back with me. I'll give you $200."

"It's not for sale—especially to someone who never stepped in the field," I insisted. "An enemy rifle is a Grunt's trophy. A REMF's trophy is a beer mug." The trucker was stunned by my remarks and said nothing more.

After the registration was completed I was somewhat relieved. Now the only way a REMF could take my rifle home would be to tamper with the serial number, which wasn't likely.

The next day Siner and I were pleasantly surprised to see Dennis Silig come in from the field. He had been recommended for promotion to Sergeant and was scheduled to appear before a promotion review board. As one of the most trusted members of our platoon, Silig deserved the advancement.

GIs typically arrived in Vietnam as PFCs and, after several months, attained the rank of Specialist, which Siner and Silig had easily achieved.

However, to advance to the leadership position of Sergeant, potential candidates needed to pass an oral exam. Siner and I immediately went to work helping Silig study. Siner made the task easy by obtaining a set of the exam questions from battalion headquarters. He told a naive clerk that he needed a copy to complete a story he was writing about combat zone promotions. The test questions covered basic infantry tactics, map reading, calling in fire support, disciplining subordinates, and more. They were exactly the topics I had learned in NCO school, so providing Silig with the answers was simple. Besides, Silig was already performing several squad leader tasks under the watchful eye of Platoon Sergeant Wakefield, who had been grooming him for the promotion.

Silig appeared before the board and aced the exam. He probably would have passed without our assistance, but our encouragement gave him the extra confidence to breeze through it. Of course the cheating helped, too. We didn't celebrate Silig's promotion because the only good aspect about his new position was the pay raise. The bad thing was that now he would be responsible for leading men into combat instead of following them.

The next morning, Silig was ordered back to the DMZ, so Siner and I went to the chopper pad to see him off. While waiting, we joked about his new position.

"Now that you and Wiknik both outrank me," Siner began, "do you think you'll allow me to be seen in public with you?"

"No way," Silig snickered. "Us NCO's have to stick together. Although, I'm a real NCO. I got my rank the hard way, not like Wiknik who is one of them Instant NCOs."

"Oh yeah?" I chimed in. "You think you made rank the hard way? For your information, NCO school at Fort Benning was pure hell from start to finish. It was harder to stay awake during those classes than it is when on guard duty here."

The friendly banter continued until Silig climbed aboard the Chinook. After the chopper roared out of sight, Siner's glance reflected a lonely feeling. The three of us had become buddies, and even though we were forced to endure the emptiness caused by Silig's departure, we tried to act as if it meant nothing.

The next day I went back to the 18th Surgical Hospital at Quang Tri to retrieve my rifle and other gear that was stored during my initial visit. Quang Tri is twenty miles north of Camp Evans, and the only travel link was Quoc-Lo 1. With no scheduled transportation going north, I would have to hitchhike. For protection I borrowed an M-16 and two bandoleers of ammo. It turned out to be just extra weight because I quickly secured a ride with two GIs in a jeep who were going directly to the hospital.

The thirty-minute trip was across a forbidding wasteland where the Army strip-bulldozed the vegetation to eliminate potential VC hiding places. There were no farms, villages, trees, or hills. The only features were the spotty scrub brush and the shallow Khe River. It looked nearly as desolate as the surface of Mars.

At the hospital I collected my gear, but with no transportation going south I walked to the Quang Tri city limits gate to hitch a ride back to Camp Evans. The traffic was unusually light, but eventually a US Marine driving a water tank truck gave me a lift. Unfortunately, he was only going to the Khe River to fill the tank with water before returning to Quang Tri. After a ten-minute ride, the truck stopped on a low bridge above the river. Before I got out of the cab, the driver asked me to stay for a while.

"A guard usually comes with me but he didn't show up today. Do you think you could cover me while I'm getting the water? Rumors are snipers are shooting at trucks."

"Sure," I nodded, still hoping he would still give me a ride to Camp Evans. "Since no one is with you, how about bringing me the rest of the way? Nobody will know."

"Sorry, but I've got to get this water back so the officers can take their showers. They'll have my ass if I'm late."

"Typical REMFs," I mumbled to myself.

The driver dropped a large hose over the railing that noisily splashed into the tranquil river and began drawing up the water through a suction pump. Since there was no screen on the end of the hose, I wondered if any fish ever got pulled in. During the twenty-minute fill up, dozens of potential rides passed by. The loading was uneventful, so after the truck drove away, I continued toward Camp Evans on foot. As American vehicles ignored me, I couldn't imagine why I was unable to get a ride. I supposed that with my two rifles and extra bandoleers of ammo I looked menacing enough that the few US vehicles dared stop, though most slowed for a look. Yelling out "Fuckin' REMFs!" as they drove past probably didn't help, either.

It was getting late and as dusk emerged, the already sparse traffic ceased altogether. The eerie stillness reminded me of the suspense movie "North by Northwest," in which the lead character is dropped off in the middle of nowhere to meet a man who doesn't exist. I was alone on that road, or hoped I was, and trying not to panic.

It was bad enough to be ten miles from the nearest friendly lines but worse still, no one knew I was out there. No one, that is, except perhaps the VC. I was a fully exposed and very inviting target. I could not safely continue walking because after dark I could meet either the enemy just as easily as a US patrol. Worse yet, the Army monitored several battery-powered acoustic and seismic sensors to warn of enemy troop movements in the area. Triggering a device could result in artillery or mortar rounds coming my way.

It was just light enough to see a mile in either direction when I took a long, last look, pleading with the horizon to materialize a truck. Nothing. I began searching for a natural depression, low shrubs, rocks, anywhere to hide for the night. Suddenly, a distant flash caught my eye. It was the headlights of a jeep speeding toward me.

I ran to the middle of the road waving my arms. The vehicle stopped three hundred feet away. Over the glare of the lights I could barely distinguish the outline of the jeep's two occupants. They had to be GIs because the average VC did not have anything to drive, but at that distance I was not recognizable as a fellow American. As far as they knew, I could be an AWOL GI, a VC, or a crazed ARVN. When I approached the vehicle, they backed up. When I stopped, they stopped too. Then I ran at them and they backed up faster and farther. I yelled, but they couldn't hear me over the engine noise. Then I remembered a hand flare in my rucksack. When I shot it skyward, the jeep inched forward until I was recognized as a GI. Finally, they pulled up to give me a ride. That was close. If those soldiers had not come along I would have been left to spend an interesting night in the middle of nowhere alone (assuming I survived to talk about it).

A few days later, the aid station doctor declared my prostate fully healed and released me for field duty. I had gotten so used to the safety of the rear that I had to mentally prepare myself before going back to the boonies. Even so, it felt good knowing that I ghosted away 21 days, probably a record for someone with a bleeding penis.

Early the next morning, I went to the chopper pad to catch a Chinook flight to the DMZ. Waiting there ahead of me was a new guy, PFC Bernson. I gave him a token nod as I sat on a stack of C-rations. I sensed him staring at me but when I glanced in his direction, he spun around to fumble with his equipment.

"Fuckin' Cherry," I whispered, shaking my head.

Bernson looked out of place. He was slightly overweight, had frizzy hair, wore glasses, and his new fatigues still smelled of mothballs. He seemed more like a library clerk than a Grunt. Yet, Bernson's goofy image reminded me of my first time going to the field: scared shitless and wondering how anyone could survive a year in the jungle. I felt the weight of his stare again.

"Nervous?" I asked, casually tightening my bootlaces.

"Boy am I," he answered, relieved I had acknowledged him without denigrating his existence. "Have you been here long? Are you a veteran . . . I mean an old-timer?"

"I've been here seven months," I said examining the horizon. I finally looked him in the eye. "So I guess that makes me an old-timer."

"What's it like out there . . . in the jungle? I mean . . . what does it take to survive? I've heard so many different stories that I don't know what to believe."

I didn't know what to say. No one had ever asked me that. I just assumed that Cherries picked up on things and, if they watched and learned carefully, became old-timers like me. But Bernson had a sadness that made me feel obligated to tell him what I had learned about the war.

"The way I see it," I slowly began, "Grunts face three wars in Vietnam. The first is against Mother Nature. In the dry season, it's so hot during the day that we hardly move for fear of heat exhaustion, and at night we use our energy staring into the darkness while fending off hordes of mosquitoes. During the monsoon, it's cold because we're wet all the time, and we end up sloshing through muddy ditches, rice paddies, or a rain forest. Bad weather also delays our re-supply causing us to miss out on mail and food."

"What about the enemy?" he asked, thirsty for information. "How bad is that part? Is there a lot of fighting?"

I laughed to myself remembering how seldom we had actually engaged the enemy. I scooped a handful of pebbles and sifted them through my fingers before speaking again.

"That's the second war," I said, pitching a stone. "In my seven months, we've only encountered Gooks eight or nine times. That may not sound like much, but just being in the field is a battle in itself, mainly because we are constantly at risk. It's tough knowing that someone is out there aiming to kill you. Although we usually come out on top, like when we kicked the shit out of the NVA on Hamburger Hill, but we still lost more than fifty guys in that battle. But that was six months ago and the Gooks haven't been fighting face-to-face like that lately. Instead, they observe our habits and strike when it's to their advantage, either by ambush or with booby traps."

"Geez," Bernson moaned, rolling his eyes, "how do you keep from getting killed or wounded? There's got to be a secret to surviving all this."

"You could be a Ghoster like me," I said grinning. "But seriously, the key to staying alive is common sense and alertness. It's that simple. You have to think about the consequences of your every move. Bad things can happen fast if you do something stupid or don't pay attention to details. That means you have to watch where you walk, sit, sleep, and even where you shit. There is no relaxing; a Grunt's workday is twenty-four hours of hunting and being hunted. When we drop our guard—that's when the Gooks are the most likely to pounce."

"You said there were three wars," Bernson said quizzically. "What could be worse than the weather and the enemy?"

"The third war is the worst war," I growled fiendishly. "It's the one between the Lifers and the Grunts. A Grunt's goal is to make it home alive. A Lifer's goal is to win the war regardless of who gets zapped. Lifers love the war for the power it gives them over people's lives. I've met only a few good ones; the rest are arrogant pricks who rarely feel what the Grunt feels. Sure, Lifers are out in the bush too, but they usually don't go on recon or LP, they never walk point or carry the machine gun, and the only guard duty they pull is radio watch from the safety of the perimeter CP."

I probably told Bernson too much too fast. He looked more depressed than before. I only wanted to educate him, not blow his mind.

"Everything you've told me sounds so bad," he lamented. "Isn't there anything good about being here?"

I brushed my hands against the seat of my pants before answering his question. "There is only one good thing about being in Vietnam. It's the day you get on a Freedom Bird to go home. But it's a long year, and the only way to get back to the World is to just finish your time. Most Grunts make it home without a scratch. The guys who get screwed-up usually did something stupid, like listening to a Lifer. But don't worry, you'll be all right. We have a lot of good men out there and everyone looks after one another. Hell, before long, you'll be teaching new guys how to survive."

A Chinook landed at the chopper pad and we climbed aboard. The hour-long ride to the DMZ was ominous but it always felt that way when returning to the field. We landed at the Mai Loc base camp and separated to two different supply choppers going to the company LZ. The slick I was in landed first. After the supplies were unloaded, Silig and two other GIs gently slid in a body bag with a dead GI. I looked at the bag and felt an emotional tug.

"Who's in the bag?" I asked Silig, knowing that it really didn't matter.

"Nobody you know," he answered in a resigned tone. "He was a Cherry who went outside the night perimeter to take a crap but didn't bother telling anyone. He got lost in the dark and was thrashing around in front of one of the other positions. Our guys assumed he was an NVA, so they shot him."

"How are the shooter's handling it?"

"Not good. The whole company is shook up over this. Friendly fire is a tough way to die."

After the second chopper landed, GIs milled around the LZ helping to move the supplies. Then disaster struck. As the chopper lifted off, a malfunction caused it to tilt sideways, ramming into a tree. A rotor blade broke loose and reeled toward the crowd like a huge sword, killing six GIs instantly. Doc Meehan was one of them. He was cut in half. Alongside Meehan lay several other GIs who met the same gruesome fate. One was PFC Bernson. An eerie chill ran through me. The deaths were horrifying in themselves, but it was unimaginable that my survival advice to Bernson should also have included freak accidents.

It was bad enough for a GI to die at the hands of the enemy, but when we killed our own, especially on consecutive days, it was difficult to accept. As the bad news circulated some men moaned and hollered over the senseless deaths. A small group threw down their weapons yelling "We quit! Fuck this war!" Others joined in, but the mutiny quickly turned

from bitterness to mourning as several GIs openly wept. The platoon leaders moved to break it up, but Captain Hartwell, disregarding normal military protocol, gave us time to grieve for the deceased. This was the first outlet for our emotions, and we unleashed months of suppressed anguish.

Our "rebellion" lasted less than an hour. We made a stand, then gradually rejoined our units. One of the men summed it up with a resigned grumble, "Fuck it. Don't mean nothin.'" We knew we weren't going to change anything by allowing ourselves the luxury of compassion. In the violent world of combat we had learned more about death than life, so the only thing to do was continue numbing ourselves and soldiering on.

When I returned to my platoon, I found that we had a new leader, 2nd Lieutenant Alexander Cramer. But before meeting him, Silig took me aside to warn me about Cramer's erratic behavior.

"You are not going to believe this new Lieutenant," Silig began, noticeably concerned. "He's a nut case who never stops babbling about killing Gooks. The first thing he did was to put the machine gun on LP to "surprise the enemy." He didn't care that the LP is supposed to be manned by rifleman for early warning; he wanted offense."

"Where the hell was Wakefield?" I asked, irritated at Cramer's audacity. "He's supposed to stop shit like this."

"Wakefield is too busy sucking-up to make any waves. Besides, Cramer is the real problem. He also tried to RIF over too big an area in thick vegetation. Two men got disoriented and were lost for nearly an hour. They were pretty shaken up when we finally found them but Cramer shrugged it off as a strategy lesson."

"I just don't understand why cherry officers have such giant egos," I said angrily, shaking my head. "They establish themselves as war authorities before experiencing it and without getting advice from who's been fighting it. No one should ever be put in danger because of some gung-ho Lifer. The time has come to stop that kind of bullshit." Silig nodded in agreement as I went to confront our new platoon leader.

Lieutenant Cramer motioned me to wait while he talked on the radio. At first glance, he appeared to be an ordinary guy about twenty-five years old with average stature. While watching him speak, I noticed his not so ordinary presence. He reminded me of the comic strip character "Pigpen," disheveled and dirty from head to toe. But Cramer wasn't just

dirty like the rest of us; he was filthy from falling in the mud so much. Both bootlaces were untied and his extra-long pants belt hung loose. Ink from a leaky ballpoint pen had found its way from his hands to the side of his face. The slob picture was complete as he constantly scratched his head.

When Cramer finished talking on the radio, he took two steps toward me then tripped on a vine and fell flat on his face. Rather than stand up where he fell, Cramer crawled to a small tree to pull himself upright. He casually dusted himself off as if his appearance and clumsiness were routine. Though I planned to form my own opinion about Lieutenant Cramer, this first impression left me agreeing with Silig's warning of incompetence. I wondered how such a klutz ever made it through Officer's Candidate School.

"I understand you're the senior NCO in the platoon," he said, shaking my hand. "Why then aren't you the platoon sergeant?"

"I like being a squad leader," I answered rigidly. "That way I know who I can trust."

"That's admirable, but the only way you'll ever be considered for advancement is to have additional leadership skills on your military resume."

"Save it for someone else, Lieutenant. The only advancement I want is back in Connecticut."

"Ah, home," he sighed wistfully. "I'm sure you've heard of Reno, Nevada. That's my hometown. I want everyone to call me Reno because that's my radio call name; it makes for a good nickname, too. I'm surprised you guys don't have nicknames for each other. That's just not right. As I get to know each of you better I'll come up with some nicknames that fit your characters."

"Lieutenant," I interrupted, trying to stop his chatter.

"It's Reno," he shot back. "Call me Reno."

"No way, Sir," I replied angrily. "Making up nicknames for the men is like taking away their identity. Some guys already have nicknames given to them by their friends, not assigned by a Cherry Lieutenant."

"If that's your way of reminding me I'm the new guy, you can keep your opinions to yourself," he scolded, then quickly changed the subject. "I don't want our relationship to start off on the wrong foot, so we'll skip the nicknames for now. Instead, I want you to know how I plan to inflict the maximum number of casualties onto the NVA, be it physical or

psychological. The first thing we need to do is make significant enemy contact. Not just a crummy firefight or ambush, but close hand-to-hand combat. You see, I hold a black belt in Karate, which allows me to legally kill a man with my bare hands."

"Lieutenant!" I nearly screamed, shocked by his outrageous remarks. "Do you know what you're saying? Do you realize how crazy this sounds?"

"Wait, just hear me out," he continued excitedly. "Every time we kill a bunch of Gooks, we'll stick one of these calling cards into their mouths." Cramer handed me an ace-of-spades deck of cards reading, "Death Dealers, Company A, Reno's Raiders: NVA and VC Extermination, 24-Hour Service."

This man was fucking nuts. No doubt about it. I was too stunned to respond. No officer in any Army could be as moronic as Lieutenant Cramer. My only hope was that he was just trying to impress me. A black belt in Karate? Death calling cards? These were just the tip of the iceberg regarding his bizarre ideas.

"The Gooks hardly attack platoon-size patrols anymore," he continued, "because they know they'll get their asses kicked. So we're going to break down into six-man recon teams to spread ourselves over a larger area. That will give us more chances to ambush the NVA and pick up some easy kills."

Easy kills? I thought I had seen and heard it all. Cramer had to be the world's biggest asshole. There was no way I could sit back and listen to any more of his lunacy. "Lieutenant Cramer," I began firmly, trying to stay calm, "there are a few things you obviously don't understand. First of all, we cannot and will not change our names to satisfy your nickname hang-up. It's just too confusing. Everyone already knows who the other guy is; you're the one who doesn't. Second is no such thing as an 'easy kill.' The Gooks have guns and bullets just like us, and they are not going to die for their country without a fight. And as far as using karate on the enemy, the first time you try any of that shit, we'll be sending you home in a body bag. This is not a training exercise and we are not making a movie. We're dealing with real life and real death. This is a not a game!" When I finished I just stood there, glaring into his eyes.

Cramer cocked his head back with a confused look.

"I don't like your attitude, Sergeant. Need I remind you that you are speaking to a commissioned officer of the United States Army?"

"It doesn't matter who I'm talking to," I responded in disgust. "You Lifers are all the same. For once, I'd like to see the war-dogs listen to us Grunts. We're the ones who get your precious body count."

Cramer didn't say anything. He didn't have to. The look on his face told me we shared the same disbelief about each other. It was the only thing we had in common.

"Before you do anything," I continued, "get rid of those stupid ace-of-spades cards. If we start planting them on dead bodies, the Gooks will do something worse to GI corpses. In other parts of Vietnam it's escalated to a mutilation contest. We cut off an ear and they cut off a pecker. There's no end to it!" Lieutenant Cramer was getting annoyed but I didn't care. He needed to be educated and it was obvious that no one else had stepped forward to do it. "And another thing," I said doggedly, "those six-man recon teams are nothing but suicide squads. North Vietnam is less than ten miles away and that means lots of Gooks, up close and personal. A small enemy force can easily wipe out those six men. You're asking us to do what a LRRP (Long Range Reconnaissance Patrol) team does, but we are not trained for that kind of duty."

"That's enough Wiknik!" Cramer finally shouted. "I call the shots! I determine the tactics! If you think being an old-timer gives you the right to run this platoon, then you will find my brand of military discipline very harsh. I will not permit malcontents to undermine my command. Do I make myself clear?"

"Like I said before, you guys are all the same. You can get yourself killed if you want, but I'm not going to let anything happen to the men on account of your sorry ideas. I'm going to do whatever it takes for us to survive—even if it means leaving here as a Private." I knew my remarks would forever taint our relationship, possibly putting us in greater jeopardy. But I had to attempt to wake up Cramer to the realities of war for the sake of the men under his command.

The next day, I was not surprised when Cramer ignored my protests by dividing us into six-man ambush and recon teams. Cramer put me in his group. Maybe he wanted to keep an eye on me, but I hoped he wanted me along for my experience.

We didn't speak to each other for nearly two days, which made the men uneasy. Cramer finally broke the silence when we came upon a hole in the ground that appeared to be an opening to an enemy tunnel.

"Sergeant Wiknik," he began, staring at me with a sly grin, "since you're the smallest man here, I think you should explore the hole."

"No thanks," I answered coolly, as if what he asked was meaningless.

"It won't be that bad. We'll tie a rope onto your leg so your body can be dragged out if anything happens while you're down there."

"I'm not going in there," I insisted. "The Army has trained teams for exploring tunnels, and none of us are qualified. We won't know what to look for."

"You are a member of the best trained army in the world," Cramer snapped, furious at my insubordination in front of the men. "You should be able to perform any task presented to you."

I didn't answer Cramer. Instead, we had a staring standoff until a new guy, PFC Daigle, broke it up by volunteering for the job. Cramer reluctantly conceded.

We armed Daigle with a .45 handgun, a flashlight, and a rope tied to his leg. He crawled down the opening and had wiggled perhaps twenty feet when we heard the dull thuds of several pistol shots. Before we could pull the rope, Daigle flew out of the hole like a human cannonball. He stood on the surface, trembling like he'd seen a ghost. It turned out that Daigle was claustrophobic but too ashamed to admit it. He volunteered to go into the tunnel just to end my standoff with Cramer.

The tunnel was a NVA bomb shelter. Once inside Daigle came face-to-face with a large snake that must have fallen in a few days earlier. When the snake came after Daigle, he emptied the .45 into it. Daigle was so terrified he didn't even remember how he had turned around to scoot back out. Since no one else was willing to go into the hole, and we weren't sure if the snake was dead, a grenade was tossed down to finish it off.

The snake episode completely psyched-out Daigle, turning him into an emotional wreck. The only thing he talked about afterward was how to get out of the infantry. For several days he bugged Cramer about getting him reassigned, but Cramer wouldn't even consent to granting a short rest in the rear. We were sure Daigle had lost his mind when he openly fantasized about shooting himself or wandering off to take his chances as a prisoner of the NVA. Eventually, Daigle quit the crazy talk when he worked out a deal with Cramer who, to our surprise, agreed to send him back to Camp Evans. When the next supply chopper came in, Daigle said his good-byes as if he would be gone forever. Little did we know, he was leaving the field for good.

After the helicopter flew away, Cramer giggled loudly. "That Daigle is such a dope," he boasted, as we gathered around. "I told him the only way to get out of the infantry was to sign up for two more years of service. So he's going in to meet with a re-enlistment officer and I'll get the credit if he goes through with it."

We were shocked that anyone could stoop so low. "What did we ever do to deserve someone like you?" I asked, as the others nodded in agreement. "Daigle wasn't thinking straight and you took advantage of him."

"What's the big deal?" Cramer asked, honestly wondering why we did not share his view. "He was no good to us anyway. The guy was a basket case."

The men looked at Cramer as if he was the enemy. That's when I made up my mind that somehow, before my tour is over, I was going to find a way to ruin him. No one as despicable as Cramer deserved a command.

During the next two days we painstakingly followed a ridge trail looking for an ambush site with an escape route. The path wound in all directions and often passed through small clearings, perfect for an enemy trail watcher to keep tabs on our movement. To our surprise, we found several pieces of US military equipment sloppily hidden in the bushes alongside the trail. Not knowing if they were abandoned by fleeing GIs or planted by the NVA, we avoided them for fear of booby traps.

We finally located a spot that gave us a clear view of the trail in both directions and, if needed, we had an escape route down the side of a ridge. Technically, we had a good ambush site. The problem was the weather. Fog and rain moved in, forcing us to be extra alert because the steady dripping of rainwater masked other sounds. After dark, the dripping made things worse. We would not know if the enemy approached unless they tripped over us. Those conditions made for some long nervous hours. Luckily, the NVA never showed.

On the third morning the sun broke through, warming the air and drying us out. We had just finished morning chow when the sound of rustling leaves and snapping branches caught our attention. The noise came from the small valley below us. We quickly positioned ourselves for action and concentrated on the foliage for a glimpse of movement.

"The NVA likes those valleys," Cramer whispered knowingly. "There must be a whole platoon digging in down there."

"Sounds like monkeys to me," I remarked nonchalantly.

"Monkeys?" Cramer blurted, spinning his head around. "Are you crazy? No wild animal makes that kind of noise."

"Last month a band of monkeys foraging toward our position sounded exactly like that."

"Don't give me that bullshit," Cramer shot back, trying hard to prove his competency. "That commotion is from the Gooks. I'm calling for an air strike."

Cramer contacted a Forward Air Controller who refused to authorize air support for noise in the trees. Instead, he had to settle for artillery. Cramer's request for fire support was surprisingly accurate. It took only two shots for the battery to hit the target. As the first rounds exploded, blood curdling screams and weird howls echoed from the impact area. Cramer was ecstatic. He must have thought he was wiping out an NVA division as he yelled into the radio, "Fire for effect! Fire for effect!"

Sure enough, as the barrage continued, a pack of monkeys swarmed through the trees past our position. We just shook our heads. Realizing his mistake, Cramer called for a cease-fire. The artillery commander radioed back to question the abrupt stop, but Cramer was afraid to tell the truth. He said the NVA troops apparently evacuated the area after the first rounds. Captain Hartwell, who was listening on his radio, ordered us to check the impact area for bodies. We didn't bother.

"I told you so," I said gloating. "Once in a while give us some credit for surviving so long." Cramer sat pitifully embarrassed and did not acknowledge my remarks.

In the afternoon we moved to a hilltop with a commanding view of a trail that zigzagged through the valley below. This gave us the chance to employ our own style of trail watching. Each man took turns carefully inspecting the terrain through binoculars. After a few hours, one of the men spotted a lone NVA soldier sitting beneath a distant tree. He was too far away for a rifle shot so Cramer called for a Cobra gunship. Helicopter pilots must love "Gook in the open" radio calls because a chopper showed within minutes.

Cramer verbally guided the gunship to where we had last seen the soldier. When the NVA broke from his cover, the pilot shot him to pieces.

"There's no stopping us now," Cramer boasted proudly. "We're gonna make them Gooks eat lead."

"Eat lead?" Freddie Shaw whispered in disbelief. "Is this guy for real?"

We came to wonder why our platoon was cursed with Lieutenant Cramer. If any of us believed in evil spirits, the day's events were a bad omen: it was Halloween.

In early November, the 38-day US Marine deployment was complete, transferring responsibility for the DMZ region to the South Vietnamese 1st ARVN Division. Accordingly, 101st units began phase-out operations in preparation for their next assignments.

"What the hell is wrong with you, Lieutenant?
Can't you tell the difference between the
enemy and a fucking pig?"

CHAPTER 9

Guns and Chain Saws

Back in the United States, opposition to the war was gaining strength. On November 15, 1969, one month after Vietnam Moratorium Day, America's capital was the scene of the biggest peace rally yet. An estimated 250,000 demonstrators gathered at the foot of the Washington Monument for "The March on Washington, DC." As big as this rally was, four days later the nation's attention was diverted from the war to outer space where the Apollo 12 astronauts successfully completed the second moon landing of the year.

To the average Grunt, neither event was cause for celebration. America's passions and priorities were clearly going in opposite directions. We knew that neither technology nor protest fervor would get us home any sooner. Our best hope for leaving Vietnam alive lay with our ability to ignore the outside world and continue sharpening the tools of our trade.

After leaving the DMZ, my company was supposed to go to Eagle Beach for a well-deserved three-day stand down. An intense tropical rainstorm canceled those plans and sent us instead to Camp Evans, where the only recreational facilities consisted of the outdoor movie theater and the tiny EM Club. The lack of organized recreation did not bother us because we were just as happy staying dry and getting drunk. However, since our superiors did not consider that kind of activity to be either recuperative or productive, we were sent back to the field after only one night under a roof, despite the persistent rain.

The storm set a record for the region, dumping more than fifty inches of rain during a seven-day period. Since we didn't dare attempt crossing the flooded terrain, our daytime defensive position became a permanent ambush site. As successive torrents deluged the AO, we were as miserable as livestock trapped in a muddy pen.

The Brass were concerned that the seven days of rain may have allowed the enemy to advance their infantry and mortars closer to Camp Evans in preparation for an attack. To counter this perceived threat, and to create a buffer between the mountains and Camp Evans, a new artillery firebase was ordered built. Located atop a barren bluff only two miles west of the base camp, Firebase Jack would be my company's new command post.

Two days into the construction, a VC sniper took several potshots at a helicopter ferrying building supplies. This first sign of the enemy quickly changed my platoon's mission from static defense to roving offense. Unfortunately, the low scrub brush and open rolling hills allowed the enemy to easily evade our patrols. To effectively pursue the VC, we moved during the pre-dawn hours to likely avenues of enemy approach, where we waited patiently in daylong ambushes. No one ever showed.

The unseen enemy and the lousy weather overshadowed the frustration of long, dull hours of lying in wait. As the storm wound down, there were rain showers everyday, sometimes heavy, and sometimes light, with only rare glimpses of the sun. Even these breaks in the clouds were never long enough to dry our clothes and equipment. After dark it was worse. We were so cold from being wet that some of the men slept huddled together for body warmth. Each day of rain caused morale and alertness to dip dangerously low, so we increased our patrols just to stay active. One squad went out in the morning; a different squad went at noon; and a third in the late afternoon. Each patrol returned with the same report: no significant signs of enemy activity.

However, we were finding an abundance of wild boar tracks. The scrub brush and rolling terrain outside Firebase Jack was ideal habitant for the boars. This quick-footed beast can weigh more than two hundred pounds and looks ferocious with woolly hair and long sharp tusks. Though the animal was not generally considered a threat to humans, I was not going to test that notion if I came face to face with one. The boars were given the same treatment as an enemy soldier.

A few nights later on guard duty I detected movement in a nearby gully. It was a boar. Initially, I was just going to shoot it, but instead I recognized this as a perfect opportunity to rattle Lieutenant Cramer. I woke the men in my position and told them we were going to kill the boar while trying to make it look like we were under attack.

As the animal continued to approach, it stopped to sniff the human scent on a claymore mine. That's when I squeezed the detonator.

KA-BOOM!

Though the blast almost certainly killed the boar, we fired our M-16s and threw grenades to simulate a real battle. Believing this was an actual firefight, the positions to our left and right started firing as well. After the shooting stopped, Cramer crawled to my position for a report.

"What's down there?" he whispered excitedly. "Gooks? How many?"

"I'm not sure, sir," I answered gravely. "It looked like a Gook trying to sneak up on us."

"Did you get him?"

"I think so," I said confidently. "After blowing the claymore we fired up the area pretty good. I didn't see anything moving after that."

"Way to go," Cramer said as he patted me on the back, elated by the prospect of a kill. "Since we already gave our position away, I'll pop a flare to see if anything is moving."

As the flare shot skyward, the flickering light made the blood splattered hulk indistinguishable as man or beast.

"All right!" Cramer cheered. "A dead Gook! We'll wait until daybreak to check him out in case he was able to booby-trapped himself. In the meantime, I'm calling this action in."

"Good idea," I encouraged him. "The Colonel will love it." This was too good to be true. In the morning our battalion commander will come out to verify the body count and instead see our gung-ho Lieutenant for the asshole he really is.

As soon as it was light enough to safely see, Cramer hustled out a squad to view the kill. When he approached the boar, he glanced at it as though it was an innocent victim of the previous night's firefight and continued searching for the enemy body. Eventually, Cramer returned to the impact area and gazed down at the carcass. His mind raced as his eyes darted from man to man. Finally, Cramer's jaw dropped and his eyes widened when he realized what had happened during the night.

"A pig!" he screamed at me. "You killed a fucking pig!"

"It looked like a Gook to me," I shrugged.

"It looked like a Gook?!" he bellowed, while charging to my position. "I called in a pig as a dead Gook!"

"Maybe it was a Hog Cong," I grinned, as some of the men laughed. "Next time be sure of what we've killed before you call it in."

"You son-of-a-bitch! You knew it was a pig all along, didn't you?!" I just smiled knowingly in reply.

Just then we heard the faint whirling thump-thump of Colonel Dynamo's approaching helicopter. Cramer lurched forward, cranking his head skyward.

"The Colonel's coming in!" yelled the RTO.

"Noooooo!" Cramer shrieked. "Call him back! Tell him it's a mistake! Tell him the VC got away!"

It was too late. A smoke grenade had already been popped, signaling the location for the chopper to land. The entire platoon snickered as Cramer ran frantically through the perimeter trying to figure out what to do. But there would be no escape. The helicopter landed and Colonel Dynamo leaped out with a triumphant smile.

"Good morning gentlemen!" he heartily greeted us. "Where are the vanquished?"

Cramer perspired as he weakly pointed down the gully at the mangled carcass. The Colonel's smile faded as he looked long and hard at the boar. Cramer stood motionless staring at the ground until the Colonel turned to him.

"Last night," the Colonel slowly snarled with his head cocked sideways, "my RTO woke me because you said you had engaged the enemy and had at least one kill. So I came out to confirm the body count and what do I find? I find that you killed a goddamn pig! What the hell is wrong with you, Lieutenant?! Can't you tell the difference between the enemy and a fucking pig?"

"Uh . . . er . . . I," Cramer sputtered, as the Colonel continued belittling him.

"I will not tolerate any officer who hallucinates in the dark. If you don't know how to recognize the enemy, dead or alive, then you need a crash course on the subject. Maybe I should send you to the Ho Chi Minh Trail to direct NVA truck traffic! Do you understand what I'm telling you? You fucked up mister!"

"Y-y-yes Sir," Cramer whimpered.

"From this day on, you will radio in a daily report of this platoon's activities. If one of your men fires his rifle, throws a grenade, or detonates a claymore, I want to know why. I also want to know who walks point and who walks drag, who takes a shit and how deep it gets buried! Now take your sorry platoon and link up with Captain Hartwell. You certainly cannot be trusted out here on your own." The Colonel stormed back to his chopper and sped away.

Cramer was so stunned at this crushing blow to his credibility, delivered with gusto in front of his men, that he was nearly despondent. I however, felt quite smug over the incident. Only now, I would have to watch my step because Cramer would surely seek revenge.

For the next several days Cramer refused to speak with me. I was even excluded from regular platoon meetings; communication between us was relayed through one of the other squad leaders. If giving me the silent treatment was the only punishment Cramer could come up with, it was great. I didn't want to talk with him, either.

On Thanksgiving Day, our entire company gathered for a traditional turkey dinner that was flown out to us by helicopter. Along with the meal came four mess hall servers to set things up, not much of a task since it was a paper plate and plastic fork affair. Surprisingly, the food was hot and quite good, causing several to joke that there must be a new cook at Camp Evans.

The best humor of the day was found watching the servers. Like typical REMFs scared at being in the field, they overloaded themselves with M-16 ammunition and hand grenades; some even had bayonets attached to their rifles. After the meal, the servers formed a mini-perimeter with their backs against one another, as if an enemy attack was imminent. They were where the war was and, true to REMF tradition, wanted no part of it. When the helicopter returned to shuttle the servers back to Camp Evans, Cramer finally broke his silence.

"Sergeant Wiknik," he began, with a contented grin, "you've been selected to participate in a special assignment. Get your gear together and grab a seat on that chopper."

My bullshit detector was spinning off the meter. "What kind of special assignment?" I asked suspiciously.

"I don't want to bore you with the details. When you get in, report to battalion headquarters. They'll tell you all about it." I surmised that Cramer's revenge for the pig shooting incident was to separate me from my friends. I was upset, but tried to look at the bright side: it was a fair exchange for embarrassing him in front of the Colonel.

At Camp Evans, the battalion Operations Officer briefed me on the newly-formed LZ Cutting Team that I would be in charge of. "This mission is the first of its kind for our battalion," he began. "The team will be inserted at strategic locations to cut a series of LZs that will be used for future combat assaults or troop extractions. You'll go in at first light, cut the LZ, and then are extracted before dark."

"What about the team members?" I asked curiously. "Who are they and where did they come from?"

"They are fifteen specially selected men who all have knowledge of demolitions and chain saws, as well as infantry training. I think that with your leadership skills and their background, it will be a great team. You'll meet them in the morning. Now get a good night's rest."

I thought it odd that I didn't meet the men right away, but the task sounded simple enough to not cause any alarm. Besides, any reasonably experienced team should be able to easily cut an LZ in half a day. I was even looking forward to the change of pace and hoped the team shared my enthusiasm.

At dawn, I went to the chopper pad where the group was already assembled and waiting. While introducing myself, I began to feel uneasy as I vaguely recognized some of their faces. Then it hit me. These GIs were not part of any organized team; they were the duds from our battalion! Each had a history of problems ranging from bad attitudes to poor hygiene to just plain stupidity. They were the useless GIs who flunked out of stateside training but still managed to get sent to Vietnam. I surmised that this assignment was the Army's last ditch effort to make something of them before resorting to disciplinary action for being so dysfunctional. I hated to admit it, but Lieutenant Cramer got the last laugh by recommending I be put in charge of such misfits.

Based on the team's makeup, I began to doubt that our function was for really cutting LZs. Perhaps our noisy activity was supposed to drive the enemy into a nearby ambush, or worse yet, we were going to be used as decoys to attract the enemy because the Army considered us expendable. Whatever the reason, I was stuck. I tried not to panic by reminding myself that the team was a tactically sound idea and that this mission could instill a renewed sense of honor and duty into the men. Before the day was over, I would never think such thoughts again.

Our LZ site was a jungle hilltop about five miles northwest of Camp Evans. Triple canopy vegetation nearly two hundred feet tall covered the hill and concealing the ground below. The only way to reach the ground was by rappelling down through the trees. As our helicopters circled the area, I expected the standard artillery barrage to scare off any lurking NVA. There was none. Instead, the lead helicopter flew at treetop level, where it hovered while nylon ropes were tossed out the door into the wind-blown leafy ocean. It was beautiful, but it was also scary as hell.

PFC Mauro was the first to rappel. With a radio strapped on his back, Mauro crouched on a landing skid and prepared for the drop. A second GI stood on the opposite landing skid to balance the helicopter. When the pilot signaled, Mauro disappeared into the vegetation as if he were swallowed. The rope was taut as he descended, but slackened each time he got snagged on a tree limb. Within a short time he was on the ground. From there, Mauro directed the pilot to move the helicopter approximately fifty feet to an area between the trees where the rest of the team could rappel down with minimal obstructions. I was next.

As I mentally prepared myself for the trip down the rope, I envisioned the enemy waiting to ambush us once we were on the ground. Two sharp tugs from Mauro signaling me to come down snapped me into action. The descent was exhilarating, with branches slapping my face and pulling at my equipment. Once through the canopy, the ride to the ground was so simple I landed standing up. It was strange to travel so swiftly from the panorama of the airborne world to a dark world of trees, shadows and no view. I quickly freed myself from the rope and assumed the anchor position while Mauro provided security.

I gave the two-tug signal and had barely positioned myself before the next GI plummeted down at me in a blur. Screaming like he fell off a cliff, the GI traveled so fast that blue smoke poured from his leather gloves. I let go of the rope so he would not land on me. The soldier back-flopped onto the ground and bounced nearly a foot high. After coming to rest, his eyes rolled back until only the whites showed. Since he was not breathing I assumed he was dead.

I could not understand why he had gone so fast because the friction of the rope looped through his gear should have controlled his descent. When I moved to release him I discovered that he never hooked up, the GI simply grabbed the rope and free fell two hundred feet. As he shot earthward, he instinctively squeezed the rope tighter causing the gloves to act like a lubricant and they got so hot they smoked.

The unlucky GI was not dead but had had the wind knocked out of him. When he got his wind back, he began thrashing and yelling, "Arrgghh! My back! Arrgghh! My hands!" When I removed the gloves, they curled into grotesque claws. In addition to burned hands, the GI injured his back and could not walk. Before the rest of the team could come down, the GI was hoisted back up and flown to the aid station for treatment. If the Gooks were watching and saw what happened, they would never bother to attack because we stood a better chance of killing ourselves than them.

After everyone was on the ground, we conducted a cursory patrol of the immediate area. There were no signs of the enemy; not even an old trail. I put six men on guard duty and the rest to work. I reminded everyone that the chain saw and demolition noise would be sure to attract attention, so the sooner we finished the job and got out of there, the better.

The best way to clear the LZ was to cut below the crest of the hill, dropping the trees down the slope as we worked our way to the top. Trees that were less than a foot in diameter were felled by chain saws. Larger trees were knocked down with a charge of C4, a powerful plastic explosive that was surprisingly safe to handle—even with this crew. As the day wore on, one by one, the saws were rendered useless as their inept operators dulled the chains by hitting rocks. One misplaced saw was crushed when a tree landed on it. Without spare chains or files for re-sharpening, we had to put the saws aside and use the C4 to knock down the remaining trees. The C4 did not last long, so I radioed in for spare saw chains, files, and more explosives.

When our re-supply arrived, it contained no files or chains but we did get explosives: five cases of surplus Korean War-vintage stick dynamite, blasting caps, and fuses. That was just what I needed, ultra sensitive explosives being handled by ultra unbalanced people. By the time we got to clearing again, it was evident the LZ would not be finished that day. Rather than call any more attention to our location, I set up an NDP (Night Defensive Position). A small knoll about three hundred feet from the LZ was chosen.

Normal guard duty rotation was arranged but no one followed it. When I woke in the morning everyone was asleep. I yelled at the men, warning them about the hazards of sleeping on guard duty, especially since our position was not exactly a secret. But they all pointed fingers at one another trying to shift the blame. I did not bother pushing the issue. I just wanted to complete the job and go back to Camp Evans.

The LZ was finished by mid-morning so I radioed in for the helicopters to pick us up. However, I was told to sit tight because all available aircraft were committed to a big combat assault operation. So we sat and waited. In the afternoon, a lone helicopter came out to pick up the chain saws, gasoline, and extra explosives and at the same time try the LZ for size. As three team members loaded equipment inside, the pilot called me to his window.

"I'm not taking that dynamite back!" he yelled over the engine noise. "It's too volatile! Use it to blow away some of the stumps, then destroy the rest!"

"Okay!" I agreed, nodding to him. "When do we get picked up?"

"Probably tomorrow morning!" he yelled back. "All hell broke loose today so most birds are tied up!"

That was not what the three men loading the chopper wanted to hear. As the engine revved for take-off, they dashed aboard. I had my back turned to avoid the rotor wash, so before I realized what happened, the helicopter was airborne. None of us on the ground could believe our eyes. Like rats deserting a sinking ship, the three cowards took their first chance for escape. I radioed the pilot to bring the trio back, but got no response. I was down to eleven men. I was furious, not just at the three who had fled, but I was also mad at battalion headquarters for experimenting with such simpletons. To keep busy, we blew apart any stumps that might affect helicopter landings and takeoffs. When we finished, there was still about one hundred sticks of dynamite left.

"I think the best thing to do with this dynamite is to dig a hole and bury it," I said, hoping everyone would agree. "No one will ever find it out here."

"Let's blow it up instead," an excited Mauro insisted.

"Can I do it?" begged a giddy GI the men called Cowboy. "Those hundred sticks will make enough noise to scare away every Gook within ten miles of here."

Why an alarm did not blast off inside my head I don't know, but it didn't. I agreed to blow it up. Our only command detonator had a seventy-five foot long cord. That would not give Cowboy much distance to buffer himself from the explosion. But he found a seemingly safe spot alongside a fallen log. After carefully stacking the dynamite over the crest of the LZ, I handed Cowboy the detonator. He dropped down next to the log grinning like a mischievous boy ready to pull a fire alarm so he could watch the red trucks whiz by. Little did we know that would be his last fun for a long time.

The rest of the team high-tailed it to the far side of the hill. I radioed a general alert of the impending explosion and yelled the standard blasting phrase, "Fire in the hole! Fire in the hole!" On that signal, Cowboy squeezed the detonator.

An awesome blast rocked the hilltop, spewing dirt, stones, and wood splinters so high that some of it landed on us. When the rubble stopped falling, we shot questioning glances at one another wondering how much debris had landed on Cowboy, and whether his proximity to the explosion had been fatal.

We ran to the LZ and discovered a hole in the ground big enough to park a car in. There was so much pulverized debris that it looked like the earth had vomited over itself. The blast so dramatically changed the familiarity of the LZ that we couldn't immediately locate Cowboy. We pushed aside branches and clumps of soil until someone heard a moan underfoot. We accidentally discovered Cowboy by stepping on him. He was alive.

Cowboy survived the blast and the temporary interment but not without side effects. Dirt was packed into every crevice of his head. His eyes opened no wider than tiny slits and dirt-filled drool ran out of his mouth. The concussion gave him a nosebleed and he mumbled incoherently. Worse yet, when we tried to stand Cowboy up, he fell down in wobbly slow motion. Cowboy needed immediate medical attention. I called for a medevac and within an hour he was taken away. I later learned that Cowboy developed an equilibrium disorder that sent him stateside to finish his enlistment.

Early the next morning, the helicopters came out to return us to Camp Evans. We arrived without fanfare. Our stupid injuries, the damaged chain saws, and all the time wasted gave our commanders little to celebrate. Never again would there be any such team comprised of the battalion misfits because we came too close to getting someone killed. A trained team from the Army Corps of Engineers would cut future LZs.

Since the LZ team was disbanded, each member was sent back to his original unit, which meant I would again fall under the control of Lieutenant Cramer. However, Cramer would have to wait because I was going out of the country on a mid-December R & R. And, if my luck held out, I was hoping to earn some extra ghost time upon my return by taking advantage of the expected Christmas cease-fire.

"Tell me, how many women and children did you murder in the My Lai Massacre?"

CHAPTER 10

R & R Hawaii

Vietnam servicemen earned a week's vacation after six months—if they survived that long. These seven days are known as R & R, or Rest and Relaxation. To a Grunt, R & R is the ultimate stand down. We could choose from among eight exotic locations: Bangkok, Hong Kong, Honolulu, Manila, Singapore, Taipei, Tokyo, or Sydney, Australia.

My first choice was Hawaii because I knew the currency and the language. I also wanted to enjoy modern American conveniences like cars, television, abundant electricity and musical lyrics undistorted by pidgin English. Most of all, I wanted to be back in the World where my girlfriend Mary and my sister Janice could visit me. The three of us had been planning this reunion for several months, hoping to create a bond we would cherish forever.

The Hawaiian R & R option was especially designed for reuniting spouses, sweethearts, and family members who had been separated by the war. However, our company clerk, Specialist Simmons, cautioned me about going to Hawaii.

"You're going for all the right reasons," he began, "but I've seen too many Grunts come back from Hawaii with a radical personality change."

"What the hell are you talking about?" I asked, disbelieving.

"It's simple. Hawaii is the World. The shock of being in America again and then being jerked back to Vietnam is too depressing. Returning GIs don't care about their Grunt friends like before; everything they do is controlled by self-preservation. I think you would be better off vacationing in an Asian country where the lifestyle is similar to what you've been used to."

"Are you nuts? The Asia I've seen is a little too primitive for me. Besides, how could I change, me of all people?"

"It's just a natural progression where the stages of your tour take on different meanings. In a war zone, soldiers change all the time because they're experiencing life ten times faster than a civilian does."

It all sounded clinical, especially coming from a clerk. I shrugged it off. Besides, Simmons knew I was not going to change destinations, especially at this late stage, so he handed me a set of R & R orders and sent me to the Camp Evans airstrip.

After a non-stop C-130 transport flight I arrived at the giant Ton Son Nhut Airbase in Saigon. I was immediately struck by the contrast of this modern R & R processing center when compared to the rudimentary setting of the one in Vung Tau. Ton Son Nhut was like a tiny piece of transplanted Middle America. The grounds featured fine trimmed lawns, hedges, and flower gardens. The paved streets were lined with concrete sidewalks and streetlights. Even the buildings were reminiscent of a stateside military post. It was hard to believe I was still in Vietnam. Gone were the familiar tents, sandbags and guard posts, and no one carried a weapon. I reported in and was assigned a locker and a bunk for the night. Like most out-country R & R travelers, I would spend the next twenty-four hours purchasing civilian clothes, toiletries, and shedding some of the anti-social behavior acquired from the war zone.

One of the first civilized acts I wanted to perform was to relieve myself in a flush toilet. After eight months of crapping over the edge of a log or squatting in the bushes with cold rain running down my ass, I deserved a slice of dignity. I flushed twice, marveling at the long forgotten gurgling sound that whisked waste away. Then I amused myself by repeatedly flipping the light switch off and on until a showering GI yelled at me to knock it off.

After securing my few belongings, I changed into civilian clothes so I could quietly blend in with everyone else. Then I tagged along with two GIs headed for the EM Club. When we walked through the club door, the flashing lights, blaring music, and huge dance floor transfixed me. On each side of the bandstand were bikini-clad Vietnamese Go-Go girls dancing suggestively to the driving beat. It was all downhill from there, for the crowd of wild, drunken GIs was yelling obscenities and throwing ice cubes at the dancers. The waitresses had it worse; they were pinched and groped as they worked their way through the tables.

A dozen MPs tried to maintain a level of civility by removing the rowdiest GIs, but it was a losing battle. The lack of self-control spread like a disease. I never understood why people behaved like obnoxious morons simply because they were far away from home. Their conduct made all servicemen look like assholes. Undaunted by the riotous atmosphere, we grabbed a table as far as possible from the ruckus.

I decided the best way to celebrate my upcoming R & R was to toast it with a few drinks. My only previous drinking experience was with beer, but I figured hard liquor was not much different. Like a country bumpkin on his first trip to the city, I decided to try whatever was on the menu. I searched for a drink that tasted good and started downing rum and cokes, followed immediately by a screwdriver. From there it was gin and tonic, then rye and ginger. By the time I worked up to scotch and soda, the noisy club had turned into a blur. I was completely blitzed. Since I had drunk different brands of beer in one sitting, I never gave a thought to the effects of mixing liquors. I supposed that being stupid was the only requirement needed for getting shit-faced. Thinking it was funny, the GIs I came in with never tried to stop me. Nice guys. Where was Freddie Shaw and his lecture on ignorant oil when I needed him?

The two GIs helped me stagger back to the R & R center and lifted me into the top bunk. I fell asleep instantly. About an hour later I woke up to a violently spinning room. I remembered hearing that the best way to stop the spinning was to put one foot squarely on the floor. Forgetting that I was in the top bunk, I rolled sideways and dropped my leg over the edge, expecting it to hit the floor. The momentum pulled me off and I landed in a heap.

"Hey you fucking drunk!" the GI in the bottom bunk yelled. "I'm trying to get some sleep! Get back in the rack and quit squirming around!"

"Yesh . . . oshay," I slurred, climbing back up.

Ten minutes later the room was spinning again, only faster this time. As the reeling intensified, my stomach rumbled. Too weak to move, I laid still fighting the urge to vomit. I lost. Without giving it a thought, I leaned over the side and spew onto the floor. The GI below was still awake and now more pissed off than ever. He yanked me out of the bunk and dropped me into the vomit.

"There you go asshole," he sneered, stepping over me. "Now sleep in it."

The sour odor burned my senses and triggered additional nausea. I did not want to throw-up in the sleeping area again, so I stumbled down the hall toward the latrine. The problem was I stopped every thirty feet to drop a fresh load, leaving behind a disgusting trail that had to be tiptoed around.

Miserable and groggy, I took a shower and washed the stench off my clothes. I returned to the sleeping area to find my mattress on the floor covering the vomit. Knowing that I was not wanted there, I found an empty bunk at the other end of the room. Unfortunately, I had to move every couple of hours as R & R travelers came and went. It seemed I was always in someone else's assigned bed.

In the morning, I had such a hangover I wanted to die. My head was pounding like an artillery barrage and the inside of my mouth felt like it had fur growing in it. How could I have been so stupid? Surviving the ten-hour flight to Hawaii in this condition would be quite a feat. Still, I thought, I would rather be miserable flying high above the Pacific Ocean than feeling good on the ground in Vietnam.

At 9:00 a.m. we boarded a DC-8 that had just arrived from the World. Everyone raved about how beautiful the plane looked, but I could not have cared less. In my condition, the only thing that would look good to me was an open commode. I stumbled aboard and groggily located my seat where two GIs had already claimed the aisle so they could watch the stewardesses walk back and forth.

"How about letting me sit on the aisle?" I asked them. "I don't feel too good."

"Oh no you don't!" one of them snapped. "We're staying right here. Those stewardesses got round eyes and tight skirts."

"Yeah," offered the other, "you can look out the window. We'll let you know if anything happens on this end." Then they giggled and poked each other like little kids.

"Okay," I moaned. "But I'm giving you fair warning. Last night I got drunk and threw up all over the R & R center, now I'm just waiting for my morning puke. How about lending me your airsickness bags? I'll give them back if I don't use them." That did the trick, and the guy sitting on the aisle begrudgingly gave up his seat while demanding I return to the window as soon as I felt better. I agreed.

The plane taxied to the end of the runway where it sat for what seemed like an eternity. When we finally got takeoff clearance, the engines revved up and we sped down the tarmac. The liftoff was smooth but shortly before reaching cruising altitude, the plane hit a downdraft and suffered a series of sinking dips. That was the last thing my stomach needed. The FASTEN SEAT BELTS light was still lit but it didn't matter. I grabbed an air sickness bag and ran to the nearest restroom and vomited for the last time. Feeling better, I offered to take the window seat, and slept there the entire way to the island of Guam, our refueling and rest stop.

At the end of World War II, Guam became a principal US defense position in the western Pacific. Although the World War II remnants were gone, Guam was still the site of extensive Navy, Army, and Air Force installations. We would only be on the ground for an hour but it was enough time for me to take a short walk around the airfield. The island did not have much to offer for sightseeing because the nearby terrain was relatively flat, but I was amazed to see so many B-52 bombers in one place. Their drab camouflage paint really made the DC-8's gleaming silver body stand out.

After we re-boarded the plane, my hangover did not nag me nearly as bad as before, so I asked the girl watchers if I could sit in the aisle seat for a while. They refused. After six hours on the plane, they still snickered and poked each other. I was beginning to think they were weird. As we crossed the International Date Line, I tried to make conversation about going from a Monday to a Sunday, but they acted more annoyed than interested. I could not figure out what their problem was, so for the rest of the trip I kept busy with magazine crossword puzzles.

Four hours out of Guam our plane touched down at Honolulu International Airport. I felt like I had just returned to planet Earth. Gone was the military backdrop I had become so accustomed to. Hawaii was a pure civilian setting with cars, modern facilities, and friendly faces.

An airport shuttle bus brought us to the R & R processing station at nearby Fort DeRussey. Our paperwork took only minutes, after which the staff commanding officer reminded us of their strictest rule: travel beyond the Hawaiian Islands in any direction was strictly prohibited. Any attempt to do so meant immediate R & R cancellation and a court martial. The harsh punishment was instituted after some homesick GIs succeeded in making it back to the States, where they either deserted or were caught for being AWOL. With only four months left to serve in the military, I saw little to gain in taking that chance.

We were also advised of the possibility of confrontations with anti-war activists. Their fervor was at an all-time high over the recent disclosure of how US soldiers had murdered South Vietnamese civilians in the village of My Lai in March of 1968. The accused GIs were from a company in the 23rd Infantry Division (nicknamed Americal Division), which was demoralized by repeated casualties from sniper fire and booby traps. They surrounded the My Lai village expecting to trap the VC; instead found only women, children, and old men. In the hours that followed, the civilians were murdered and their homes were destroyed. The news of the atrocity and the alleged cover-up sent shock waves through the American public and the US military command.

The reporter who initially broke the My Lai Massacre story received the Pulitzer Prize for journalism. In the aftermath of the award, much of the media gorged themselves on the sensationalism of isolated disgraces of the American military. No longer did it matter how well GIs performed or how many continued to die for their country. Instead, we were portrayed as drug-crazed psychopathic killers. This unfair label was much more than a black mark on GIs. It was a disgraceful image that ultimately led many homeward-bound soldiers to deliberately return unnoticed and quietly slip back into society as if they had never been away. I did not want to hear any more about the atrocity—even if it was true. I came to Hawaii to forget about the war, not to be reminded of its ugly brutality. When we were finally released to our loved ones, the My Lai incident was far from my mind.

I stepped into the R & R greeting room where my sister Janice was waiting. We ran to each other and embraced. Then I anxiously looked around, expecting my girlfriend to surprise me by suddenly jumping out.

But she was not there. I realized from my sister's pained expression that Mary had not come to Hawaii.

An empty feeling shot through me. My mind started to race over why Mary did not come. Was her absence part of a cruel joke, or does she simply no longer care? As those thoughts raced through my mind I felt even more discouraged watching wives and lovers dash into each other's arms. Their happiness made me feel out of place, unloved. I was certainly glad to see my sister, but the number of times I could hug and kiss her was limited.

"Why isn't Mary here?" I finally asked Janice, afraid of what the reason might be.

"Um . . .," she hesitated, "her parents wouldn't let her come."

"Why not? It was all planned. Nobody said there was a problem."

"They didn't want us all sleeping in the same room," she winced.

"So, who said we were all staying in the same room?" I asked, questioning the logic of what I'd gone through in the war and not being trusted overnight with my girlfriend of two years, and with a chaperone no less.

Janice did not answer. Instead, she changed the subject by talking about her flight over, how Mom and Dad were doing, and the car she had recently bought. I was so depressed that it was an effort to show genuine interest. The only thing I wanted was to telephone Mary to find out the real reason why she had not come, but I could not even do that. It was after midnight in Connecticut, so my call would have to wait until the next day.

Meanwhile, Janice and I walked the busy sidewalks of downtown Waikiki buying postcards and corny souvenirs at curio shops. After dark we wandered through nightclubs, sampling exotic drinks and listening to live music. The variety of activity was amazing. Unlike the Vietnamese strips with only a few bars, Waikiki has so many lounges and cabarets that it was difficult choosing which to patronize. There was no doubt about it: this was Hawaii. I was back in the World! As badly as I felt without Mary by my side, it was a good place to be. I was finally free of the Vietnam time warp, if only for a week. However, contentment is a fickle companion, and my initial sense of ease was about to disappear.

The next day I phoned my parents. My mother cried when she heard my voice. Her emotional release caught me by surprise and made it difficult for me to hold back my own tears. I suppose that servicemen almost always miss their mother more than a lover or a spouse.

Second to my being in the war, my mother's greatest concern was for Jerry, my younger brother. He had just received his driver's license and was terrorizing the neighborhood in a beat-up 1959 Dodge sedan. I told her not to worry about it, remembering when I had done the same thing, but just thinking of riding in a car with the radio blasting made me homesick. We spoke for nearly an hour and I promised to call her again before going back to Vietnam.

I called Mary next. I was nervous as her mother answered the phone.

"Is Mary there?" I asked, not sure of what I was going to say to her.

"Just a minute please," she answered cheerfully. I heard her yell in the background, "Mary, it's him! It's him!"

Mary picked up the phone and delivered that sweet hello I had been dreaming about for the past eight months.

"Oh Mary," I cooed. "It's so good to hear your voice. I've missed you so much!"

"I've missed you too, but I didn't think you'd be able to call me. How did you ever get to a phone?"

"Are you kidding?" I laughed. "There's a phone in my hotel room. I couldn't very well call you from the beach."

"The beach?" she stammered, sounding confused. "Where are you?"

"Where am I?" I asked her back, wondering why our conversation was not making any sense. "I'm in Hawaii. Where did you think I was?"

"Hawaii?" she paused. "Wait a minute, who is this?"

"This is Artie! Who did you think it is?" My heart began pounding, but not in a good way.

"Ha!" Mary scoffed. "That's a good one. Artie is in Vietnam. Now who is this?"

"This really is Artie. I'm in Hawaii on R & R. You were supposed to come here with Janice. Don't you remember? This trip was all planned. I even sent you the plane fare. Why didn't you come?"

The phone went silent when Mary realized it really was me. At the same time my heart sank because I just realized that her mother had not yelled "It's him!" She had said, "It's Jim!"

What a lovely R & R surprise. I was just initiated into the pitiful club, whose members know the despair of losing the one thing that kept GIs going: a sweetheart. I expected Mary to have a few dates while I was gone, but not find someone to take my place. Perhaps her past letters about drug abuse had something to do with her guilt for taking a new boyfriend. I had lost Mary months ago and never knew it. I felt betrayed, empty, and alone.

We slowly resumed conversation, but it was muddled and strained. I did not bother asking about the other guy because it would not change anything. Mary was back in the World, free to do as she pleased; I was trapped in the military, forced to take whatever came my way. We said good-bye on friendly terms and she promised to write more often. Big deal, any future letters would be from someone who used to love me, so there would be no joy in receiving them.

After hanging up the phone I sat motionless, as if I was in a trance. I agonized over what I had done to deserve such a heartbreaking punishment. I was so devastated I no longer wanted to be in Hawaii. I was ready to go back to Vietnam and direct my misery against the Army and the war. Mary cut me deep, and at that moment I did not care if I lived.

If these are the emotions felt by servicemen who have been dumped while on overseas duty, I wondered how many combat deaths could be blamed on the infamous Dear John letters GIs receive. I told Janice what happened; she was not at all surprised. My family had known of the situation and had wisely planned for me to hear the news in Hawaii with my sister instead of alone in Vietnam. It was a nice thought, but it did not ease the pain.

During the next few days I found it hard to spend time with Janice, though I am sure that hurt her feelings. It was not that I did not enjoy being with her. I just thought my depression would spoil her vacation, too. Eventually I wasted three days moping around before reminding myself I was in Hawaii and the war is thousands of miles away. Only a fool would perpetuate his own misery in a place like this. I had to cure my heartache, and I knew just what would do the trick: female companionship!

Waikiki Beach swarmed with bikini clad maidens from which I figured on having my pick. After surveying the sunbathers, I spotted a lone blond beauty lying on a blanket so I confidently sat down beside her.

"Hello," I cheerfully began. "My name is Artie. Do you mind if I join you?"

She turned slowly, looking at me with a hollow stare that made me feel invisible.

"Are you talking to me?" she asked indignantly.

"Well . . . uh . . . yes."

"Listen buster, I've got a jealous boyfriend who is supposed to meet me here. If you don't want to get flattened, just head on down the line."

Hmm, tough customer. I gave her a timid smile before silently turning away. Undaunted, I continued searching until I came across an attractive girl listening to a radio. She was chewing gum and bobbing her head to the music.

"Hello," I greeted her. "Do you mind if I join you?"

"Sure, sit down," she said with a big smile. "So what's happening?"

Now this is more like it, a friendly female. We talked for several minutes, with her giggling through the entire conversation. I was not sure if I excited her or whether her bathing suit was too tight because she kept pulling on it. A short time later her parents, who were swimming nearby, rejoined their daughter. I stood up to introduce myself, but before I could say anything, her father started yelling at me.

"How old are you?!" he demanded.

"I'll be twenty-one in a few days sir," I answered respectfully.

"Really? I'll have you know that our daughter isn't even fifteen, and she is not allowed to date. Just what were you hoping to accomplish?"

"I . . . I didn't know," I stammered, now completely embarrassed. "She certainly looks old enough."

"Well, she's not! There are plenty of other girls on this beach. I'm sure you can find one closer to your own age. Good-bye."

What a bummer. I had been away from home so long that I was unable to recognize jail bait. I could have told her father that some of the whores in Vietnam were only fifteen years old, but that probably would not have changed his mind. Instead, I left peacefully to look for someone else.

My next target was a gorgeous Hawaiian girl who looked like a model from a travel brochure. Her bronze body and long black hair contrasted beautifully with her bright yellow bikini. She sat majestically on a blanket reading a book, looking up occasionally to gaze at the ocean. My instincts told me to stay away, but she was even more tantalizing up close. I just had to speak with her.

"What are you reading?" I asked with an adoring smile.

She looked up to give me a cursory once-over.

"Why do you want to know?" she asked in an aloof tone.

"I just want someone to talk to," I answered meekly. "Can I sit down?"

"Sit down if you want to. It's a public beach."

This meeting was not going as well as I had hoped, but I was determined to see it through.

"Sure is a nice day," I offered, expecting a similar response but she was not interested in discussing the weather.

"You don't have much of a tan," she said, examining me closer. "Only your arms and face have any color. Are you from the mainland or are you in the military?"

"I'm in the Army," I answered proudly. "I'm on R & R from Vietnam."

"Vietnam . . . I see. What do you do in Vietnam?"

"I'm in the infantry. It's not very glamorous. Mostly humping through the jungle, trying to stay alive."

"Oh . . . the infantry," she sneered, throwing her head back. "Tell me, how many women and children did you murder in the My Lai Massacre?"

The question caught me off guard. "What?" I exclaimed, overwhelmed by the accusation. "That happened over a year ago. I wasn't even in the Army then."

"You are part of the war machine, that's all I need to know. Warmongers like you thrive on bullets and blood."

I was too shocked to respond. I just sat there watching as she gathered her things and walked away. I was doubly confused when everyone within earshot stared as if I had done something wrong. Embarrassed, I quickly left the area.

I never dreamed of a war protester confronting me like that. I wondered what she hoped to gain by lashing out at soldiers who have no control over the mandates of the government. We had become targets for the anti-war crowd simply because we were unable to obtain a draft deferment. In the aftermath of My Lai, the American military, not the communists, was viewed as the bad guys. It was as if war protesters thought GIs liked being in Vietnam; nothing could be further from the truth. No one hates war more than those forced to experience it firsthand. Now I understood why some GIs were reluctant to pursue the enemy with the same vigor as in the early years of the war. The public's perception of the American soldier was becoming the war's controlling influence.

Knowing I had done nothing in Vietnam to be ashamed of, I refused to be discouraged by the bikini-clad protester. I was still determined to find a girl, but it was time to change my strategy. I had to ignore the attractive females in their skimpy swimsuits in favor of someone that most guys would only give a cursory glance. The time had come to find a girl with character, a girl of intelligence, a girl as desperate for companionship as me.

After a careful search, I spotted a young woman who looked like she had just arrived from the back woods. She wore a two-piece bathing suit straight out of the 1940s. The girl was plain, yet oddly appealing, but the feature I found most attractive was her white as a ghost complexion that matched mine. Since our skin tones would not clash, I ventured closer.

"Hi," I cautiously greeted her, thinking if she turned me down that I might just give up. "Can I join you?"

"I don't see why not," she answered with a curious smile, "you've got the same farmer's tan as me. People will naturally think we're a couple." I could not help but laugh at her remarks.

Her name was Cynthia. She was a nineteen-year-old Canadian visiting her retired grandmother. As we spoke, I discovered Cynthia had a refreshingly friendly down-home attitude, much different from my previous encounters. To avoid another possible anti-war showdown, I told her about my role in Vietnam.

"Oh you poor thing," she said sympathetically, "you guys are getting such a bad rap from the press. I don't think your sacrifices are being properly recognized."

"Well, thanks," I responded, pleasantly surprised. "I haven't met too many people who share your feelings."

"That's too bad. Canada has some men fighting in Vietnam too. It's wrong not to support the soldiers."

That was all I needed to hear. I convinced Cynthia that I was a harmless, lonely GI, thousands of miles from home, and that we should go back to my hotel room to privately discuss how the war was affecting me.

Cynthia's acceptance had me hoping that I was going to get some free love to help ease the pain of Mary dumping me. When we arrived at the hotel, my sister, who had been waiting patiently, was there to greet us, so any thoughts of intimacy quickly vanished. After introductions Janice invited Cynthia and her grandmother to dinner. To my dismay, Cynthia

thought it was a good idea and called her grandmother, who also agre
to join us. Now I knew nothing intimate would happen.

I expected Cynthia's grandmother to be a stuffy old lady, but Lillia
turned out to be an enlightened woman who had been around. She was s
impressed with Janice and I traveling halfway across the world to reunit
that she treated us to dinners and shows for the rest of my stay. Lillian's
generosity made me feel that there was still some good in the world.

Nothing romantic happened between Cynthia and me. Love did not
bloom and the only physical contact we had was a few embraces and
innocent kisses. With Janice and Lillian around most of the time I could
not do much anyway. Besides, no one could take Mary's place that fast. I
was just happy that someone was there to help turn a hopeless start of the
week into something special.

When the time came for me to return to Vietnam, the last thing I
wanted was fanfare, so I asked Cynthia and Lillian not to see me off.
However, I could not do that to Janice, although I told her there was not to
be an emotional farewell. I wanted our good-bye to be nothing more than
a simple hug. I did not want any tears shed for me until the day I walked
through the front door of our parent's home.

As I climbed aboard the airport shuttle bus, the sheer thought of the
DC-8 looming in the distance, and the return to Vietnam that it
represented, slipped my mind into oblivion. The mixed bag of emotions
that was my R & R would forever alter my perception of the war. The
company clerk who warned me about going to Hawaii was right about
my attitude change. Suddenly, I no longer cared if I had an impact on the
war or not, vowing to focus on survival more than ever before. And if
survival meant having to stoop so low as obeying the Lifers, I would do
it.

Well, maybe.

"Make it easy on yourself and play the game a little
longer, or I'll have you defusing booby traps
until you go home. Is that what you want?"

CHAPTER 11

Return to Vietnam

If war is hell, then the devil was at home in Vietnam and I did not
want to be his guest anymore. The return trip from Hawaii was a blur. All
I could think about were the endless miseries waiting for me in the jungle.
After the Chinook shuttle left me at the Camp Evans chopper pad, I could
hardly remember how all my travel connections had been made.
However, upon hearing the all-too familiar rumble of distant artillery and
breathing the putrid mix of diesel fuel and burning shit, I knew I was
back.

With no one to greet me I stood alone, cursing the bitter loneliness of
this place. Then, as if on cue, a passing rain shower poured down on me.
Feeling adequately insulted, I conceded my fate and trudged to the
company headquarters to let the Army know I was back. Specialist
Simmons was there to greet me.

"How was Hawaii?" he asked, testing his theory that a GI's attitude
usually changed after being on American soil again. "Did it turn out like
you expected?"

"It wasn't anything like I expected," I said with a mocked grin. "I lost my girlfriend, I was taunted by a war protester, and the only women I spent time with were my sister, a Canadian virgin, and her grandmother. The whole thing was like a soap opera. I can't wait to see what happens next."

"It's Christmas Eve," Simmons offered, trying to cheer me up. "Most units are in the rear for a 48-hour cease-fire, so you've got a little time to get back in the groove. Did you know that Company A is going to Camp Eagle tomorrow to see the Bob Hope Christmas Show?"

"The Bob Hope Show," I mused. "That ought to be something."

"Not for everyone," he winced. "You're back under Lieutenant Cramer's control. Since you just returned from R & R, he put you on the list of volunteers to stay behind in defensive reserve in case the Gooks don't honor the cease-fire. I guess Cramer's dislike for you hasn't softened much." I nodded knowingly and rejoined my platoon.

The men were eagerly preparing for the show by shining boots and getting haircuts and clean fatigues. As they paraded through the company area drinking beer and joking around, it was difficult to hide my jealousy. After all, I was exposed to the same dangers as everyone else and felt just as deserving to attend the show as the next guy. As I stepped into the hooch, an unusual number of new faces startled me.

"Hey, Sergeant Wiknik!" Dennis Silig yelled, as he waded through the crowd to greet me. "We've been waiting for you! Meet the guys!"

The banter suddenly stopped as all eyes turned in my direction. I gave a hesitant wave and nodded as the unknown men began talking again while still looking me over.

"What the hell is going on Silig? Why was everyone staring at me?"

"It's all part of my public relations campaign. Since you've been gone, we've gotten a lot of Cherries, so I've been telling them all about your exploits."

"My exploits?" I said, shocked at the very word. "What kind of exploits?"

"I told them how you were the first to the top of Hamburger Hill and that you prevented an attack on Firebase Airborne by single-handedly discovering an NVA weapons cache. I also explained that you are one of the few NCOs who thinks its more important to survive on a mission than follow stupid tactics and get killed."

"What the hell did you do that for? I don't need to impress new guys." I was actually a bit pissed about the whole thing.

"Yes you do," he said in all seriousness. "This is a new breed of Cherries with bad attitudes. They know that the war is winding down with the Vietnamization program, so none of them plan to be the last to die here."

"No shit," I replied, now at least understanding Silig's twisted strategy to win them over to the right way of thinking. "But we've got plenty of guys to help break them in."

"Not anymore. After you left for R & R, Shaw, Alcon, Keoka, Scoggins, Smith, and the others were shipped home. Even guys who were supposed to stay until the middle of January received an early-out Christmas gift. I guess the Army is willing to do anything to get more support for the war. You should have seen their faces when they found out they were going home."

As he spoke, I felt an awful loneliness. My friends left and I never knew it. Would I ever see them again? "Did you get their home addresses so we can keep in touch after the war?"

Silig gave me a funny look. "Who the hell wants to be reminded of this fucking place after they get home?" I nodded in agreement.

"But you have other things to worry about," Silig continued. "Lieutenant Cramer has been bragging how he shipped you off to the LZ cutting team. He said you're the problem child of the platoon and needed to be taught a lesson, and if you didn't change, he would do it again for good. If you want to stay in the platoon, I think you should offer him an apology."

"I would rather kiss Ho Chi Minh's stinking dead ass than ask forgiveness from that bastard."

"So lie," Silig suggested. "Cramer doesn't have to know you're faking it."

Rather than take any chances, I took Silig's advice to swallow my pride and tell Cramer what he has probably wanted to hear for a long time. I sought out the lieutenant and edged my way up to him and saluted.

"Lieutenant Cramer," I began, hoping to get through the apology without making myself sick. "I was wrong to question your authority and tactics. I'm going to work hard at making sure it never happens again. I also want to apologize for the pig-shooting incident. That was supposed to be a joke, but it went too far."

"Well isn't this something," Cramer said with a smirk, thinking he had finally broken my will. "My brand of punishment has finally taught Sergeant Wiknik the error of his ways. From now on, it would be in your best interest not to complicate the war by questioning my strategy or trying to embarrass me."

"Yes sir," I faintly conceded, "but my goal still has not changed. I plan to finish my tour with as little risk as possible to me and the men. If I question you in the future, sir, it is only because I am trying to offer something constructive, and it will not be anything malicious."

"That's more like it," he said with a handshake, believing my comments were honest. "I've always thought that you'd be a productive member of the platoon. When we get back to the field, let's get started on that body count. We haven't killed anyone lately."

What a jerk.

Now that I had apologized to Cramer, trying to control him would be harder. I did not think Silig and I could do it alone. To succeed, we would have to enlist Howard Siner who, several weeks ago had been mulling a return to the field. I hoped he had not changed his mind.

The next morning, I watched the men excitedly board the Chinook shuttle for Camp Eagle. It was good to see them so cheerful, especially knowing that whatever entertainment they would see had to be far better than what was offered at the Camp Evan's theater. As soon as the Chinook left, I got together with Siner to ask for his help.

"I want you to come back to the field," I said with all the honesty and sincerity I could muster. "With most of the old-timer's gone the platoon's experience level is too low for me and Silig to handle—especially when it comes to dealing with Cramer. What do you say? Will you come back? I think you'd make a big difference."

"Thanks for your confidence but I'm way ahead of you," Siner smiled. "I requested field duty two weeks ago and I'm just waiting for my replacement."

I almost screamed with joy. "Great! What made up your mind?"

"Several things," he frowned. "I just got so sick of listening to the REMFs whine about how rough it is in Camp Evans when they have no idea of how much worse it could be. Then they bitch and moan when Grunts come in from the field, calling them gun-toting crazies who have nothing better to do than shit-up the place. Being in the rear is a reward in itself, but when I found out that more REMFs than Grunts are going to the Bob Hope Show, I just didn't want to be associated with them anymore."

"Fuck it, don't mean nothin.'"

"It gets worse," Siner added. "The Brass knows all about Lieutenant Cramer's leadership troubles. The problem is no one is willing to do anything about it because young officers, good or bad, are getting harder to come by. But I think you, me, and Silig can straighten him out."

"Just straightening Cramer out isn't good enough for me," I said in grave determination. "We need to get him removed from the field."

When the men returned from the Bob Hope Show, most were rejuvenated from the first-rate entertainment. In addition to Bob Hope, the ninety-minute show included singer-actress Connie Stevens, The Golddiggers all-female song and dance troupe, astronaut Neil Armstrong, Les Brown and his Band of Renown, and Miss World, Eva Reuber-Staier. However, some men were visibly depressed. The show represented a little piece of the World, a life we all missed so terribly. Worse than that was Christmas Day at Camp Evans. There were no seasonal decorations, no familiar Christmas carols, no exchanging of gifts—not even a cheap Santa Claus costume for a few laughs. Aside from being in the rear for the cease-fire, Christmas was like all the other holidays that passed unnoticed. The only significance was that it brought us another day closer to going home.

The next morning we returned to the field, working the flatlands about five miles northwest of Phong Dien. During my absence from the platoon, I hoped Lieutenant Cramer would mature as a leader or at least realize he was not going to win the war by himself. I was sadly disappointed. Cramer had not changed at all. He was the same incompetent jerk he always was, except now a new level of ineptitude emerged: without well defined terrain, he could not read a map.

One afternoon, Cramer decided to call in artillery on a hedgerow about a quarter of a mile away. Following proper procedures, he asked for a first-round white smoke marker. The marker landed on a hilltop so far off that the smoke blended in with the clouds. Rather than request another marker for adjusting the fire, he simply radioed in new coordinates and asked for two high-explosive rounds.

At first, the familiar screech of the approaching shells sounded like they would sail harmlessly past us. However, as the noise intensified, it was quite obvious that the rounds would land far short of the hedgerow.

Silig and I exchanged panicked glances and yelled, "Incoming! Hit the dirt!"

Cramer stood watching the target while the rest of us sprawled on our bellies. An instant later, two deafening explosions ripped into the earth a few hundred feet away, sending shock waves through the ground below us. "Cease-fire!" I yelled to Cramer. "That's too close, Lieutenant! Cease-fire!"

I had just finished screaming those words when chunks of hot shrapnel noisily landed in the bushes just a few feet away. Cramer never moved. He just stood staring at the impact area as if he were on a street corner.

"Lieutenant!" I called to him, "what the hell are you doing!"

"Wow," he calmly answered. "Did you see that? I guess I'll have to adjust before firing again."

Luckily he had only asked for two rounds. "You're damn right you're going to adjust, but let's look at the map first!"

I checked his coordinates and discovered we were about one thousand feet away from where he thought we were. His error could have been tragic, but luckily no one was hurt. It was difficult to hold back my anger, but since I had just returned from exile I said nothing more and hoped this was an isolated incident.

Three days later we set up an ambush next to a VC trail that skirted a shallow river. After dark, Cramer radioed in for harassment mortar fire to keep the VC off balance and possibly chase them into our line of fire. The problem was, Cramer failed to tell us that he requested the mortars. As a result, when an errant mortar shell exploded less than a hundred feet away, we thought the VC had fired it at us.

Pandemonium broke loose as everyone quickly gathered their gear on Cramer's order to evacuate the area. Rather than calm us down and admit that he called for the mortar round, Cramer played it as if the VC really did fire at us. Within moments we were headed for higher, more defensible, ground. Moving like phantoms in the dark always made us jittery, even more so now because we thought the VC were close. There was no talking allowed, so if we drifted apart only the dull thuds of our equipment pulled us back together again. We were always afraid our movement would attract a wandering VC who might mix in with us. But our biggest fear was that we would stumble into another platoon and get shot up. Luckily, neither concern came to pass.

Several minutes after we retreated from the river I began wondering why only one enemy mortar round had been fired. That was when I figured it out. We were not under attack but instead running away from another map fuck-up. I halted the platoon and told the men to set up for the night. When things calmed down I took Cramer aside.

"Lieutenant," I began, barely restraining myself from grabbing him by the shirt front, "you asked for that mortar round, didn't you?"

Cramer did not know what to say. His puzzled look was all I needed to confirm my suspicion.

"Do you have any idea of how much danger you just put us in? If you're going to call for fire support, keep us informed. We've been lucky with some of the mistakes you've made, but one of these days it's going to catch up with us, and the platoon won't take it lightly. Being out here is supposed to be a team effort; no one will think any less of you for getting a second opinion on map reading and tactics."

"Now Sergeant Wiknik," he responded calmly, as if trying to patronize me. "I know you mean well and you think I have a few kinks to work out, but really, I know what I'm doing. Trust me."

Cramer's attitude was unbelievable. He should have been removed from the field long ago, but I guess Howard Siner was right when he said young officers, even incompetent ones, were hard to come by. Rather than waste any more time trying to get through to him, I had to find a way to get Cramer to self-destruct before he killed one of us. Simply getting him removed from the field was no longer good enough; I want him bounced out of the Army as well. I would just have to find a way to capitalize on his stupidity.

A few days later, when Captain Hartwell arrived for a routine visit, the opportunity I was so desperately seeking fell into my lap. As Hartwell and Cramer walked the perimeter to review our defenses, Cramer waved his M-16, using it as a pointer. As they approached a nearby position, a shot rang out. Everyone except Cramer hit the dirt.

"Lieutenant!" shouted the Captain. "Get down! We're taking sniper fire!"

"Hey everybody," Cramer sheepishly announced. "There is no sniper. Heh, heh, heh. That shot was mine. Heh heh. My weapon went off by mistake."

Captain Hartwell could not believe what had just happened. "Lieutenant!" he shouted at the top of his lungs. "What the fuck is wrong with you? Why wasn't your weapon on safety?"

"Don't worry about it Captain," I chimed in before Cramer could respond. "His weapon goes off like that all the time, but we're getting used to it." I nodded softly to Cramer as if I was trying to support him in front of the Captain. Cramer almost jumped out of his skin at my comment.

Hartwell's eyebrows arched up in disbelief as he waited a few seconds for Cramer to deny my remark. Cramer was speechless and his silence only infuriated the Captain all the more until he could hardly maintain his composure. Finally, he spoke slowly and deliberately.

"Lieutenant, have your RTO get me a chopper so I can get back to Camp Evans where it's safe. Then I'm going to figure out a punishment that fits your level of ineptitude. You'll be hearing from me real soon." That was it. There was no other conversation.

Cramer's jaw dropped and it looked as if someone had just kicked him in the stomach. He was in shock as he agonized over what Hartwell was going to do to him.

"Don't worry, sir," I said with false consolation, "the worst thing Hartwell could do is put you in charge of a mine-sweeping detail."

"Why did you tell the Captain that my weapon goes off all the time?" moaned Cramer.

"I just wanted to ease the tension with a little humor. Did I do something wrong?" I asked, feigning surprise.

Cramer was too depressed to argue. Instead, he went back to the CP and stared into space. I was ecstatic. I could not have dreamed up a better scenario myself. However, Cramer had not survived all this time without someone covering for him, and that someone turned out to be our own Platoon Sergeant Wakefield.

Wakefield was a classic case of an Instant NCO gone bad. He started his tour as a seemingly regular GI, but during the last few months had been brainwashed by Cramer, who had recently promoted him to Staff Sergeant. Since they were always protecting each other's ass, it was my job to torment Wakefield as well. The next day, while Cramer was still reeling from Captain Hartwell's visit, I got the chance.

We were patrolling along a high ridge when Cramer was notified that a supply chopper was inbound and that we needed to locate a natural LZ in order for it to land. From our lofty position, a good LZ was spotted at the bottom of the ridge, so we headed for it on an old VC trail. However, our movement was slowed by thick brush that choked the path. We were not even halfway down when the chopper pilot, thinking we were in position, radioed us to mark the LZ with smoke. Rather than ask the pilot to return in an hour, Cramer yelled a ridiculous and dangerous command, "Everybody run! The first guy to the LZ can pop smoke!"

I thought that this could not be happening, but sure enough the lead squad disappeared, running down the trail while the guys in the back bunched up behind me because I stopped.

"Maintain your intervals!" I shouted at them. "Nobody runs! We're going down this trail as if we are walking point!"

I took only a few steps before Sergeant Wakefield bellowed, "Wiknik! What the hell are you walking for? You heard the Lieutenant! Now step it out!"

"Come on Wakefield," I said, appealing to his sense of judgment, "don't you think it's a little dumb to go blindly running down a trail? It's too easy to set off a booby trap or get ambushed. Besides, look at the helicopter circling up there. They think we're somewhere near the LZ. If they spot people running toward it, what's to stop them from thinking we're Gooks and start shooting at us? We can't even call in our position because Cramer took off with the radio. So we're walking."

"Like hell you are. Everyone runs to catch up with the others."

"Fuck it, man," I said firmly. "My squad walks or we park our asses right here." I glared directly at him, challenging his authority.

"What did you say?" Wakefield asked, implying he had not heard me right.

"I said 'fuck it!'. We are not going anywhere until someone at the LZ pops a smoke and that helicopter goes in for a landing."

Everyone's attention was on Wakefield, who knew he had to keep the upper hand.

"Sergeant Wiknik," he said, giving me one last chance, "hustle your men down that trail. And I mean now!"

"Sure, I said. You go first."

Wakefield did not know what to do. No one had ever stood up to him like that. He nervously glanced at the men staring at him and then turned back to me. Before he could speak, I pointed to the LZ and casually announced, "Hey look, smoke is out. Let's get moving, guys."

As the men started down the trail, Wakefield stopped me when they were out of earshot. "Just what were you trying to pull back there, Wiknik? I don't like being fucked with, especially by a malcontent like you. Don't ever pull any shit like that with me again."

I merely looked at him, shrugged, and walked off without replying. That only pissed him off all the more.

Three days later we were sent to Camp Evans, where Captain Hartwell began Lieutenant Cramer's punishment by placing him in charge of the SERTS rifle range. The in-country replacement training school had recently moved from the relative safety of Bien Hoa to Camp Evans to put the new guys closer to the action. It was poetic justice to have Cramer responsible for teaching Cherries about the firing, maintenance, and safety aspects of personal weapons. Also in camp was one of our other battalion companies for a mandatory weapons and tactics refresher course. The Brass felt that the additional training would increase our confidence and make Grunts more effective in jungle warfare. Not too many old-timers wanted to practice what we had been doing for real, but we figured this exercise would help the new guys benefit from our experience as well.

The training was fairly basic: how to deploy the M-60 machine gun; how to make maximum use of a claymore mine; how to recognize terrain that offers a military advantage; and different ways to identify and avoid booby traps. We also practiced rappelling from a fifty-foot tower, climbing up and down a rope ladder hung from a hovering Chinook, and everyone's least favorite—bunker line guard duty. Between training sessions I was summoned to battalion headquarters for a talk with Edgar Boyce, our First Sergeant,.

All First Sergeants liked to be called "Top." The unofficial title was customarily given to senior enlisted men who had made a career out of the Army. Boyce had more than two decades of dedicated service to his country and was highly respected for his uncanny common sense and knowledge of the military. His present job was to keep a logistical and administrative watch over the battalion from the rear.

One thing Boyce hated was a bad officer, but he was on a first name basis with the good ones, Generals included. Another thing he hated was NCOs who argued among themselves, like Wakefield and I did. Just having to face him on this issue was scary. His square-jawed, imposing figure reminded me of a tough football coach.

"Well now, Sergeant Wiknik," he began, glaring at me, "what's this bullshit I hear about you telling Sergeant Wakefield to go fuck himself?"

"Me?" I asked innocently, trying to look like I had no idea what he was talking about. "I never told him to go fuck himself."

"What exactly did you say?"

"Er, just . . . fuck it."

"Hmm," he said, rubbing his chin. "According to Wakefield, you said 'fuck it' to him three times. To me, 'fuck it' still means 'fuck you.'"

"But Top, if you knew what he wanted us to do . . ."

"I don't give a damn about the circumstances! I don't care if you were one hundred percent right! You don't challenge a superior—especially one of my Sergeants—in front of subordinates. That only makes you both look like assholes. Respect for the chain of command is essential if we expect to be successful. When you don't agree with someone, you discuss it privately, otherwise the system breaks down. Do you understand what I'm telling you?"

"Yes, Top," I answered weakly, feeling like my father had just chewed me out.

"Listen Wiknik, you only have a few months left to serve and I know you won't be re-enlisting, so make it easy on yourself and play the game a little longer. If you can't get with the program, then I'll have you defusing booby traps until you go home. Is that what you want?"

"No, Top," I said, trying to sound apologetic. God, that was the *last* gig I wanted during my final few months in this place. "I don't know what came over me. Sometimes I get a little crazy from being out in the boonies too long. It won't happen again."

"It better not. Now get your ass down to the training area and help Lieutenant Cramer at the rifle range."

"Lieutenant Cramer?" I protested. "Come on Top, that guy is bad news. Can't I do something else while we're in the rear?"

"Sorry kid. Cramer brought this shit on himself, and you just got pulled in with him."

I dreaded this rifle range assignment because Cramer's ideas for running a training exercise were as bizarre as his field tactics. He was so worried about doing a good job that he had spent the previous night creating a script for his class. As his assistants, Silig and I acted out the roles he invented. Cramer began each class with a brief history lesson on the evolution of the M-16 rifle. Speaking softly and using a range of hand gestures, his voice steadily rose until he yelled out: "TO KILL THE ENEMY!" That was the cue for Silig and me to menacingly charge out of a nearby bunker and fire several well-placed rounds into a pair of straw VC dummies that looked like scarecrows. Then we attached our bayonets, fired a few more shots, stabbed the dummies, and finished with a vertical butt stroke to knock their heads off. The class knew that our phony routine had nothing to do with what really took place in the boonies, but Cramer stuck to his script just the same.

Silig and I looked like idiots as we performed our act three times each day, so we decided to liven up things a bit. Before the next class, we loaded our rifles with tracer rounds and doused the dummies with lighter fluid. When Cramer yelled out his line, we charged out and shot into the dummies. Within seconds they were completely engulfed in fire. Unfortunately for Cramer, he had his back to us and did not know what was going on. While Silig and I admired the flames, the class erupted in laughter. Cramer turned around to see what was going on, spotted the fire, and began yelling hysterically, "Get some water! Get some water!" Then he knocked the dummies to the ground and stomped on them as if they were salvageable.

After the smoke cleared, Cramer looked even more foolish when he got on his hands and knees to push the charred remains into a pile. Rather than continue, he dismissed the class. The oddest thing was that when it was over, there was no punishment except we had to make new dummies.

At the end of each training day, Silig and I got together with Howard Siner to have a few beers and listen to some music. One afternoon, an aid station doctor noticed us hanging around and asked if we would be interested in providing security for a medical team going into Phong Dien village the next morning. Recognizing the opportunity to avoid the rifle range with Lieutenant Cramer, we agreed to go.

Medical teams visited villages throughout South Vietnam as part of the on-going pacification program designed to show the civilians that Americans are more compassionate than the Communists. Our team was comprised of one doctor and two medics who carried only basic examining equipment; antibiotics, rubbing alcohol, and first aid supplies. Since this would be a peaceful mission we left our grenades and bayonets behind and only took along minimal ammunition. If we looked too intimidating, the villagers might feel threatened and not be as eager to take the free medical care.

Early the next morning a truck drove us to what looked like the village square, which was nothing more than a water well and a cluster of banana trees surrounded by straw huts. Word spread fast announcing the doctor's presence as the elderly and young mothers with children quickly formed a line. Conspicuously absent were the teenaged boys and able-bodied men who had been drafted into the military. When the examinations began, Silig, Siner, and I stood a short distance away and watched for trouble. There was none. Aside from the weapons we carried, the peaceful tranquility of the village nearly made us forget there was a war going on.

To get the children to cooperate, the medics promised each a candy bar, then teased and tickled them until they giggled. The long forgotten sound of children innocently laughing caught us by surprise and made us wish we were kids again and not part of this damn war. After the kids were examined, some wandered over to us, perhaps hoping for another treat. But as they gathered around, their interest was in something other than candy.

Siner never went anywhere without something to read, and on this day he carried the latest issue of *Life Magazine*. The kids were awestruck by the photographs. They pointed and gawked at the turn of each page. In their sheltered lives they had never seen, even in pictures, the skyscrapers of New York City, the beauty of Yellowstone Park, snow covered ground, or Caucasian girls with flowing blonde hair. An entirely different world was right in front of them. Curiously, the mothers kept their distance, but acknowledged us with approving smiles.

When the medics called for us to leave, Siner handed the magazine to a little girl, "Here, you'll get more use from this than I will." The kids howled with gratitude and scampered back to their mothers.

Siner and I walked toward the truck, but Silig did not move. He stood erect, staring sadly into the village where the children had disappeared.

"Hey Silig," called Siner. "What are you looking at? Let's get going."

"I hate this fucking place," he said in disgust. "Being around those kids reminds me of how much I miss my nephews."

We had become so accustomed to the GIs cold-hearted image that Silig's emotion was a surprise. It opened a little crack of our otherwise dormant tenderhearted side.

"We all miss somebody," I answered slowly. "I guess it comes with the territory."

"Oh yeah?" barked Silig. "Don't ever ask me to go on one of these goddamn missions again! I'll stick to the boonies where there are no reminders of home!"

"Listen Silig," added a consoling Siner. "We all hate this place, but you can't let it get to you. If it'll help to let your feelings out, go ahead. Anything said stays between us."

"Fuck it," Silig uttered with his voice trailing off as he trudged toward the truck, "it don't mean nothin.'"

But we knew it did.

Time away from the war and the boonies was welcome, but this week long training gig at Camp Evans was starting to get to us. Having already done these exercises under life and death situations, doing them for fun grew old really fast. As the grumbling continued, a troubled Grunt reached his limit.

We were milling around the mess hall after lunch one day when Specialist Henry Nelson, an otherwise good-natured guy, calmly announced, "The food here sucks." We all nodded in agreement as he walked off and disappeared between the hooches. He returned a couple minutes later with a loaded M-16, two bandoleers of ammo, and several hand grenades hanging from his web gear. No one paid much attention; we see guys dressed like this all the time. Some of us thought he was preparing for more training. Nelson looked back at us with an odd look on his face that told me something was really wrong. Without a word he stormed into the mess hall and fired three shots into the roof. Seconds later, the cook nervously walked out with his hands raised followed by Nelson holding his collar and pointing the M-16 at his head.

"Nelson!" a shocked Silig called out. "What the hell are you doing?"

"Me?" he answered unsteadily. "I can't take this shit anymore. I'm going home and I'm taking this lousy cook for a hostage."

An unknown GI joked, "Don't take him, take me. The next cook might be worse!"

Everyone chuckled, but there was nothing funny about what was going down. It was too insane to be real and yet, no one really tried to talk Nelson out of it. We simply watched as he guided the cook to the chopper pad, where they waited for the next helicopter to land. The MPs were summoned, but unsure about Nelson's state of mind they kept their distance.

When a chopper came in, Nelson chased the door-gunners away and demanded to be flown to Da Nang, where he planned to catch a flight out of Vietnam to the United States. We quietly watched the helicopter lift off and fly out of sight. No one said much of anything as we walked to the training area. A few guys smirked that finally someone had the guts, or was crazy enough, to pull a stunt that many of us only dreamed about. The next morning, however, any humor anyone saw in this event vanished when we learned that after the hijacked helicopter landed in Da Nang, there was an unsuccessful standoff that ended only when US Marine snipers killed Nelson.

We didn't know for sure if Nelson had been killed or we had just been told that to keep others from trying the same kind of escape. Given how it had all gone down, it was likely he had been shot and the news shocked us. All of us took his death personally because we silently rooted him on without trying to stop the insanity. Maybe, with just a few words, the outcome might have been different. Obviously Nelson was out of control, but the thought of him dying in a shoot-out with other GIs was devastating. To keep us from dwelling on his dumb sacrifice, the refresher training exercises were canceled and all units were ordered back to the field. However, Nelson was not so easily forgotten because we all shared his frustration over a Grunt's bleak life and how it could lead to tragic consequences.

As for the cook, he was assigned to a different mess hall. His food really did suck.

"They've been trailing this platoon for nine months just waiting for the chance to capture me."

CHAPTER 12

Insanity to Go, Please

At the end of his tour of duty, Captain Hartwell called the company to Firebase Jack for an informal farewell. After a brief speech, he walked the perimeter saying good-bye to selected soldiers. I was surprised when he took me aside to talk privately.

"Sergeant Wiknik," he sternly said, "the time has come for you to stop fucking with Lieutenant Cramer."

"What do you mean, sir?"

"Cut the dumb act. I've watched the two of you to go head-to-head long enough and your new company commander won't be as tolerant of rebel NCOs as I have been. So, for the remainder of your tour, end the feud before you get into something you can't worm your way out of. Got it?"

"Captain," I began, "Cramer doesn't have his shit together. He's so intent on impressing the Brass that he creates dangerous situations by his own stupidity!"

"That's enough!" Hartwell commanded. "Lieutenant Cramer is a commissioned officer and will be respected as such. He's come a long way, and now you will cut him some slack, mister."

"Yes sir!" I answered, feeling somewhat betrayed but not defeated. What a bummer. The Captain turned Lifer just before going home.

"There's one more thing, Wiknik," he said in a much calmer tone. "I understand you're from Connecticut."

"Yes, sir," I nodded, somewhat puzzled.

"I'm from Connecticut, too. If you like, when I get home I'll call your folks to tell them that you're well and getting along alright."

"Really?" I said, feeling flattered. "Thanks!" Maybe Hartwell is not so bad after all.

The first thing I had to do was send a letter home to alert my folks that Captain Hartwell would be getting in touch with them. Parents with sons in the war zone who receive a phone call from the Army instinctively fear the worst. Unfortunately, Hartwell got home faster than the mail and his surprise phone call had my parents reeling.

Initially, my mother was glad to talk with someone who had just seen her son, but since I had never mentioned Captain Hartwell in any of my letters, my mother became suspicious. Hartwell's natural style is slick, like a salesman, so as the conversation continued, my mother remembered a newspaper article exposing a scheme where con men called parents of sons serving in Vietnam. The callers promise that through their military contacts, they could get infantrymen into safe jobs in the rear. The cost was a large cash payment whose size depended on the time each soldier had left to serve.

My parents were frantic. They were also embarrassed to tell anyone they might be targets of a scam. Worse still, they worried that if Hartwell had the connections to get me out of the field, then he would also have the ability to keep me in the field longer if they failed to cooperate. However, Hartwell did not imply any such thing and of course never asked for money, so my parents now began worrying that he was withholding information on my health or status, and that this call was an initial contact to gain their confidence. The fact that my tour was nearly over and my parents were anxious for my return only increased their concern.

Of course, none of their wild fantasies were true, so when my parents finally received my letter notifying them of Captain Hartwell's impending phone call, they were ecstatic. Now they could happily tell friends and relatives of the nice things the Army had to say about me. They were proud, but also felt sympathy for parents who were indeed victims of fraud.

Back at Firebase Jack, our new company commander prepared for his first combat command. As Captain Giroux was introduced to us, a few GIs whispered insulting remarks because he looked cherrier than most Cherries. Giroux's pressed fatigues and polished boots already called attention to him, but the dozen grenades dangling from his web gear completed the recruiter's poster boy look. New guys were often the butt of jokes, but Giroux's officer status naturally invited sarcasm.

Captain Giroux began his first day visiting each squad and reciting the same worn-out sermon about how we are going to crush the Communist threat and make South Vietnam safe for democracy. Some of the guys still believed that drivel, but the months of humping the boonies and getting shot at should have made it clear that the war was going nowhere.

As dusk approached, the firebase quieted noticeably. The bunker line guards settled in while artillery soldiers melted into the safety of their hooches. As Captain Giroux checked our defenses, he was shocked to learn that there was no LP going out and that there had not been any LPs for the last month. Captain Hartwell did not believe an LP was needed because the wide-open scrub brush terrain did not offer a likely avenue of enemy approach. After dark, the bunker guards used starlight scopes to see farther, and cover more ground, than an LP ever could.

Giroux did not care how our former commander ran things, so he immediately decreed that an LP would go out every night. In addition, he wanted the most experienced man (which was me) to perform LP on-the-job training of the new guys. Hoping to avoid a steady diet of this potentially dangerous job, I protested.

"Captain Giroux," I said, mindful of his inexperience, "I'd like you to reconsider sending out an LP."

"Are you kidding?" he asked, looking at me as if were crazy. "In a war zone, early detection of enemy movement is essential to the security of any military installation. That's basic defensive strategy, Sergeant."

"Yes, sir it usually is. But in our situation, there is just too much ground to cover," I countered. "We'd be better off dropping random harassment mortar rounds outside the firebase."

"That's ridiculous. Do you have any idea what mortar rounds cost? The LP is going out. That's final."

"In that case, sir, I'm requesting to be excluded from LP duty."

"Excluded?" he asked in disbelief. "Nobody gets excluded. What's the problem. Are you afraid?'

I hesitated for a moment, realizing that I really was scared.

"Yes, I'm afraid," I answered candidly. "I am especially worried about being out there with only Cherries. I have forty-eight days left, and I don't want to take unnecessary chances."

"Sergeant, a scared soldier makes for an alert soldier. I'll see you in the morning when you back come in." The discussion was over.

Completely disgusted, I gathered the LP members and led them to a position with an adequate view of the surrounding terrain. We were only three hundred feet from the firebase, but being outside the wire was so spooky I stayed awake most of the night—more afraid of a Cherry pulling the trigger at a shadow than the Gooks. As the night wore on, I was surprised at the amount of noise coming from the firebase. I heard sounds of people talking and laughing, metal clinking, and I even saw someone light a cigarette. They made perfect targets for a VC sniper. If nothing else, the LP would serve as a teaching aid to show the new guys how not to act after dark.

The night was uneventful, but when it was my turn for guard I got an unexpected surprise. To keep track of guard time, Grunts passed around a wristwatch with a luminous face. However, on this night one of the Cherries handed me a large pocket watch that glowed with the Walt Disney cartoon character Mickey Mouse. The mere sight of the smiling Mickey Mouse in a war zone stunned me. With all the chaos and loneliness of Vietnam, here in my hand was a tiny piece of my childhood. It painfully reminded me of how much I hate the war and of how bad I wanted to go home.

At first light we returned to the firebase. The Cherries did okay on their first LP but it did not matter much to me. In fact, nothing seemed to matter. Over the next several days I found my behavior in the grip of erratic mood swings. I was becoming nervous, suspicious, and obsessively cautious of the people and activities around me. I felt as if my life was in greater danger then when I first came to Vietnam.

My sudden attitude change was known as STS (Short-Timer's Syndrome), a condition where the subconscious mind thinks it is time to go home, but the reality of still being in Vietnam created a psychological conflict. To us Grunts, STS simply meant that a guy was getting burned out. The Army only acknowledged it if it rendered a soldier useless in the field. The most common symptoms of STS are agitation with new guys over things as minor as eye contact, excessive talking, or too many questions. A soldier with this neurosis also hands out merciless warnings for honest mistakes and often fanatically check and recheck each man for ample ammunition, clean weapons, and basic combat readiness.

The commonly accepted cause of STS, other than having a lifetime of ordeals crammed into a relatively short period of time, was that GIs arrived and left Vietnam alone. If soldiers came in as a unit, they would be counting the days together like a class of high school seniors waiting for graduation. The way a GI's tour was arranged, there was no one who shared the same feelings about being close to going home. Each GI's DEROS became an individual event.

Commanders who recognized STS sometimes removed the soldier from the field and allowed him to finish his tour performing mundane tasks in the relative safety of the rear. I knew I would have no such luck with Lieutenant Cramer, but I had not forgotten the escape successfully used by Specialist Harrison back in June. His goofy antics convinced everyone he was too unstable to remain in the boonies, so a similar performance enacted at the right time might also work for me.

A few days later, a supply chopper brought Siner back to the field. Silig and I breathed a sigh of relief upon his return. Not just because Siner was our friend, but also because he was experienced and kept his cool no matter how frustrating or dangerous things became. Siner was sacrificing a lot to be back with us, but as a true Grunt he knew Lieutenant Cramer had to be stopped once and for all. If it could be done, the three of us would find a way. In the meantime, the war went on.

In addition to putting out LPs each night, Captain Giroux also sent out ambush patrols. When it was our platoon's turn, the target area was a rarely used VC trail junction that began showing signs of renewed activity. Captain Giroux was so sure our ambush would be a success that he assigned us a Kit Carson scout for interrogating any VC we might capture.

Under the subdued light of a full moon, we zigzagged across the mile of open terrain outside Firebase Jack, walking primarily in gullies and draws to hide our movement. The moonlight also helped us pinpoint the ambush location by the sighting of a nearby stone cliff. Once we were at the ambush site we quietly melted into the brush on a knoll that provided a commanding view of the trail junction and possible enemy escape routes.

Lieutenant Cramer placed his CP on top of the knoll, giving him an observation advantage over the rest of us. I had no sooner finished checking my squad when Cramer scurried over to Silig's position. In a loud whisper he announced, "I just saw movement by the cliff!"

That shot the platoon into high alert status. We readied for action while I joined Silig and Cramer to determine what was out there. Because there was a full moon, we did not bring a starlight scope. Cramer left his binoculars at the firebase, so we had to depend on our night vision. We watched for thirty minutes but nothing happened. We eventually shrugged it off because the cliff was not close to the trail junction and it did not make sense for the VC to be anywhere near it.

About twenty minutes later, Cramer again told Silig he saw activity around the cliff, only this time he radioed for five rounds of mortar fire. The short barrage landed with exceptional accuracy and, as the dust settled, we watched intently for signs of life. Nothing moved, but now we needed to focus our attention on both the trail junction and the cliff.

Another twenty minutes passed when Cramer again claimed to see something moving on the cliff. He requested and received another mortar volley. The results were identical: no movement and no return fire. In the meantime, Captain Giroux radioed Cramer and gave him hell for scaring away every VC within five miles and told him that he better have something to show for it in the morning.

Perhaps ten minutes passed when, for the fourth time, Cramer again claimed to see movement near the cliff. This time, instead of standing on the perimeter, Silig and I climbed to the CP to share Cramer's view. We watched for a short while until, sure enough, we saw something moving too. But the movement was peculiar, as if it shifted in one direction, and then the other direction. When it started again, we watched more intently.

"Lieutenant," Silig groaned, realizing what the movement was. "Are you for real? Stay here and watch the cliff while I go down to the perimeter edge."

Silig walked about fifty feet away just below the crest of the hill, where he grabbed a skinny tree and shook it. The tree stood about three feet higher than the surrounding vegetation and was in Cramer's line of sight with the cliff. Whenever the perimeter guard leaned against the tree, the branches and leaves wiggled back and forth. In the moonlight, and in Cramer's mindless world, the illusion was enemy movement.

"Well, it could have been something," Cramer shrugged, walking away. The remainder of the night was uneventful.

Whenever mortars or artillery are requested, it is standard procedure to check the impact area for enemy casualties. We knew such a search would be fruitless so in the morning, instead of admitting to an error, Cramer radioed in a story about finding several blood trails that disappeared into the brush.

When we returned to Firebase Jack, Captain Giroux asked Cramer for a detailed account of the previous night's events. Perhaps Giroux knew about Cramer's tendency to exaggerate because he also spoke with several platoon members to see if everyone's versions were consistent. They were not. As a result, Captain Giroux ordered our platoon to patrol an area far from the remainder of the company; a move not based on strategy but rather on punishment. The only positive aspect of our being exiled was that it was not likely we would be used to reinforce another platoon if it got into trouble. The problem was, if we needed assistance, there was no one close to help us, either.

The rainy season was ending and the dry season's renewed heat restricted our humping to the early morning and late afternoon. Most of our day was spent relaxing on a trail edge or in a bamboo thicket. During these hours our most popular pastime was playing cards. Hearts was our favorite, and we played for a nickel a point. Even Cramer tried his luck but, after losing a few dollars, he grew tired of a game because "it is not much of a challenge for men of intellect." His remark gave us an idea: an officer gambling with enlisted men was strictly taboo. Win or lose, if we could lure Cramer into some serious gambling, it could be the opportunity we had been seeking for so long to rid ourselves of him.

Since Cramer needed "a challenge for men of intellect," we figured that the best game to beat him at was chess. Howard Siner was a successful amateur player who just happened to have a traveling chessboard. When asked if he was interested in playing a thinking man's game, Cramer quickly accepted, bragging that he was the captain of his high school chess team.

The stakes were set at $20 a game, and it did not take long for Siner to discover that Cramer was not the chess player he claimed to be. He easily beat him, but kept the games very close to keep him playing. When Siner sensed Cramer was about to quit, he purposely lost several games by an ever-widening margin. This tactic prompted Cramer to raise the stakes to $50 a game for a better chance of winning his money back. Siner reluctantly accepted and Cramer promptly began losing. Still convinced he could win, Cramer foolishly wrote $50.00 IOUs that he also signed and dated. The games continued with Siner dropping one on occasion, until he was ahead $220 in cash and $1,100 in IOUs! In a desperate attempt to break even, Cramer begged Siner to play one last game for double or nothing.

"C'mon Siner," Cramer whined. "You've won almost three months of pay from me. I at least deserve a chance to break even."

"The games are over," Siner said with finality. "I think we need to cool it a bit. You didn't play very well toward the end. Perhaps we can try a rematch in a week or so."

"A week?" Cramer blurted out, getting everyone's attention. "I'm not waiting a week! You've got my cash and IOUs! I demand more playing time!"

"Let's give it a rest," Siner insisted. "A week without gambling won't hurt us."

Cramer was stunned and possibly a little suspicious now, but he said nothing more because the men were staring at him. As Siner put the chess game away, he gave me a wink because the IOUs were all the evidence we would need to nail Cramer. The only problem we had now was to figure out a way to get them back to battalion headquarters. In the meantime, we needed to get Cramer refocused on the war. That was my job.

"Lieutenant," I began, looking nervously into the jungle, "for two days we did nothing while you and Siner played chess. Since we never sent out any patrols, there's a chance when we leave here that we'll walk into an ambush or a booby trap. I think we should cut our own trail and head straight into the jungle."

Cramer thought about it for several moments. "Okay," he agreed with a sneer, "but Siner is walking point."

Silig and I looked at each other in disbelief, knowing that Cramer was trying to punish Siner for winning—or get him killed so the IOUs would be worthless.

After several hours of hacking through the brush, Siner broke out to a freshly worn trail that looked like the VC used it only moments before. After checking it in both directions, we felt an eerie sensation of being watched or that we were close to something evil. We decided to proceed with our Kit Carson scout at the point because he would be able to spot danger easier than we would. After hiking to a trail junction, we stopped to rest and consider which direction to go.

Silig and I climbed a nearby knoll for a better view. On the far side of the knoll were three rectangular dirt piles similar to the cache site I had discovered in the A Shau Valley. We dug feverishly into one, expecting to uncover hidden weapons or food. When we hit a plastic covering, I eagerly tore it out of the ground. When I saw what it was my whole body lurched backward in shocked disgust. I had opened the shallow grave of an enemy soldier's decomposing body. The rotting stench was so putrid it gave me the dry heaves. We hastily covered it back up. Neither of us had any desire to dig into the other mounds. Whenever they could, the VC carried their dead from the battlefield and secretly buried the bodies to keep US forces from tracking the exact number of enemy soldiers killed. However, in this case it did not work. Although already dead and buried, the last earthly deed of these three VC was to become part of our body count when Cramer radioed in the location of the grave.

Our scout was nervous hanging around the bodies of former comrades, so we left the knoll to follow the trail that led to higher ground. As the path took us deeper into the jungle, the scout slowed his pace, taking deliberate, cautious steps. He was rounding a turn when his foot tripped a hand grenade booby trap. The explosion killed him instantly.

The scout's specialty was the detection of booby traps, so the one that got him must have been cleverly hidden. Cramer assumed the explosion was command detonated and signaled the beginning of an enemy attack. "Ambush!" he yelled, firing fanatically into the jungle. A few Cherries shot along with him until Siner ran up calling for a cease-fire. Cramer was flat on the ground yelling into the radio that we were in a firefight and may soon need artillery support.

"Lieutenant!" Siner shouted. "What the hell are you guys shooting at?!"

"The Gooks blew an ambush on us! We were taking small arms fire!"

"Really? Then how come when I yelled 'cease-fire' the Gooks stopped shooting, too?" Siner stared hard at our commanding officer.

Still lying on the ground, Cramer didn't respond. "That was no ambush," Siner continued, the disgust dripping from his words. "It was a booby trap and you know it."

"Our scout was killed by an enemy explosion and there was rifle fire," Cramer replied, though without his usual conviction. "I radioed in that we were ambushed and that's how it's going to stay."

"Who are you trying to impress?" asked Siner. "The only thing you accomplished was to let the Gooks know where we are."

Cramer quietly stood up and walked away. He radioed in to cancel the artillery and request a medevac for the scout's body. To satisfy my curiosity, I took a squad up the trail to the spot where the VC had supposedly launched their attack. The search revealed nothing to support Cramer's claim of an ambush. The medevac arrived soon thereafter and hovered above the treetops, sending down a rescue basket for the scout. The body was loaded and the chopper flew away without incident.

Cramer decided we would watch the trail for the next several days, hoping to ambush any VC who might come around to investigate our shooting. Each squad would take a turn lying in wait with the remainder of the platoon in a nearby support position. The close high ground would conceal us, but to get there we would have to hack through thick undergrowth. Once again Cramer ordered Siner to take the point and cut the trail. Bad blood was rapidly developing between these two.

With Silig close behind for protection, Siner slashed through the jungle as the rest of us slowly followed. Our column moved ahead ten feet, sat for two minutes, then moved again. Eventually we were stretched out so far I could no longer hear the steady whack of the machete. Since the man in front of me had not moved for several minutes, I assumed the point had reached the top and that Cramer was checking the area for defensive positions.

Without any warning there was a loud blast at the top of the hill: another grenade booby trap had detonated! Seconds later we heard the dreaded words, "Medic! Medic!" When I did not hear his trademark panic rifle shots, my spirits soared in the hope that Cramer had finally gotten zapped. For an instant, I felt embarrassed realizing how we had played right into the VC's game plan. The first booby trap on the trail killed our scout. Then, knowing how predictable GIs are in heading for higher terrain, the VC set a back-up booby trap at the hilltop. The Gooks might be miles away, but they continued to kill and maim without firing a shot.

We were unnaturally quiet while the medic was at the point position for what seemed like an eternity. Waiting to find out who was hit often brought on a feeling of helplessness. No one felt much remorse over the loss of the Kit Carson scout because he was a former VC, and probably had wounded or killed GIs. Finally, word was passed down on who was wounded. It was like a message from hell: the shrapnel had hit both Siner *and* Silig. The news paralyzed me. How could this have happened to my two best friends? With machine-like quickness I headed for the top.

I found Siner sitting with his back against a tree. The left side of his face was splattered with blood and partially covered by a field dressing tied around his head like a turban. A chunk of shrapnel had ripped into his scalp above the forehead. He had no other wounds, but was in pain and had blurry vision. Silig was hit in the buttocks and the back of both legs. In his own silent agony, tears trickled down his dirty cheeks as the medic attended to him.

"Are you guys all right?" I asked, knowing even before I was through speaking that the question was a stupid one.

"We'll be okay," Siner winced. "Just tell the guys to watch for trip wires and to keep their helmets on. If I had kept mine on, I wouldn't have gotten hit. Tell them!"

"Okay, I'll pass the word along. Do you know what happened?"

"When we reached the top, I didn't bother to look for wires. I just dropped my rucksack and threw my helmet down. I began clearing a spot for the CP when I tossed a branch aside, tripping the booby trap. It was something only a Cherry would have done."

Siner and Silig's wounds were serious but not life threatening. I just wished Cramer had gotten it instead because he seemed to revel in the fact that Siner was hurt. Cramer also wasted no time reporting the action to whoever was willing to listen on the receiving end of the radio.

"Yeah, we're onto something big," he bragged. "The Gooks are trying hard to slow us down. That means we're getting close. Real close."

"Hey!" I yelled at Cramer. "Did you call for a medevac?! These guys are hurt! Let the fucking war take a break!"

"The chopper's on its way," Cramer waved at me. "So take it easy."

His attitude infuriated me. "I'll take it easy after these guys get picked up. But until then, you better get your shit together! If we're so fucking close to the Gooks, then let's check for more booby traps so we can get the rest of the platoon up here into defensive positions. When that medevac comes in, we've got to give it protection."

"You're right," Cramer sheepishly agreed as he signed off the radio. "I'll have Wakefield conduct a quick sweep of the area."

Siner and Silig knew that getting wounded as they did was a blessing in disguise. Once they got back to the rear with Cramer's IOUs, they could expose him as an out of control officer who neglected his military duties while gambling with subordinates.

The same medevac returned and the rescue basket still had the scout's blood smeared on it. Silig, the most seriously injured, went up first. Siner followed shortly after. There were no goodbyes because somehow I knew I would see them both again. As the chopper sped away with its engine noise echoing off distant hills, I looked around at the remainder of the platoon and felt a terrible void. No one was left from Hamburger Hill, the A Shau Valley, or the DMZ. Except for Cramer and Wakefield, everyone had less than six months of field experience. Humping the boonies with a platoon of Cherries under Cramer's twisted command was something I wanted no part of. The time had come to enact my escape plan; to convince everyone that I had finally lost my mind.

To put things in motion, I set up a meeting with the newest guys to pass along some "little known facts" I had been saving for months. Most new guys believe anything an old-timer says because they figure that surviving for such a long time must mean we have done something right. It also helps when the new guys are gullible.

"I got you guys together because I've got some health tips that just might make life a little more bearable in the jungle," I began in a serious tone. They edged closer as if I was a football coach preparing to give them final instructions before a big game. "Everyone is always complaining about the tropical heat and humidity. The best way to tolerate it is by letting your fingernails grow long because they'll act like cooling fins to lower your body temperature." The Cherries shot confusing glances at one another until I added, "and long fingernails make it easy to pull leeches off."

They nodded knowingly until one of them inquired about my fingernails.

"Sergeant, why aren't your fingernails long?"

"That's because, I've been climacteric for a long time." I said it with an all-knowing exasperation in my voice. No one dared ask what it meant.

"Another thing we don't do in the field is wear under shorts," I continued. "Guys who wear shorts often come down with crotch rot because their balls can't get proper ventilation. But worse than that, there's a greenhouse effect in your pants that can cause uncontrollable pubic hair growth. That would be mighty embarrassing when you get back home." I knew that story was a winner when a few minutes later I spied a guy stretching his pubic hair to check its length while he urinated.

Besides coming up with silly statements, I also marched around the perimeter with a fixed bayonet on my rifle and grenades hanging from all over my web gear. Acting jittery, with my eyes darting about, I repeatedly checked each man for loose and noisy equipment, telling them, "The Gooks are out there. I've seen them." Then, to completely astound them I added, "Don't forget to leave Vietnam as you found it by not littering or carving initials into trees. After the war you may want to come back for a camping trip." With that, everyone looked at me as if I had finally lost it—everyone except Wakefield.

"I know what you're doing," he sneered, pulling me aside. "You're not fooling me with your bullshit. But the thing is you're such a bad influence on the men that I want you out of this platoon, too. So do what you want, but stay out of my way."

"You better be careful Wakefield, I'm unstable and I might snap at anytime." I raised my eyebrows and widened my eyes.

"Fuckin' flake," he mumbled, walking away.

The only platoon member I felt bad about fooling was Specialist Mike Perdew, who had been with us for five months. Perdew was one of those quiet individuals who would never dare question an old-timer, no matter how bizarre he acted. But he was also the one person I felt certain would continue the fight against Cramer if Siner, Silig, and I failed in our effort at getting him removed.

My antics continued for two days before the men finally complained that I was driving them crazy. That left Cramer with two options: get me to stop or send me to the rear. Since he would never willingly let me out of the field, he called me to the CP for an attitude adjustment speech. I gave him my best performance. Better than an Oscar, the rest of my lifetime would be my award for the act of a lifetime—if I could pull it off.

In military fashion I marched to Cramer's position and snapped to attention.

"Sir! Sergeant Wiknik reporting as ordered, sir!"

"Cut that out!" he yelled, scanning the jungle around us. "If the Gooks are watching, they'll know I'm an officer and try to kill me first."

"Don't worry, sir," I assured him. "It's not you they're after. It's me."

Cramer's eyes narrowed. "You? What the hell are you talking about?"

"The Gooks have been watching us for a long time," I answered. Cramer suspiciously eyed the jungle above both my shoulders. "They've been trailing this platoon for nine months just waiting for the chance to capture me."

"Capture you?" he asked, jerking his head back. "What makes you think they want you?" He was serious, and he thought I was, too.

"It all started one night last May. We ambushed and killed the daughter of a VC Colonel outside Phong Dien village. I didn't shoot her, but in the confusion of my first enemy contact I continued firing after the other guys stopped. Everyone was shouting at me to cease-fire, so the Gooks that got away heard my name and memorized it. I was safe when we went to the A Shau Valley because the NVA had never heard of me. Then, when we came back to Phong Dien, we ambushed and killed a VC Colonel's son and the same thing happened. Everyone was yelling at me to stop firing, so the Gooks heard my name again. They've been after me ever since. Hell, the villagers said the VC have a bounty on me."

Cramer stared blankly at me. If he considered the recent booby trap incidents together with my story, it could make perfect sense in a Lifer mind as warped as his. Then quite seriously, and to my pleasant surprise, he asked me how I knew the Gooks were watching us. It was all I could do not to burst out laughing.

"At night," I whispered, while darting glances beyond Cramer, "they sneak up close, calling my name and telling me to give up. They promise that if I surrender, they will stop setting booby traps. I don't trust them." Then, practically sobbing, I leaned in close and grabbed Cramer's shoulders. "You've got to protect me. The VC are not going to wait forever. One of these nights they're going to attack and drag me off. What am I going do?" I looked at him with pleading eyes.

"I . . . I . . . well, I don't know," he said slowly. "Go back and check on your men while I think about it."

I returned to my position to wait for Cramer's next move, which didn't take long. After hearing my story he radioed for advice on what to do with me. Less than an hour later he gave the order to start cutting a LZ for the next morning's resupply. As the men worked, Cramer gave me the good news.

"I'm sending you to the rear," he began as I listened without expression. "You're eligible for a seven-day leave and I just received word that it was approved. Isn't that the dumbest luck? Besides, it would be better for the platoon if you rested, you know, to forget about the Gooks looking for you. That kind of talk makes the new guys nervous."

Actually, Cramer was the nervous one. He always knew I hated him, and now my antics convinced him I was unstable. That's where the seven-day leave idea came from. By sending me to the rear, Cramer showed that he was more concerned for his own safety than the platoon's. Regardless, I was happy that my plan succeeded.

Since that night might be my last in the bush, some of the guys offered to pull my guard duty as a going-away present. I refused. If we had enemy contact during my last night, I wanted to be on top of it right away. Besides, I needed to pull guard duty to reinforce my story about being singled out by the enemy.

Guard duty that night was long and maddening. It seemed darker and quieter than usual. With my close friends gone from the platoon, I felt terribly alone. That's when I made myself a vow to never step into the field again. With only thirty-two days of service remaining, I would do anything to stay in the rear—even if it meant becoming a REMF. The night was uneventful, and the only attack we endured came from the pesky insects.

The next morning I was packed and ready to go before most of the men were awake. While saying goodbye to the few people I was friendly with, I sensed their feeling of abandonment as well as the all too familiar envy of watching someone escape the field. However, I was pleased with one accomplishment: I was living proof that a Grunt could endure a year of combat duty with hardly a scratch. Of course, my ghosting was a big help.

When the supply chopper came in, two Cherries scrambled off and, in their typical clumsiness, stood gawking at their new surroundings. I felt a twinge of pity knowing what miseries lay ahead for them—especially with Lieutenant Cramer. Yet nothing could prepare them, the war was something they would have to experience personally. Each man had to find his own way.

As the chopper crew tossed supplies to the ground, I headed for the open door. In a final display of goodwill, Cramer came over to shake my hand.

"Good luck, Wiknik!" he shouted over the engine noise. "As bad as things have been between us, I want you to know that I've enjoyed the challenge! When you get back to Camp Evans, don't go into any crazy talk about the Gooks wanting you to give up! That was some joke! You almost had me going there for a while!"

I couldn't resist testing his stupidity once again. "After last night, I won't have to worry about the Gooks anymore!"

"What do you mean?" yelled Cramer, tugging on my shirt as I climbed into the helicopter. "What happened last night?"

"The Gooks said an officer is more valuable than an NCO, so I gave them your name!"

Cramer's mouth fell open and he took two steps backward and stood motionless as if he had just received a death sentence. As the chopper lifted off, I smiled and waved goodbye. Cramer was already peeking over his shoulder to scan the tree line.

I grinned from ear-to-ear all the way back to Camp Evans.

"Susie's is the ultimate massage parlor and the
best place in the city to find a woman.

CHAPTER 13

Vacation Time

Camp Evans never looked so good, not just because I was out of the
field but because my tenure as a GI was nearly over. As far as I was
concerned, the last of my military days would be treated as a formality.

I reported to our First Sergeant, Edgar "Top" Boyce, to get my
seven-day leave in order and also to find out how Siner and Silig were
doing. Silig was at the 18th Surgical Hospital at Camp Evans and would
soon be released for light duty. Siner was at the 95th Evacuation Hospital
in Da Nang because it was the nearest facility capable of handling head
wounds. Since Top had no information on Siner's condition or recovery
rate, I asked to start my leave that afternoon and visit Siner at the hospital
along the way.

"You can visit your friend," Top said, glaring at me. "But you're not
going anywhere for at least two days."

"What?" I asked, startled by his restriction. "Why so long?"

"Because you have been recommended for promotion to Staff
Sergeant and you have to appear before the review board. But if it were

up to me, I'd bust your ass down to PFC and send you back to the goddamn boonies where you belong!"

"Gee, Top," I asked, acting oblivious to having done anything wrong. "What did I do?"

"Come on, Wiknik!" he shouted, pointing an accusing finger. "That story you told Cramer about the Gooks trying to get you was bullshit!"

"You're right," I smiled. "It was bullshit. Those Gooks didn't fool me. If I surrendered like they wanted, they'd still put booby traps out. It's a good thing I didn't fall for that, huh?"

Top shook his head and looked skyward as he rolled his eyes. "Draftees like you make the Army look bad. When are you going to get serious?"

"Look, Top," I countered, trying to stay on his good side. "I don't want to appear before the review board. Hell, I don't even want the promotion. I'll be out of the Army in a month, so just give that sergeant stripe to someone who can use the extra money."

"That suits me fine," he shot back. "I don't like the idea of promoting a flake anyhow. Now get your sorry ass out of here and don't let me see you again until your leave is over!"

Top just didn't understand. He thought I committed an unpardonable sin by acting crazy when all I wanted to do was stay alive as the end of my days in Vietnam were drawing to a close.

The next morning I took a C-130 shuttle flight to the US airbase in Da Nang. The out-of-country R & R processing center moved its operations there to ease the overcrowding of the Ton Son Nhut airbase in Saigon. However, the vacation destinations for seven-day leaves were still the same as for R & Rs. This time, however, I had no intention of going to Hawaii again. I opted for Sydney, Australia, because returning GIs bragged about free women with round eyes and no language barriers.

As usual, there, was a problem. Seven-day leaves were considered a second R & R and Sydney was in such high demand that first-time furloughs took priority. As a result, I was placed on the bottom of a standby list behind thirty people. Since I would not secure a seat that day, I visited Siner at the hospital.

Aside from the thick bandage on his head, Siner looked fine and seemed quite normal. Unfortunately, his spirits were down because he felt his head wound was relatively minor and did not deserve the same attention as men with more serious combat injuries.

"Listen Howard," I began, sounding uncharacteristically sympathetic. "You should be proud to be with these guys no matter how minor you think your wound is. You got hurt in combat and have earned the right to be here. When I came to this hospital a few months ago it was to stop my penis from bleeding because I was convinced I had masturbated once too often. That had nothing to do with combat and every doctor examining me thought I was a weirdo. Try living that down!"

We had a good laugh and Siner felt better. That is, until he told me how Cramer's gambling IOUs were lost. Then I got depressed.

"As soon as the medevac brought me to the Camp Evans aid station," Siner explained, "the medics removed my clothing to check for additional wounds. While being treated, someone went through my stuff and took the IOUs."

"That means Cramer has a friend working for him in the rear."

"Right," Siner sighed. "It looks like our efforts were for nothing."

I groaned out loud as we both shook our heads in disgust.

"I don't know how a guy like Cramer could have someone willing to stick their neck out for him," Siner added.

"Not only that," I answered, "with me going on leave and you and Silig out of the picture, there's nobody out there to threaten his command or keep him in line. I should have never played like I was crazy. I feel like I ran out on the platoon."

"You've got nothing to be ashamed of," Siner said profoundly. "After spending eleven months in the bush you've taught guys how to watch out for the Lifers and the Gooks. The example you set will probably save lives."

I nodded a silent thank you.

After a two-hour visit I returned to the R & R center to check my flight status. I had advanced only four spaces. At that rate I could be hanging around for a week—a definite plus for earning more ghost time! The next morning I checked the list again to find that I had not moved at all, so I went back to the hospital.

When I arrived, Siner was preparing for transfer to Japan for further tests. This final round of examinations would determine whether he finished his enlistment in the States or would be given a medical discharge. Either way, he was leaving Vietnam for good.

I was always glad for anyone who got out of Vietnam alive, but this departure was bittersweet at best. Together, Siner and I had survived the battle of Hamburger Hill as well as countless ambushes and patrols. We were not only a team, but had become close friends. We exchanged home addresses and promised to meet someday after the war. I tried to say goodbye, but it was too awkward with the hospital staff pushing me to leave. Instead, we simply shook hands and nodded, purposely hiding any display of emotion. If anything good came from my Vietnam experience, it was having Howard Siner as a friend.

It would be ten years before I saw my friend again.

My return to the R & R center left me feeling empty and alone. With no reason for me to continue waiting for a chance at Sydney, I changed my plans and took the next flight to any location that did not have a standby waiting list. My new destination was Bangkok, Thailand, and that afternoon I was on my way with 200 other GIs. The commercial flight was uneventful except for a detour around Cambodia because our fat jetliner would be too tempting of a target for the NVA surface-to-air missiles located there.

The capital city of Bangkok is only five hours away by air, but as a society it was light-years from the blight of Vietnam. Thailand's economy was among the most prosperous of the Asian nations, making Bangkok one of the busiest commercial and transportation centers in all of Southeast Asia.

The city was also the center of Thai culture and education with six universities, several museums, and hundreds of richly decorated temples. The busy streets were modern and filled with automobiles, streetcars, and billboards. Aside from the prominent Thai writing style on signs and advertisements, Bangkok was not much different than a stateside metropolitan area.

Since Bangkok's economy was not fully dependent on vacationing US servicemen, our visit here would bring us closer to the everyday Thai people. As a result, the R & R directors offered some behavior guidelines to prevent us from offending the citizens by a thoughtless act. We were also encouraged to buddy-up with at least one other GI because the Thai way of doing business was to offer group discounts, thus minimizing transportation and entertainment costs.

As GIs paired off, a lanky fellow with a confident swagger approached.

"Hi there," he said with a smile, stretching out his hand. "I'm Eddie Landell. Do you want to pair up with me?"

"Sure," I answered, feeling comfortable with his friendliness. "What do we do first?"

"After we check into the hotel, we're going to Susie's Bath House to celebrate freedom from the war."

"A bath house?" I asked indignantly. "I don't need a bath."

"You'll want this bath," he laughed.

"Why will I want this bath?" I asked, acting almost as dumb as a Cherry.

"Susie's is the ultimate massage parlor and the best place in the city to find a woman," he answered with a hint of reverie.

It finally dawned on me what he was talking about and began to laugh.

"I ought to know," he continued. "I came here for R & R two months ago and had such a great time that I had to come back. I found a terrific girl at Susie's. Her name is Uwe. She was beautiful and treated me so good that I stayed with her for the whole week. In fact, I'm here to get her again."

As Landell reminisced about his misplaced romantic feelings for a prostitute, I could not help from thinking about my girlfriend Mary. I still loved her and since I only had one month left to serve, I foolishly held to the hope that we might get back together again when I got home. Then I reminded myself of how much Mary hurt me and how she tried to soften the blow by promising to write more often. I only received three letters during the last two months, none of any substance. It was clear no one would be waiting for my return.

"I'll be going back to the World soon," I lamented to Landell, "so I don't want to catch anything from these massage girls. How did you stay clap-free the last time you were here?"

"Are you kidding?" he asked in disbelief. "Prostitution is such a big business here that the US military requires each girl be tested once a week. They even carry an identification card to prove they're healthy. It's the Army's way of giving prostitution a stamp of approval." That suited me just fine.

After checking into adjoining hotel rooms we headed for Susie's Bath House. The place looked like an exotic pleasure palace from a Hollywood movie. After we entered we were served complimentary cocktails and seated in front of a closed curtain. The house lights were dimmed as the curtain opened, revealing thirty beautiful girls behind a large window. They were dressed like high school cheerleaders, each with a numbered tag on her lapel. Sitting on blue velvet covered bleachers; they smiled coyly and crossed their legs several times. A few arched their backs to show off their physique, while others slowly rotated from side to side. It was a scene that could setback the women's liberation movement by 100 years, but it made me feel like a kid outside a candy store. It was all I could do not to press my face against the glass.

Landell spotted Uwe and immediately called her number. When she appeared from behind the curtain they both howled with delight and went directly back to the hotel, bypassing the customary "get to know each other" bath and massage. My decision was not so easy. The choices were so overwhelming I drifted from girl to girl. Finally, the manager politely asked me to make a selection or leave. Since I was unable to choose, I called out number 21—my age.

A fragrant, slender young girl with soft features, almond eyes, and long black hair appeared. Her name was Molly. She led me to a cubicle furnished with a massage table and a bathtub large enough for two people. The floor had thick red carpeting and the walls were etched sheet-plastic through which shadows could barely be seen. Soft music played throughout the building and the muffled laughter of other patrons added to the peaceful atmosphere. The tranquil setting was worlds apart from the distractions of the whorehouses I had visited in Vietnam.

Molly's experienced hands undressed me in seconds, causing me to get an erection so fast that I thought it would hit me in the face. As I climbed into the tub, she put her hair up and stripped down to a bikini bathing suit. She ignored my aroused condition and expertly washed every crevice and appendage on my body.

The bath was followed by an intense fifteen-minute massage that left me incredibly relaxed—but more stimulated than ever. The cure for the sexual agony she so expertly induced cost extra, which was all part of the bath house strategy. With my moral resistance turned to putty, I relinquished $200.00 to keep her for the next five days. When Molly and I got back to my hotel room, I was so horny I nearly tore her clothes off. Our lovemaking was intense, but in my zealousness it lasted all of two minutes. Her sensual passion made me feel fantastic and we happily indulged with more of the same each night before turning in.

The next day, Molly and I got together with Landell and Uwe to see the sites. There were many places to visit around Bangkok and the cheapest way to do it was to rent a taxi for the week. The most reliable cab drivers worked out of the hotel and the girls knew most of them. They recommended a cabby known as Big Sam. Oversized by Asian standards, Big Sam was a friendly man with a perpetually smiling face. Initially I was suspicious when he demanded his $100.00 fee in advance, figuring that he would take my money and disappear. However, my confidence was quickly established. Big Sam proved to be more than just a chauffeur; he was also our financial advisor. Everywhere that first day he made sure we paid a fair price for souvenirs and steered us clear of beggars and shady street vendors.

During the day we toured historical sights, went on boat rides, took countryside drives, and visited local attractions. At night it was bar hopping and dancing, or watching American movies with subtitles. A few times Big Sam took us to secluded restaurants to meet Uwe's and Molly's friends. An added bonus was that no matter where we were or what we did, Sam, Molly and Uwe rarely spoke in their native tongue—a thoughtful gesture that allowed Landell and I to be a part of everything that was going on. Their overall consideration and professionalism not only made us feel special, but also helped loosen my purse strings.

I arrived in Bangkok with $500.00 but it was almost gone after just five days. With no intention of lowering my extravagance for the rest of my stay, I contacted the local Red Cross office and wired home for an extra $100.00. The Red Cross told my parents I needed the money for food and shelter. My parents believed them. Twelve hours later the money arrived and I gladly squandered it on Molly just like before.

My week in Bangkok was a vacation I would never forget. Now I knew why Landell returned for a second time. The mood of the Thai people contrasted so starkly with their Vietnamese counterparts because nothing hung over them to choke their spirit. There was no anguish over loved ones away at war, no flood of refugees, and no threat of terrorism. Their economy was thriving, Americans were well liked, and the government was stable. As a result, I left Bangkok with a renewed respect for Asian people.

There was no sorrow or emotional attachment when the time came for Molly and me to part, even though I felt our relationship was a little more than just a successful business arrangement. But any GI who experienced a similar furlough would undoubtedly feel the same. At any rate, when I returned to Vietnam I recommended Bangkok to future R & R travelers. I also made it clear that their stay would not be complete without a visit to Susie's Bath House, and a massage from number 21 . . . Molly.

> "The Army fucked-up and promoted
> you in spite of yourself."

CHAPTER 14

Countdown to Freedom

My return to Vietnam from Bangkok was far less depressing than my previous return from R & R in Hawaii, especially since my tour of duty has been whittled down to just twenty-five days. Now it would be easy to focus beyond the war all the way to home. There was also a rumor that short-timer's were getting an early-out by up to ten days. The Army already used early releases before Christmas as a gimmick to bolster public support, so if the rumor is true, it was one I heartily endorsed.

I arrived at Camp Evans with my attitude refreshed, but I was still in the Army and Top Boyce was right there to remind me. As usual, he was pissed off. This time it was because I had stretched the normal ten days of vacation and travel time into sixteen ghost days.

"Well, well, look who's here," he said sarcastically. "The prodigal NCO returns. I've been waiting for you, Staff Sergeant Wiknik."

"Staff Sergeant? Me?" I couldn't believe my ears.

"That's right. The Army fucked-up and promoted you in spite of yourself. That means you can spend the rest of your tour as Lieutenant Cramer's Platoon Sergeant."

That hit me like a ton of bricks. "Wait a minute, Top! What happened to Wakefield?"

"He went home on emergency leave, so we won't be seeing him again. Now get your shit packed because you're going back to the field tomorrow."

"Please don't make me go," I moaned, not sure if he was serious about sending me out again. "I'd be no good in the field anymore. I've lost my edge. My desire to fight is gone. I'm just too short for that shit. Can't you find work for me here in the rear? I'll do anything."

He studied me for a few moments before smiling slyly. "I hate to see a grown man beg, so I'll make an exception in your case. You can stay and work for me, but if I hear so much as a whimper about any job you're given, your ass goes back to the field if I have to drag you there myself."

"Okay, Top," I grinned ambitiously. "Just tell me what you want me to do?"

He did not answer right away, as if relishing the moment. Then he leaned in close to emphasize my new duties. "Each morning, it will be your responsibility to make sure everyone falls out for roll-call. After breakfast, you'll organize a litter clean-up of the entire battalion area. That means all around the chopper pad and the bunker line. You will also set up the mess hall duty rosters and schedule all able-bodied personnel for various details that come from brigade headquarters."

"I can handle all that," I nodded, thinking he was finished. Man, I have it made, I thought to myself. Piece of cake.

"You're not getting off that easy," he smirked. "Your most important job will be to personally clean and maintain the battalion latrines. That means both the enlisted men's and the officer's. Everyone deserves a pleasant place to shit, so I expect you to make those toilets something to be proud of. You got any questions?"

"No, Top," I answered dejectedly. I was relieved to be staying in the rear, but was unsure of what I had gotten myself into. I did find it rather ironic that I arrived in Vietnam burning shit and now I would leave burning shit. At least it's safer than being shot at.

The duty rosters and litter pick-up required only token effort, but the latrines were a different story. The buildings were in horrendous condition. No one had cleaned or repaired anything in nearly a month. The shit buckets were overflowing, newspapers and magazines were scattered on the floors, window screens were torn, and several had missing toilet seats.

The repairs took several days because the needed materials were not readily available, forcing me to commandeer items from different latrines around Camp Evans. I must have looked especially impressive lugging around stolen toilet seats. I also tore boards and screens off vacant hooches and borrowed the latest magazines from the mobile library on its weekly visit.

After completing the repairs, I easily fell into a daily routine and found that life as a shit burner was not half-bad. My nights were free, giving me plenty of time to spend with Silig. However, he was not as optimistic about the future as I was. Silig's wounds were nearly healed, which meant he would soon return to the field, and he was not looking forward to it.

"I've got forty days left," Silig lamented, "but that doesn't make me short enough to stay in the rear. I guess I can deal with going back out to the field, but I hate the idea of being with Cramer again. It was his fault Siner and I got wounded. If Cramer does one more stupid thing, I think I'll shoot him myself!"

"Don't get too radical," I laughed, brushing aside his idle threat. "Look at the bright side, with Wakefield gone you'll be the new Platoon Sergeant. That will give you a role in the decision-making."

"Maybe," he grumbled. "I just wish you and Siner were there to help."

"Let's get a beer," I said, trying not to be reminded of Siner's departure and how I abandoned the platoon. "I'm sick of hearing about Cramer."

"Yeah," Silig muttered. "Fuck it. Don't mean nothin.'"

As each day clicked by, Top continued searching for the ultimate revenge job before I would slip from his grasp forever. To my dismay, his perseverance paid off.

"Do you know what this is?" he asked, waving a typed form in my face. "This is an authorization to release a GI prisoner to your custody. I want you to fly down to Da Nang and escort him back to Camp Evans for a court martial hearing."

"Uh . . . Ok . . .What did he do?" I stammered, wondering if the prisoner was a harmless nutcase or a hardcore NCO murderer. "Do I know this guy?"

"His name is Private Leroy Clifton and he's been AWOL for almost a year. The dumb shit was living with the Vietnamese when the Marines caught him. They've got him locked up at the 524th Quartermaster Depot."

"Why don't the MPs just bring him back?" I asked.

"Because," Top announced with a spiteful grin, "as a Staff Sergeant this is the kind of job you're getting paid to perform. Now get over to the supply shed and sign out a .45 pistol and a set of handcuffs. I expect you back here with Clifton by noon tomorrow."

"Okay," I nodded confidently. "See you tomorrow."

The task sounded easy enough. I imagined that Private Clifton was a passive soldier who became emotionally attached to the Vietnamese and stayed with them to help rebuild their lives. Or, he went AWOL to escape the war but got tired of hiding and was now ready to accept his punishment. Whatever his story was, I just figured Clifton was a hapless slob caught in military red tape and that my escorting him back was just a formality.

Late that afternoon, I arrived at the 524th Quartermaster Depot in the center of the sprawling Da Nang air base. The Marine compound, with only eight hooches, two supply sheds, a wooden headquarters building, and a small mess hall, was tiny compared to the surrounding military city. A dirt driveway circled behind the hooches to a motor pool where several jeeps and large trucks were parked. I thought it was odd that there were no bunkers or fighting positions.

When I walked into the office I barely got the chance to announce myself when a strangely exuberant 2nd Lieutenant greeted me. He acted so giddy that he never noticed my failure to salute. Perhaps the .45 slung low on my hip and the handcuffs hanging from my belt made him think I was a tough guy who commanded unquestioned respect.

"Hi ya, Sarge," he said with a silly grin. "I'm Lieutenant Butch Reinholtz. Are you here for Clifton?"

"That's right," I nodded officially, trying to act the part of a bounty hunter. "I plan on us leaving first thing in the morning. Now, can I see him?"

"Sure, this way," he pointed as we started walking. Then he proudly boasted, "This is my first command."

"Is that so?" I remarked, trying not to laugh at the announcement while glancing at his pressed fatigues and flattop haircut. "I would have never guessed."

"Yup, this compound is my responsibility."

"It must be tough running things around here," I added, wondering if Reinholtz just arrived in-country that morning. "Just what does your outfit do?"

"We're a housing unit for Marines who work on the air base. We've got truckers, freight handlers, communication operators, cooks, all kinds of people."

"So why do you have a jail?"

"It's not really a jail. It's just a temporary lockup for troublemakers and criminals."

"Criminals?" I asked sarcastically. "Are you telling me that you've already judged Clifton and found him guilty?" Reinholtz was obviously embarrassed by the question, but did not respond.

When we turned the corner, the sight of their lockup shocked me. It was a metal freight container with the words "The Big House" neatly painted above the door. Steel bars were welded across rough-cut window openings and a huge padlock held the door shut. The only comfort it offered was the shaded location; otherwise, the daytime temperatures inside would have exceeded human limit. I peered in the shadowy box for a closer look, only to see a set of white teeth, flared nostrils, and a pair of eyes that glared back. Private Clifton was the biggest black man I had ever seen.

"I figure dey send some honkie to fetch me, but not someone as scrawny as you be," Clifton laughed as he sauntered to the window. "I guess da Army be runnin' outta assholes who wanna die. I is goin' tell you now, as soon as we leave here, I gonna choke you wif you handcuffs then shoot you wif you weapon."

Try as I did, I could not swallow the giant lump stuck in my throat. "Shit, I'm in trouble," I thought to myself. "Clifton is not some poor slob regretting a bad decision about going AWOL; he's a hardcore outlaw with nothing to lose." I knew enough to know that if he even remotely suspected I was afraid of him, I would be as good as dead. I had to do something quickly so he would think twice before trying to kill me. That's when I dug deep for one last absurd performance.

"Heh, heh, heh," I cackled with a demonic stare. "Go ahead you piece of shit, help me save the Army the aggravation of dealing with you." Then I eased the .45 pistol from the holster and caressed it. "Look here, boy, I've killed plenty of Gooks during my tour, but no niggers. If you fuck with me, you'll be my first. Heh . . . heh . . . heh."

Clifton's eyes narrowed and he slowly backed off to sit silently in the corner. I gave him a death scowl then briskly walked away with Lieutenant Reinholtz following close behind.

"Sergeant?" he asked in disbelief. "You wouldn't really shoot him, would you?"

"You better god-damn believe I'll shoot him!" I shouted for Clifton to hear. "I'm not going to let some stupid nigger fuck up my record. He can go back to Camp Evans under his own power or in a body bag. The choice is his."

The Lieutenant stopped, unsure of what to do. I kept walking without looking back. Once I was out of sight I leaned against a tree, trembling from head to toe at the thought that this was probably my last day on earth. I was lamenting my predicament and cursing Top under my breath when the company clerk approached.

"Excuse me, Sergeant," he began timidly. "Do you need a bunk for the night?"

I nodded yes, looking away to hide my fear. As we walked toward the NCO hooch the clerk kept looking at me. "Excuse me again, but do you mind if I ask how old you are? I mean, you look really young to be a Staff Sergeant. Did you have a high-ranking relative help to get you promoted?"

"I'm twenty-one," I answered, half-laughing and half-thinking that I might not make it to twenty-two. "I've got no one looking out for me and this assignment proves it."

"No shit? You're only twenty-one? Man, it's hard enough just to make Corporal in the Marines. You must be one tough bastard."

"I'm not so tough. I've just been lucky," I remarked off-handedly. "Rank sometimes comes easier in the infantry."

"Why don't you stay with us peons tonight? If you bunk with the NCOs, you'll be stuck with Lifers who sit around every night talking about the good old days fighting the Korean War."

His invitation sounded good and I figured I might as well spend the night with people I was comfortable with. Without much else to do after dark we played cards, drank a lot of beer, and made fun of Lieutenant Reinholtz. When things quieted down I fell asleep fantasizing about different ways to handcuff Clifton; left wrist to right ankle or left ankle to right wrist. If I had another set of handcuffs, I could do it both ways.

Just before dawn our sleep was interrupted by whistles and men running and shouting. At first, I thought we were under enemy attack but after the panic subsided I learned to my delight that Clifton had escaped!

What a relief! I could hardly keep a straight face, because I figured Clifton would have happily killed me. I didn't question how he got loose and I didn't care. I suspected at the time that Lieutenant Reinholtz believed I was serious about shooting Clifton and had let him go since a dead prisoner might reflect poorly on him. Either that, or Clifton believed I really was crazy enough to kill him and busted out to save himself.

I immediately called Top to tell him of Clifton's escape. He gave me hell, saying something about not being able to do anything right. After I thanked him for his comments, Top ordered me to help the Marines search for Clifton. I agreed, but I had no intention of doing anything. If Clifton were found, I would be in danger again. Instead, I spent the better part of two days drinking at the NCO club, figuring that would be the last place Clifton would show up. I don't know if they ever found him and I did not want to know.

When I got back to Camp Evans Top was waiting for me with his usual glare. "Staff Sergeant Wiknik," his lecture began, "I have never in my career known anyone to dick around and waste time like you do. You fuck up every assignment, and always find a way to turn it into ghost time. You've fucked with my NCOs, pissed off every Lieutenant we've ever had, all the while knowing that you have the potential to be a model NCO. What have you to say for yourself?"

"Just doing my job," I shrugged seriously. "Trying to save lives."

"Well, your job is done," he laughed, patting me on the shoulder.

Top was laughing? What was that all about, I wondered.

"While you were in Da Nang, supposedly looking for Clifton, the Army did us both a favor. They moved your DEROS up by nine days. So you might as well start cleaning your gear and get it turned into supply."

It took a few seconds to sink in. "Yes sir, Top!" I cheered at the top of my lungs. I was ecstatic. Only a few days separated me from freedom.

"There's one more thing," Top added. "Since you've done such a fine job with the latrines, you will continue as the custodian. Tomorrow you'll start training the walking wounded so they can assume the task after you leave."

"Top, I'll do whatever you want! I'm super short!"

Time didn't drag anymore; the burden of war had been lifted. I had jealously watched so many other GIs go home and now, with my turn so close, I felt justified treating the last of my Army days as a military aberration. Wanting to end my tour with a final symbolic gesture in contempt of Lifer's, I deliberately looked for an authoritative figure to antagonize. My unwitting victim was a cherry 2nd Lieutenant just assigned to our battalion. When our paths crossed, I welcomed him to Vietnam with a wink and a smile.

"Hi ya, Wilson," I cheerfully said, as if we were old friends.

He did a double-take. "Hold it right there, Sergeant!" he commanded. "What kind of greeting was that? Where's my salute?"

"A salute for you?" I asked, as if his question was absurd. "I don't have one."

"What do you mean you don't have one? Military protocol demands that a salute be rendered when an enlisted man approaches a commissioned officer! You must salute or suffer the consequences!" A small group of nearby soldiers curiously watched to see what would happen next.

"Lieutenant," I explained. "Camp Evans is located in one of the most hostile regions of South Vietnam. The enemy has increasingly terrorized the villagers living right outside our gates. At this very moment, a VC sniper may be watching us, and a salute would make you a target because an officer is a bigger trophy than an enlisted man. So in effect, I'm could easily be saving your life by not saluting."

We were locked in a brief stalemate until Wilson leaned in close and whispered, "I don't care. I've got to establish my authority to those soldiers watching us. Just do it."

"Yes, sir!" I said, snapping to attention and presenting him with a left-handed salute.

"That's more like it, Sergeant," he nodded, unaware, or unwilling to admit, that by military standards he had just been insulted.

As the rainy season ended in the mountains, my company was sent to help build a new firebase in the northern A Shau Valley near the Laotian border. Reports from the valley were ominous. The new firebase, named Ripcord, suffered mortar attacks, snipers, nighttime probes, and ambushes from just outside the wire. Although the attacks were initially sporadic and unorganized, the NVA's constant presence magnified the spookiness and danger of the A Shau. The fighting around Firebase Ripcord would continue for the next 134 days and be the most costly US operation, in terms of lives, during 1970.

As field casualties increased, some GIs advanced a ghastly dimension to the war called "fragging." It involved the swift and anonymous killing of gung-ho superiors who needlessly risked their men's lives. Hand grenades were the weapons of choice since shooting a victim carried the evidence of a bullet. Fortunately, fraggings were extremely rare since highly competent officers led the majority of GIs. But now, in my own platoon, a fragging was being planned. A member of my old squad, Specialist Mike Perdew, was in Camp Evans to appear before the promotion board when he confided his plans to me.

"Sergeant Wiknik," he began seriously. "I need to talk with you."

"Hey Perdew," I smiled. "Why so glum? By tomorrow you'll be a Sergeant in charge of your own squad. How's it feel to be important?"

"Don't ask me, I don't want it. There's too much responsibility being a squad leader. I don't know if the guys will listen to me."

"That's too fucking bad," I shot back gruffly, disappointed by his attitude. "I did it, you can too. Sometimes it's hard being in charge, but if you don't take the promotion some other asshole will and you'll have to follow him. Is that what you want?"

"No, of course not," Perdew sighed, looking toward the mountains. "The real problem is Lieutenant Cramer. Since you left the platoon he's become more bizarre than ever. He's got these ace-of-spade cards to put on dead bodies and he keeps talking about getting into a firefight so we can win some medals. I'm afraid he's gonna get someone killed."

"Jesus Christ," I sputtered in disbelief. "I told Cramer to get rid of those cards back in October, and now he's talking about winning medals? There's no time to lose, get together with Silig so when he gets back to the field the two of you will have a solid plan for working around Cramer. That's the way we did it before."

"And where did that get you?" he asked knowingly. "You were always getting into trouble because everything you tried was a flop. I'm not waiting for Silig. When I get back to the boonies, Cramer will be finished."

"Really? What are you going to do that's so different?"

"I'm going to kill him," he answered softly, but with grim determination.

I wasn't sure I heard him right. But I had. I assumed he was kidding. "What do you want from me," I laughed, "my permission?"

"No. After all the things you've been through, you deserve to know what's going to happen."

I studied Perdew closely for several seconds. He was serious. On the one hand I was appalled because his drastic solution was something I never considered. On the other hand, it was only a matter of time before Cramer drove someone to such an extreme measure. "You need to cool off, Perdew," I lectured. "Fragging is not the way we operate. You'll have to find another way to get rid of Cramer."

"Listen, Sarge," he said, looking me in the eye. "I can do this because I can live with it. When Siner, Silig, and you were out there we were protected from Cramer's lunacy. But now, the platoon won't put up with him anymore; a couple Cherries are even talking about blowing Cramer away, but they'll probably botch the job. I'll make it look like a combat death."

I was stunned by such a casual approach to murder. Though Cramer was stupid enough to get himself zapped, he would probably cause someone else to get killed with him. I was uncomfortable with the prospect but began to understand how eliminating Cramer could be justified as a life-saving measure. I thought about threatening to expose the plan but somehow Perdew knew I would not.

"You do what you want," I warned Perdew, hoping he would reconsider. "But don't do a fucking thing while I'm still in Vietnam. I've only got two days left and it's no secret that I hate Cramer. If he ends up dead, the Army may think I had something to do with it and I'll be stuck here until it's cleared up. If that happens and I'm delayed going home, I'll hunt your ass down if it takes me the rest of my life."

Perdew nodded and walked away. That was that.

I didn't know what to think. My tour ending should have been upbeat, not shrouded in death and plots of murder. God, I hated this place.

I never found out if Cramer survived and I really don't care. For me, that part of the war is over.

"Gentlemen, I never get tired of making the
same announcement: 'Welcome home!'"

CHAPTER 15

Going, Going . . .

The morning was like so many others. The rain came down in large
heavy drops that saturated everything and everyone. But it didn't matter
because this day was the first day of a brand new adventure: I was going
home.

The last official act each infantryman performed before leaving
Vietnam was to thoroughly clean his M-16 rifle. The task was second
nature for me but now, after carrying the weapon through one year of
war, I felt unnaturally connected to it. I wanted the next owner to
understand what the rifle meant to me, so I tied a brief testimonial to the
barrel that read, "This M-16 has been to the top of Hamburger Hill and to
the bottom of the A Shau Valley. It has survived the DMZ and the rice
paddies of Phong Dien. Take care of this weapon and it will take care of
you. SSG Arthur Wiknik, Jr."

I never thought that leaving an instrument of death behind would
depress me, but it did.

Typically, when a Grunt goes home there is no farewell party, no amusing speeches, and no heartfelt goodbyes because the only people who care about him are still in the field. By mere coincidence, Silig was the only friend I had in Camp Evans because he was still recovering from his ass wound. The only official send-off I got was a stiff handshake from Top Boyce followed by a dry remark that did not deserve a response: "Thanks for coming."

I was not the only GI going home; five others from Camp Evans were leaving as well. We waited together for truck transportation to LZ Sally, our initial processing station. It was insulting that our "bus stop" was next to the latrine, especially since we had to huddle inside to keep out of the rain.

Silig stayed with me until the truck came. We didn't talk much; we couldn't, because all the things we had meant to each other were about to end. When the truck pulled up we shook hands and squeezed each other's shoulder. It was another bittersweet goodbye, but I felt fearful about leaving Silig behind. When Siner left for Japan it was easier to let him go because I knew he was going to a safe place. Silig's situation was far different; he would soon return to the field and face the war with no true friends. When he lowered his head and silently limped away, I understood just how intimate our relationship had been.

I never saw him again.

I sat among unfamiliar GIs. All REMFs and because I was infantry, I could not help but feel a little superior to them. Though we were strangers, there was no mistaking our common destination: home. We each carried the only baggage required for this trip, a large sealed envelope containing our military records. A few men had duffel bags cradled between their knees while others held shaving kits. I was the only person with something unique: the Chicom SKS rifle. They all stared at it, but no one was willing to ask how I got it.

As the truck pulled away, my last impression of Camp Evans was a picture framed by the truck's flapping canvas top and rusty tailgate. We were two miles down the road when I realized I had not asked Silig for his home address. It wasn't that I didn't care; I just wanted to forget everything associated with Vietnam. Perhaps not asking made it easier to leave. I knew I would miss my friends, but I would never miss that place.

As the truck lumbered along I downheartedly gazed at the distant mountains. An eerie sensation came over me. I felt the unearthly presence of GIs who had perished, some whose deaths I had witnessed, others I didn't even know how I remembered. I wondered if there could be such a troubled spirit world in this evil place. Just thinking about it was depressing. In the field, our war dead never received the proper farewell of a wake or funeral. We simply soldiered on, hoping none of us was next. As their faces flashed through my mind like a mournful roll call, the truck hit a bump, abruptly returning my thoughts to home.

The atmosphere in the truck was upbeat, but cautious. One GI wondered aloud why we were not flown to LZ Sally, thus avoiding road mines or snipers. Although a truck had not been attacked on Quoc-Lo 1 in recent memory, his remark kept our exhilaration in check.

We arrived at LZ Sally without incident though there was no need for us to have rushed to get there. After completing some minor paperwork we spent the remainder of the day waiting for more DEROS personnel to trickle in. It soon became obvious that we would spend at least one more night in-country.

In the morning, our DEROS group, about thirty-five strong, was trucked to the Phu Bai Airport. At the terminal we entered under a yellow archway that read, "DEROS AND ETS PERSONNEL REPORT HERE." I remembered looking enviously at the sign on other trips through Phu Bai, but on that day it was finally meant for me. While we waited, a Chaplain offered a brief sermon.

"Gentlemen, Gentlemen," he pontificated. "You are nearing the end of a long hard journey. And now, by the grace of God, you are going home. Your faith in our Lord gave Him reason to protect you from the enemy's bullets . ." As the Chaplain droned on I turned away, not wanting to hear anymore. His remarks were too hypocritical coming from a servant of God. I saw enough horrors to be reasonably sure that God did not plan the war, let alone that He took sides.

When the Chaplain finished, we boarded the C-130 transport plane that would bring us to our last in-country stop at the 90th Replacement Battalion at Cam Ranh Bay. The flight was a noisy hour and forty minutes, but the time went fast as our enthusiasm gained momentum with each passing milestone of the DEROS process.

After landing at Cam Ranh, we were bused to a complex of four buildings where briefings and final processing of our records was performed. Although only a year had passed since I last visited the compound, it felt like a decade. And yet, the atmosphere was familiar.

Small groups of clumsy Cherries, dazed at their misfortune of being in Vietnam, gawked at us with the same awe I once had when looking at old-timers. Behind them, the black smoke of a burning tub of shit rose skyward, completing the scene. I smiled knowingly.

More than 200 homebound GIs from all over Vietnam converged at the replacement station everyday and, although the processing was the usual maze of forms and long lines, the mood was surprisingly relaxed and cooperative. Though somewhat boastful, and with every reason to celebrate the end of our tour, we had yet to leave Vietnam and so avoided doing anything rash that might delay our departure. Still, the spirit of the moment was reflected on every GI's face. Glancing anxiously at the other men I could see they all radiated the same silent message: "This is really it!"

After hours of processing we were bused to the airport and detained in a restricted section away from the terminal. We were not put there to prevent escape, but to prohibit stowaways from trying to join our crew of happy evacuees. Our boundaries excluded even the latrine, but no one minded because we did not want to miss the sweet sound of the call to our flight.

And then it happened. The magnificent silver Freedom Bird, a McDonnell Douglas DC-8, dropped out of the sky and roared down the runway. We watched in awe as the plane, seemingly unaware of its importance and audience, rolled to the end of the runway and majestically taxied back to stop directly in front of us. Never before had a symbol of American technology meant so much to me. The Freedom Bird, an angel descended from heaven, had come to take me home.

It seemed too easy then, to just walk out and board the plane, but there was nothing else to do. As we crossed the tarmac a tropical breeze blasted us with hot, humid air—a final reminder of what we were leaving behind. As I approached the passenger ramp, the navigational lights flashed surrealistically, and I floated up the steps as if I was in a movie.

Smiling round-eyed stewardesses greeted us at the door, directing enlisted men to the rear and officers to the front. I dashed to a window seat with child-like enthusiasm when one of the stewardesses asked for my SKS rifle so it could be secured safely in the galley. I handed it to her, realizing how odd I must look carrying an assault rifle onto a civilian airplane.

As the seats filled I looked out at the sand dunes of Cam Ranh Bay and wondered how such a beautiful country came to be so dreadful. Meanwhile, the excitement on board was building as GIs celebrated by shouting out military slang. "Short!" was the favorite followed by, "Take off, one round will kill us all!" Others yelled, "Hot LZ!" and, "Fuck the Army!"

As the plane's engines began to spool up, our merriment dropped off to whispers. Then the aircraft nudged forward and slowly taxied to the end of the runway where it turned around and stopped. At that moment, all talking ceased and time stood palpably still while we waited for clearance to take off. Then, after what was an agonizing wait, the engines revved faster and louder as the event we had only dreamed about was about to begin.

The pilot released the brakes and the plane lunged forward. The accelerating takeoff roll glued us to our seats. Rumblings and vibrations echoed louder and louder until . . . AIRBORNE! The moment we lifted off the ground every GI let out a war whoop that out-roared the aircraft itself. As we climbed out of South Vietnam's airspace the men cheered with delirious joy. To us, leaving Vietnam was like being released from prison for a crime we had not committed. Whatever misfortune brought us there, we were now safe from the war.

When the commotion tapered off the Captain announced, "Gentlemen, you have spent one year in Vietnam and may never see it again."

More cheers erupted.

"I've been requested to circle back and give everyone a final look at the country."

Our loud reply was a unanimous "FUCK YOOOOUUUU!" With that, the plane continued straight across the South China Sea.

After the aircraft leveled off, a Paymaster 1st Lieutenant worked his way down the aisle exchanging MPC for good old American greenbacks. The money felt like a long lost friend. As the exchange continued I leafed through my military records to see what the Army thought of me. The paperwork consisted mostly of routine forms except the Article 15 I wrongly received for sleeping on guard duty at the beginning of my tour. The document, with its $50 fine, had not been processed, so I removed it from the file and flushed it down the plane's toilet.

The first six hours of our journey brought us to Haneda Airport in Tokyo, Japan, where we refueled, changed crews, and took a stretch, although we did not dare lose sight of the plane. Within an hour we were airborne again, flying over the 6,000-mile expanse of the Pacific Ocean. The mood on board was festive, yet relaxed, so I was able to sleep for several long stretches. Oddly, the stewardesses stayed hidden for much of the trip, appearing only for meals. The cocky attitude of the more boisterous GIs obviously scared them off.

Even though I understood their bravado, the war had gotten so much publicity that I wondered how things might be when I got home. Would I ever see my girlfriend again? Would my family and friends expect me to resume civilian life as if nothing significant had occurred? Or would they think I might go berserk at the slightest irritation? I knew I had changed in some significant ways. A lifetime of extreme ordeals had been crammed into a year. Who would not have changed? I tried not to think about it.

GIs wandered freely around the plane talking about everything and anything. However, most conversations focused on the same issue. Everyone was glad to be out of Vietnam, but resentful of the several months of stateside duty facing them. They rightfully felt that Uncle Sam had already gotten enough of their time. As for me, I listened quietly to their lament, feeling smug that the extra time I had put in during my stateside training prior to leaving for Vietnam left me only hours away from becoming a civilian.

As the day faded to night, the sunset at 30,000 feet was breathtaking. When it was too dark to see outside most of the men migrated to their seats to nap or read. Meanwhile, against the backdrop of the engine's steady droning through the blackness, I imagined that the airplane could easily have been a spaceship bound for planet Earth. After all, we were going back to the World.

Several hours later, the calm was broken when the FASTEN SEAT BELT sign flashed, signaling our decent to the American West Coast. Everyone quickly found their seats and silently buckled up. A lone stewardess walked down the aisle spraying insecticide to destroy any exotic insects we might be carrying.

"Do we have cooties?" a voice asked.

"It's probably Agent Orange," another whispered.

The Captain broke the silence, announcing that the State of Washington shoreline was directly ahead. We craned their necks toward the windows, straining for a first glimpse of our homeland in nearly a year. Suddenly a voice proclaimed, "I see lights!" Others joined in. "Lights! Lights! It's the World!" A flurry of cheers and bobbing heads confirmed that we were only moments away from landing.

The Captain spoke again, "Gentlemen, in a matter of minutes we will be landing at McChord Air Force Base."

More cheers erupted.

"Please remain buckled in your seats until the aircraft comes to a complete stop."

"Cold LZ!" a lone voice yelled, exciting another round of cheers.

As the plane descended, the cabin was once again eerily quiet. Everyone sat still trying to sort out the myriad of emotions racing through our minds. For a moment it was as if every GI sent out the same silent prayer: "Please God, let this be real."

Then, like a giant phoenix, the DC-8 touched down with a simultaneous thump, screech of tires, and howling deceleration of reverse thrust. Before the plane had even slowed to ground maneuvering speed, pandemonium erupted. The joy of landing on American soil was celebrated with euphoric war whoops, hats tossed in the air, and the popping of airsickness bags. GIs ran up and down the aisle, climbed over seats, and stomped their feet.

The enormity of surviving emotionally overwhelmed more than a few as they sat half-grinning with tear-filled eyes. Others shook hands, hugged, or raised a victory fist skyward. It was the single most moving experience I had ever witnessed. We were strangers by name, but as war veterans we were linked through savoring this moment of absolute survival.

"Gentlemen, Gentlemen," came the Captain's stoic voice over the intercom. "This is my seventh return trip from Vietnam and I never get tired of making the same announcement: Welcome home."

At his words, everyone hesitated as if to say, "Thank you, Lord." I know I did.

March 28, 1970, 7:25 p.m., Pacific Standard Time.

Home at last.

"After my experience, I have come to hate war."

– Dwight D. Eisenhower

Epilogue

There is a telling quote borne of the Vietnam War: "You've never lived until you've almost died. For those who fought for it, life has a flavor the protected will never know." This quote exemplifies the unique bond and perspective on life shared by wartime veterans. But the meaning of the quote also reflects the feelings of those who waited at home, for both soldier and civilian witnessed the grim reality of life's fragility. Both learned that the cost of protecting our freedom, or freedom of the oppressed, carries with it the highest cost of life itself.

We should not debate over which war was right or which was wrong. To do so only clouds the meaning of sacrificing one's life. Anyone who dies in the service of our country deserves our utmost respect and gratitude. For it is we as a nation, we as a community, and we as family and friends sending men and women off to war who are fully aware of what the consequences may be.

Most GIs arrived in Vietnam as boys, and left Vietnam as men. A lifetime of experiences compressed into a year snatched our youth and left some emotionally scarred. Yet, to serve in combat alongside these brave young men was a unique life-experience that created a bond shared only by those who have "been there."

When I was still in Vietnam, I read stories and heard rumors of how badly some GIs were treated upon their arrival home. As a result, many GIs chose to return under the cover of darkness, shedding their military garb as quickly as possible before re-visiting their old haunts. I assumed these were isolated incidents, and not in any way possible in my home state of Connecticut.

I arrived at Bradley International Airport in uniform, my chest full of campaign ribbons and bursting with pride befitting a soldier returning from war. I sat in a large waiting area while travelers filtered in. I was the only soldier in the room. As the area filled, empty seats near me were left vacant until, eventually, people stood against the wall rather than sit beside me. The room was eerily quiet as nervous glances were exchanged. I was the center of attention and suddenly realized that what I had heard was true: Vietnam veterans were as looked upon as though they had the plague. Although I never experienced being spit upon or heckled, this quarantine in the airport was, to me at least, even more telling. I was just as alone and vulnerable coming home from the war as when I left to fight in it! I was both sad and disappointed that this treatment of returning GIs was typical of our national abandonment.

Luckily, the rest of my homecoming was a better experience. When the Army gave me the nine-day early release, I decided not to tell my parents I was leaving Vietnam ahead of schedule. I thought it would be more memorable to surprise them by me unexpectedly walking through the front door. As it turned out, we all got a surprise.

My cousin Donald secretly picked me up from the airport and on the way home we fantasized on how I would make my entrance. When we arrived at my house, it was locked and no one was home! My family had taken a trip out of state and was not expected back until late that evening! Unsure of what to do next, I decided to get out of my uniform and change into civilian clothes. I did not have a key, so the only way I could get into the house was by crawling through an unlocked window. Once inside, a warm and inviting feeling rushed over me: I was really home! I fondly inspected the familiar surroundings and was happy to see that nothing had changed; even the clothes in my closet were just as I had left them. The only thing different was a map of South Vietnam hanging on the kitchen wall identifying all the places I had written home about. I still wanted to keep my arrival secret, so I decided to spend the night at Donald's. I was careful not to disturb anything or leave any evidence that someone had been in the house.

Shortly after midnight, my tired parents shuffled into the house and my mother suddenly proclaimed, "Artie is here! He's home!"

Whether or not there is there is such a thing as mothers' intuition, she had somehow detected my presence. Knowing that I was not due home for at least a week, my father laughed at the notion and told my mom she was simply tired from the road trip. She insisted I was hiding in the house and called for me to come out. When there was no response, she began searching every room. After checking the closets, under the beds, and even in the attic, mom finally gave up and agreed I was not home, but she was unable to shake the sensation that I was near.

Her antics put the family on edge. Although no one said anything, they shared the eerie feeling that perhaps I had come home—but not in the flesh. They began to worry that I might have been killed and that my spirit returned to say goodbye. Their night was a restless one.

Early the next morning, Donald called my parents to make sure everyone was awake because he wanted "to drop something off." When I triumphantly walked through the door, my father, sister and brother gawked at me without speaking a word.

"Hi everyone," I cheerfully sang out, only to be confused by their silence and darting glances as they recalled mom's announcement of the previous evening.

"What's the matter with you guys?" I asked, noticing that my mother was not in the room. "Hey, where's mom?"

"Still sleeping," my father sputtered, choking on the words as his eyes followed me down the hall.

The moment I stepped into my mother's room her eyes opened and she tilted her head back as if she was expecting me.

"I'm home, mom." I almost whispered the words.

Mom gently replied, "I know. You were here last night."

Before I could ask how she knew, she leaped from the bed and crushed me with a giant hug to make sure I was real. Tears rolled down our faces as she cried. "I knew you were safe. I knew it all along."

Though I had accidentally given them one more night of agony, my parent's year of torturous waiting had ended far better than 58,209 other parents whose sons and daughters served in Vietnam.

America's role in this long, sad war became more confused and painful as it dragged on. When our involvement officially ended on January 27, 1973, there were no parades, no heroes welcome, and no monuments. The country collectively closed the door to slip into a state of amnesia, preferring not to see or hear about Vietnam.

More than nine years later and despite a divided nation, Vietnam veterans rallied their resources to build the Vietnam Veterans Memorial. It was dedicated on November 13, 1982. This marble legacy known as "The Wall" has become a focal point for helping to heal the scars of the most nationally disruptive war modern America ever fought.

Glossary

Definitions and Combat Slang

AFVN: American Forces Vietnam Network.
AK-47: Communist infantry rifle.
AO: Area of Operation.
Article 15: Official reprimand.
ARVN: Army of the Republic of Vietnam.
AWOL: Absent With Out Leave.
B-52: Long range, high altitude bomber.
Bandoleer: Cloth belt with pockets for carrying rifle magazines.
Body count: The number of enemy killed, used to track the war's success.
Boom-Boom girl: Vietnamese whore or prostitute.
Boonie Rat: Grunt, infantryman.
Boonies: The bush, the field, the jungle.
Brass: High ranking officers.
C-130: Military transport airplane.
C-rations: Military canned food.
Charlie: The enemy (taken from Victor Charles in the phonetic alphabet).

Cherry: New combat soldier.

Chicom: Chinese Communist.

Chieu Hoi: Vietnamese for "open arms," to defect.

Chinook: Twin rotor transport helicopter.

Claymore mine: Anti-personnel explosive (command detonated).

Cobra: Bell AH-1G Huey helicopter gunship.

Concertina wire: Spooled wire with razor barbs.

Conex: 4x4x8 foot metal container for freight storage or transport.

CS: Chemical Substance, tear gas.

CP: Command Post.

DDP: Daytime Defensive Position.

DEROS: Date Eligible for Return from Overseas.

DMZ: Demilitarized Zone.

Door-gunner: Machine gun operator posted at a helicopter door.

Enlisted Man: All ranks below Sergeant.

Entrenching tool: Compact folding shovel used by infantrymen.

ETS: Elapsed Time in the Service.

Firebase: Artillery or mortar support camp.

Fire fight: Brief infantry battle.

FNG: Fuckin' new guy.

Frag: Fragmentation hand grenade.

Fragging: The killing of officers/NCOs by their own men, usually by hand grenade.

Freedom bird: The plane taking a GI home from the war.

G-2: US Army Intelligence.

Ghoster: An infantryman who passes time without being in the field (a goldbrick).

GI: American soldier from the World War II expression "Government Issue."

Gook: Dehumanized name for the enemy, also called Dink.

Grenadier: GI who carries the M-79 grenade launcher.

Grunt: Infantryman, ground-pounder, boonie rat.

Hooch: Sleeping quarters, jungle hut, poncho tent.

Hump: Trudge in the boonies.

Instant NCO: A GI who jumped from the rank of Private to Sergeant after a 90-day training course.

Jungle rot: Festering body sores.

Kit Carson Scout: A former VC or NVA who defected to the allies rather than fight with the South Vietnamese ARVN.

KP: Kitchen Police.

Lifer: Derogatory nickname for a military career man.

Loach: Nickname for the Hughes OH-6 Cayuse light observation helicopter.

LP: Listening Post.

LRRP: Long Range Recon Patrol (elite observation team) pronounced "Lurp."

LZ: Landing Zone.

M-16: Standard US infantryman's rifle (light-weight, magazine fed).

M-60: US portable machine gun (weighs 23 lbs., belt fed).

M-79: US grenade launcher (single shot).

Magazine: Detachable bullet holder (an M-16 magazine holds 20 rounds).

Medevac: Air ambulance.

Montegnard: Vietnamese hill-people or tribesmen (French for "mountaineer").

MP: Military Police.

MPC: Military Payment Certificate (GI money).

NCO: Non-commissioned officer, a sergeant.

NDP: Night Defensive Position.

Numba one: Vietnamese expression meaning good, best.

Numba ten: Vietnamese expression meaning bad, worst.

NVA: North Vietnamese Army.

Old-timer: A GI with more than six months of combat duty.

PFC: Private First Class.

Piasters: Vietnamese money.

Point or Point man: The first man in a patrol.

PX: Post Exchange (military store).

Quoc-Lo 1: Vietnamese Highway (Route 1).

R & R: Rest and Relaxation (vacation).

Rappel: Exit a hovering helicopter by sliding down a rope.

Rear: Base camp (out of the field, a safe area).

Recon: Reconnaissance.

REMF: Rear Echelon Mother Fucker, derogatory term for soldiers stationed at base camp.

RIF: Reconnaissance in force.

RPG: Rocket Propelled Grenade.

RTO: Radio Telephone Operator.

Rucksack: Backpack.

SERTS: Screaming Eagle Replacement Training School.

Shake-n-Bake: A GI who jumped from the rank of Private to Sergeant after a 90-day training course.

Short: The downhill side of the required tour of duty.

Short-timer: Less than 100 days left to serve in Vietnam.

SKS: Communist assault rifle.

Slick: Bell UH-1D utility or assault helicopter.

Smoke: Smoke grenade (emits various colors).

Socked in: Closed in by bad weather.

Specialist: Specialist Fourth Class, equivalent to a Corporal ("Speck 4").
Spider hole: Concealed one-man fighting position below ground level.
SSG: Staff Sergeant.
Stand down: Company size rest period.
Starlight scope: Night vision rifle scope.
Steel pot: GI helmet.
STS: Short-timer's Syndrome.
Supergook: An enemy soldier who seems impossible to kill, always escapes.
Tet: Vietnamese lunar new year.
Tracer: A bullet that leaves a luminous trail.
US: United States.
USO: United Services Organization (provides troop entertainment).
VC: Viet Cong.
VD: Venereal Disease
Viet Cong: Local communist irregular, guerilla fighter.
Web gear: Woven belts that hold canteens, grenades, pouches, etc.
World: The United States, home.

Bibliography

In writing this book, I referred to a wide variety of sources to refresh my aging recollection as to topography, geography, dates, and so forth. Below is a partial list of those I found the most useful.

BOOKS

Bonds, Ray. *The Vietnam War*. New York: Crown Publishers, Inc., 1979.

Drake, Hal. *Pacific Stars And Stripes: Vietnam Front Pages*. New York: Hugh Lauter Levin Associates, Inc., 1986.

Esper, George and The Associated Press. *The Eyewitness History of the Vietnam War 1961-1975*. New York: Ballantine Books, 1983.

Jury, Mark. *The Vietnam Photo Book*. New York: Grossman Publishers, 1971.

GOVERNMENT DOCUMENTS

Appendix 1 (May 9-10, 1969) to Annex A (Execution) to After Action Report, APACHE SNOW, 101st Airborne Division.

Appendixes 2 thru 11 (May 11-20, 1969) to Annex C (Execution) to After Action Report, APACHE SNOW, 101st Airborne Division.

MILITARY PUBLICATIONS

Bryan, Maj. Richard L. *The 1968-1969 Pictorial Review of The 101st Airborne Division (Airmobile).* 101st Airborne Division, San Francisco, 1969.

GENERAL ARTICLES

"America Gathers under a Sign of Peace." *Life.* October 24, 1969.

"The Battle for Hamburger Hill." *Time.* May 30, 1969.

"The Embattled White House." *Life.* October 24, 1969.

"The Faces of the Dead in Vietnam—One Week's Toll." *Life.* June 27, 1969.

"History of Camp Evans." *Ripcord Report.* October, 1989.

"The Siege of Firebase Ripcord," by Hawkins, Charles F. *American Sentinel.* August 2, 1992.

"Teddy on the Stump." *Newsweek.* June 2, 1969.

"Woe to the Victors." *Newsweek.* June 2, 1969.

SELECTED MILITARY ARTICLES

Borders, Spec. 5 Robert. "Dong Ap Bia." Rendezvous With Destiny. Summer 1969.

Editors. "Screaming Eagle Vietnam Diary." Rendezvous With Destiny. Summer 1969.

Higle, Spec. 4 Roger. "Screaming Eagle Vietnam Diary." Rendezvous With Destiny. Winter 1969.

Horvath, Maj. Richard L. "Armor In The A Shau." Rendezvous With Destiny. Fall 1969.

Horvath, Maj. Richard L. "Mystique of the Valley." Rendezvous With Destiny. Summer 1969.

Kendall, Spec. 5 Anthony. "Mai Loc." Rendezvous With Destiny. Winter 1969.

Lackeos, Spec. 4 Nick. "No Room for Emotion." Rendezvous With Destiny. Fall 1969.

McLaughlin, Spec. 5 J. Michael. "Going Home." Rendezvous With Destiny. Spring 1969.

Pitchford, PFC Gary. "The Girls Who Wear the Screaming Eagle Patch." Rendezvous With Destiny. Summer 1969.

Posner, Spec. 4 Calvin S. "Kit Carson Scout." Rendezvous With Destiny. Summer 1969.

Siner, Spec. 4 Howard. "Sixty Classes Improve Bn's Airmobile Skills." The Screaming Eagle, Vol. III, No. 5, Feb. 16, 1970.

Smith, Spec. 4 Terry. "Screaming Eagle Vietnam Diary." Rendezvous With Destiny. Fall 1969.

MOVIES

"Stalag 17," Billy Wilder and Edwin Blum, Paramount Studios, 1953.

"North by Northwest," Ernest Lehman, MGM Studios, 1959.

"The Wizard of Oz," L. Frank Baum and Mervyn LeRoy, MGM Studios, 1939.

SONGS

"I-Feel-Like-I'm-Fixin-to-Die Rag." Words and music by Country Joe McDonald. Vanguard Records, 1967. Published by Tradition. Also by Cotillion Records, 1970, a division of Atlantic Records.

"Bad Moon Rising." Words and music by J. C. Fogerty-Jondora. Fantasy Records, 1969.

"You Keep Me Hanging On." Words and music by B. Holland and L. Dozier. Motown Records, 1966; Atlantic Records, 1967.

INDEX